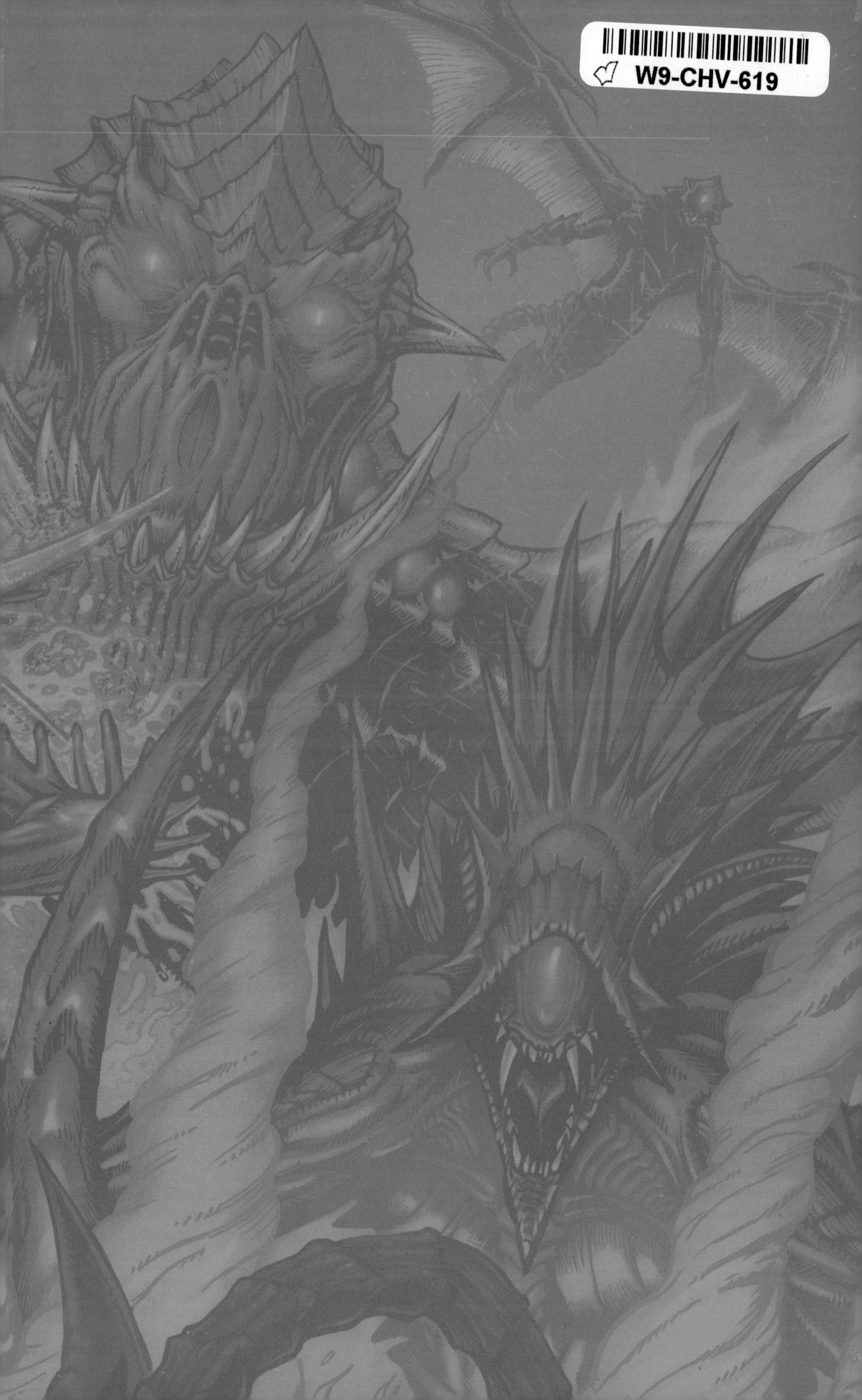

Tyler Chin-Tanner: Co-Publisher
Wendy Chin-Tanner: Co-Publisher
Justin Zimmerman: Director of Operations and Media
Pete Carlsson: Production Designer
Erin Beasley: Sales Manager
Jesse Post: Book Publicist
Hazel Newlevant: Social Media Coordinator

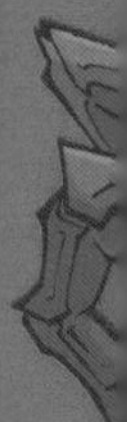

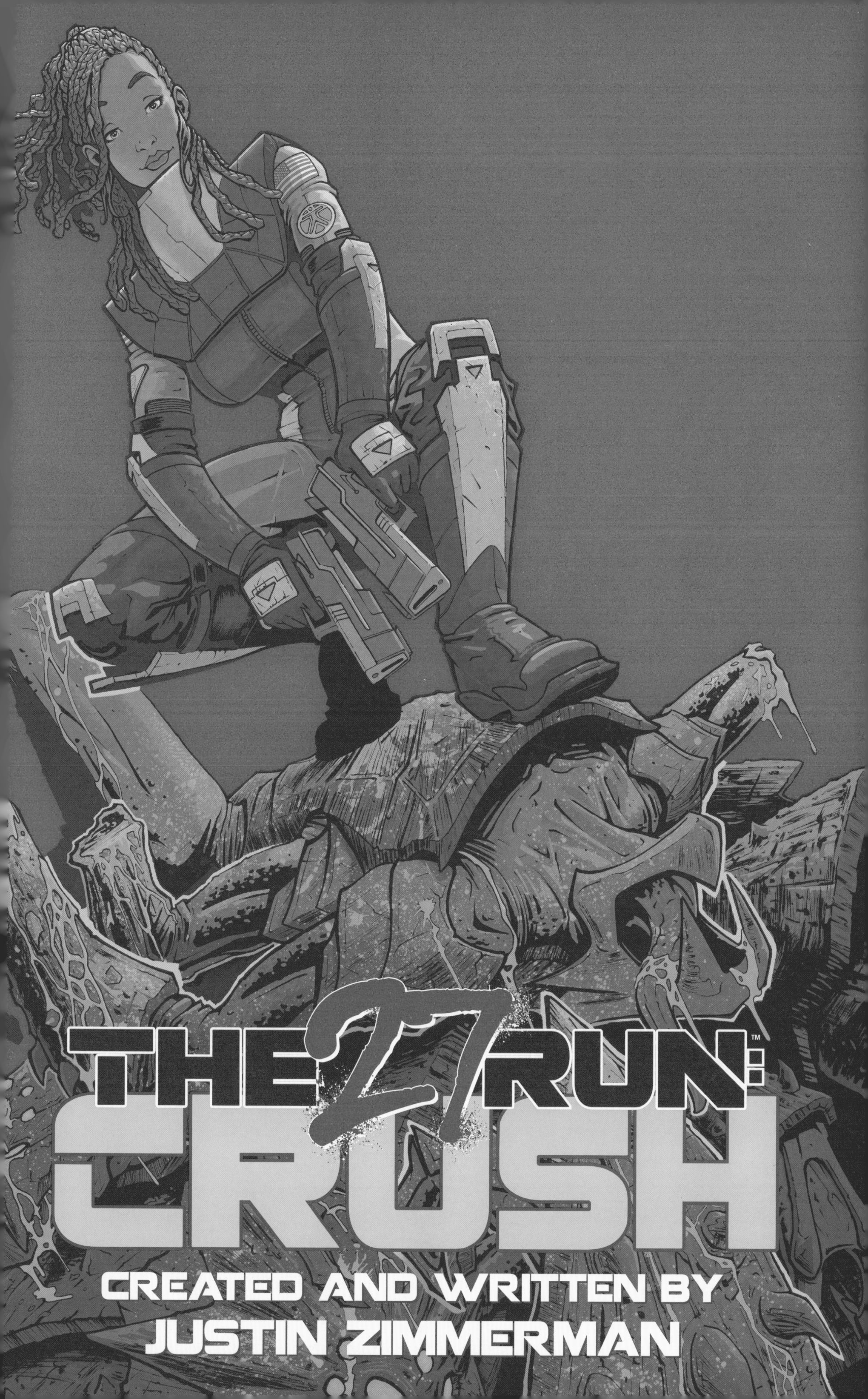
THE 27 RUN:™
CRUSH
CREATED AND WRITTEN BY
JUSTIN ZIMMERMAN

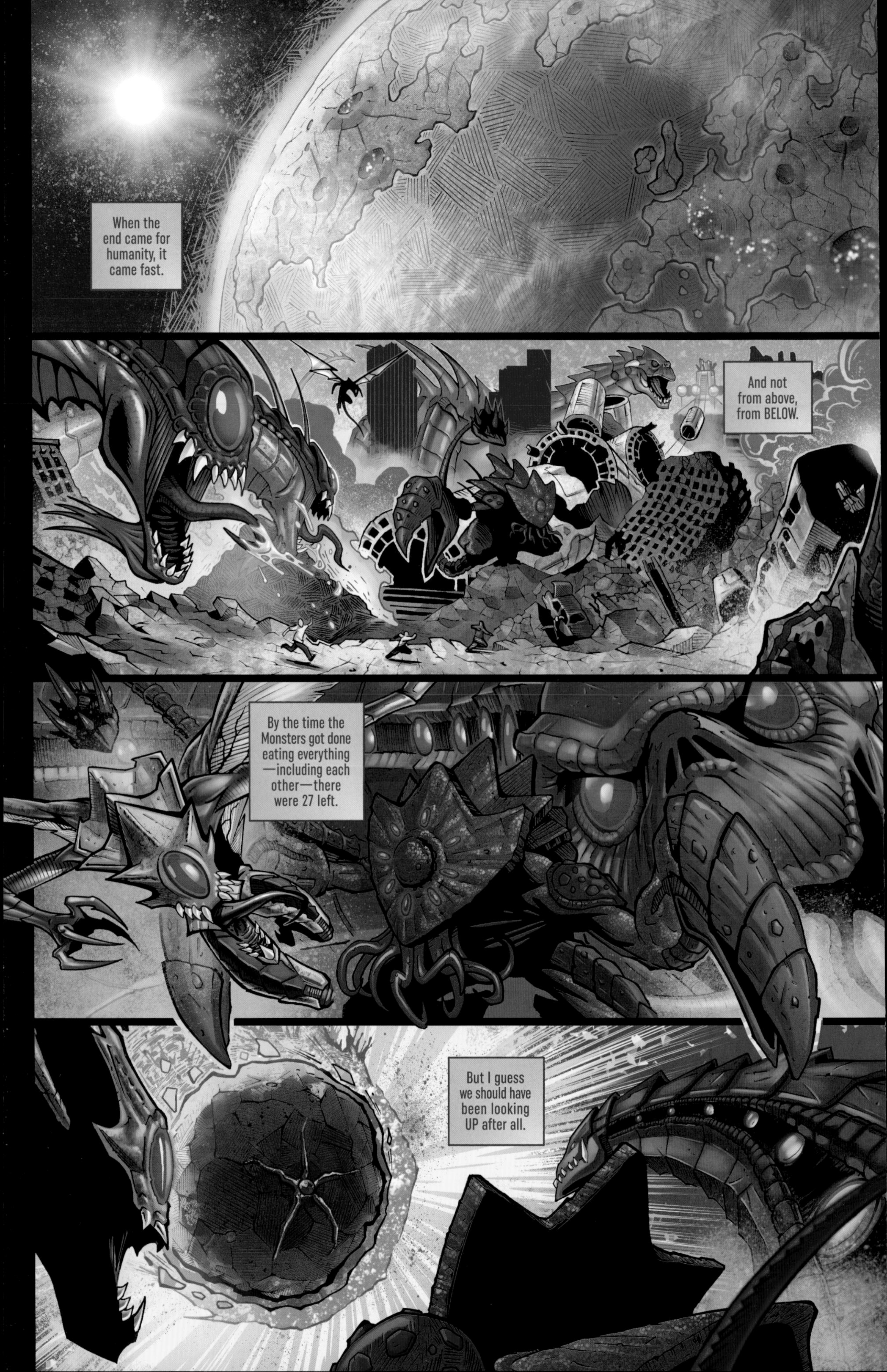
When the end came for humanity, it came fast.
And not from above, from BELOW.
By the time the Monsters got done eating everything—including each other—there were 27 left.
But I guess we should have been looking UP after all.

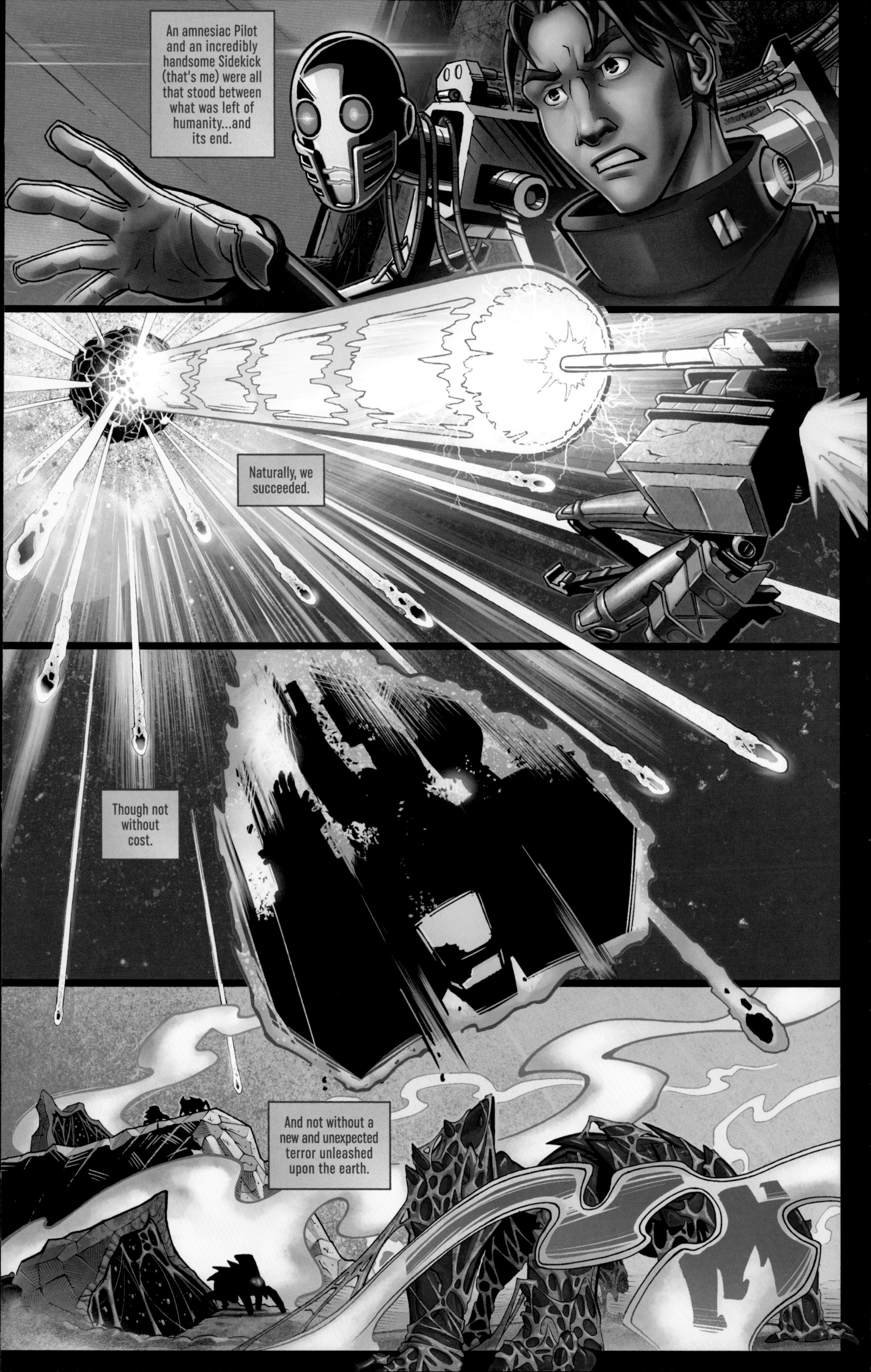
An amnesiac Pilot and an incredibly handsome Sidekick (that's me) were all that stood between what was left of humanity...and its end.
Naturally, we succeeded.
Though not without cost.
And not without a new and unexpected terror unleashed upon the earth.

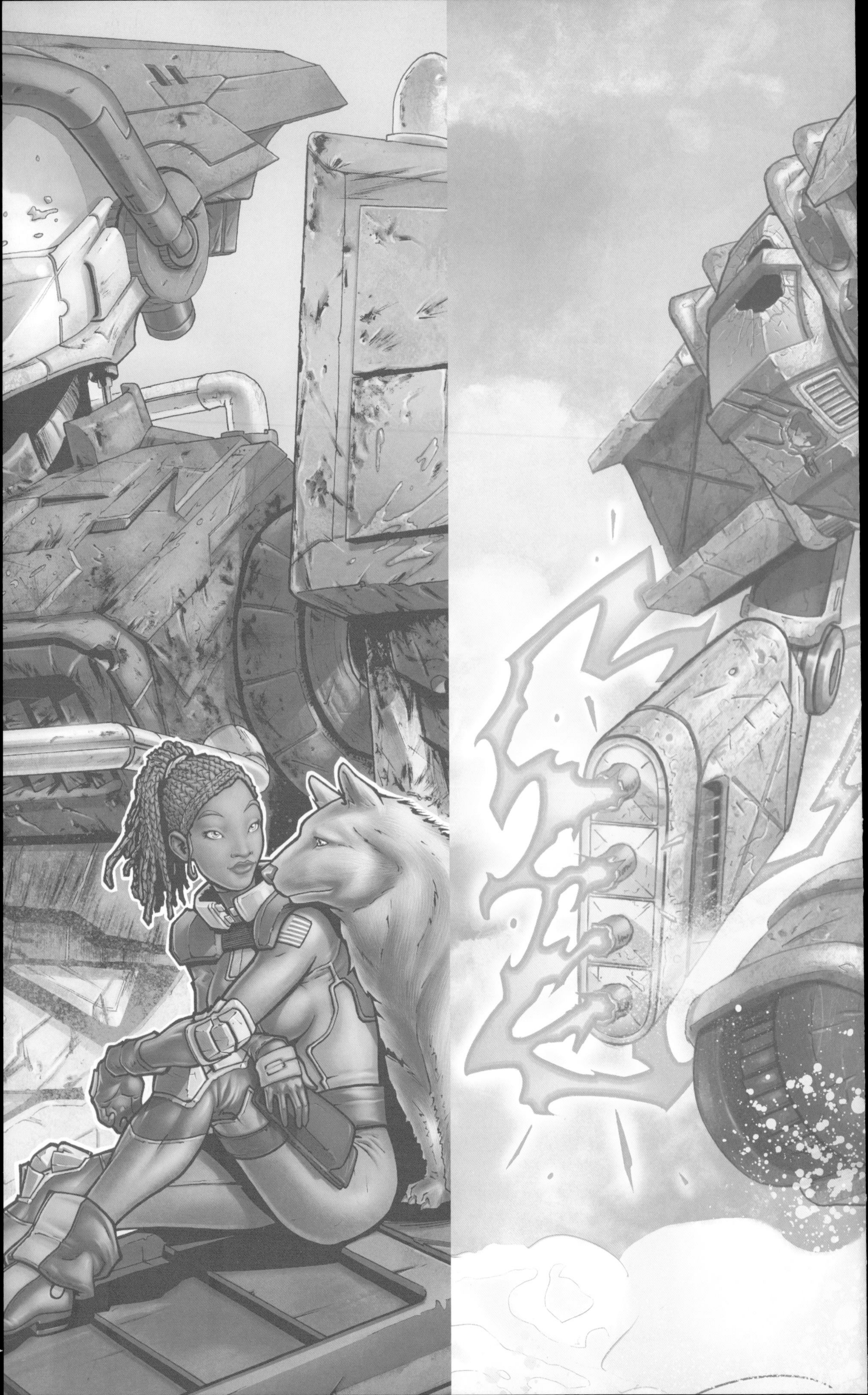

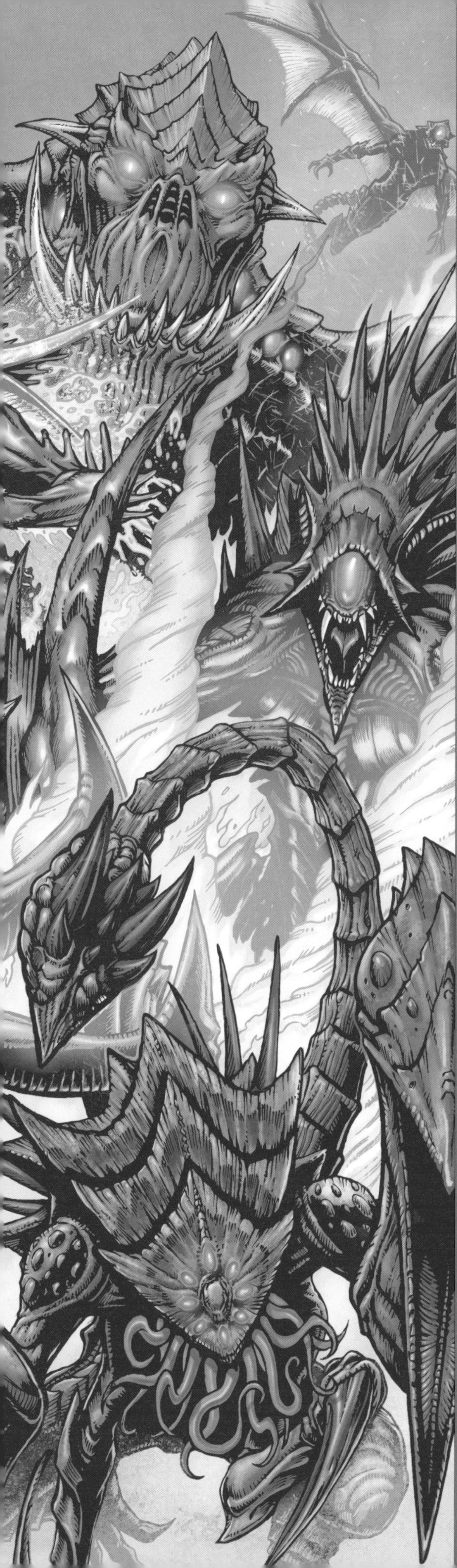

THE 27 RUN™: CRUSH

PROLOGUE
ART: ETHAN CLAUNCH

CHAPTER 01
ART: RUSSELL BROWN

CHAPTER 02
ART: RUSSELL BROWN

CHAPTER 03
ART: ETHAN CLAUNCH

CHAPTER 04
ART: ETHAN CLAUNCH

COLORS:
FRAN GAMBOA

LETTERING:
THOMAS MAUER

EDITOR:
TYLER CHIN-TANNER

FLATS:
J.C. RUIZ

FOR:
ASHANTÉ,
BETELEHEM,
ABENEZER,
GABRIELA,
CARA,
ZIA &
A'JAY.

INSPIRATIONS, ALL.
- JUSTIN ZIMMERMAN

CHAPTER 01

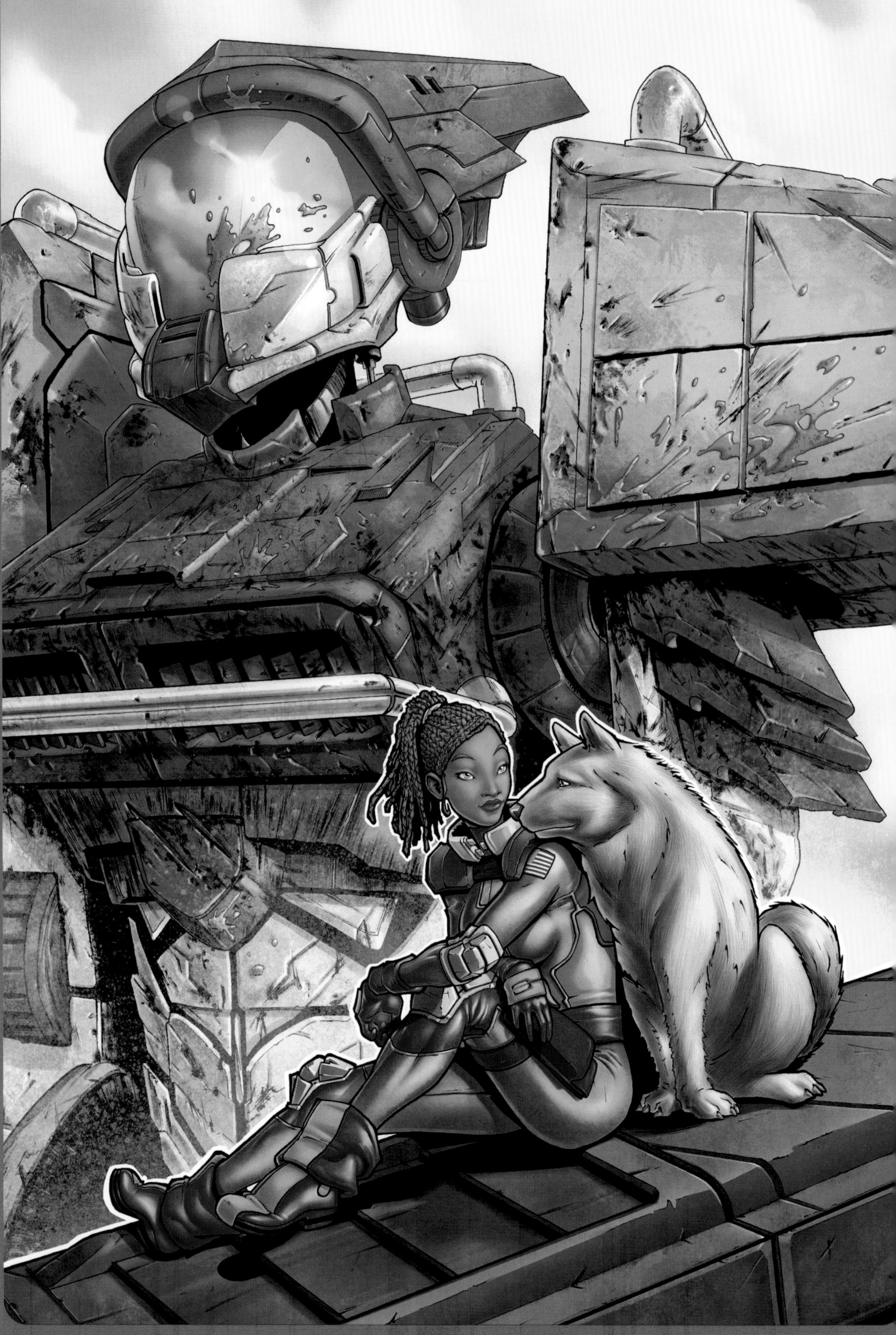

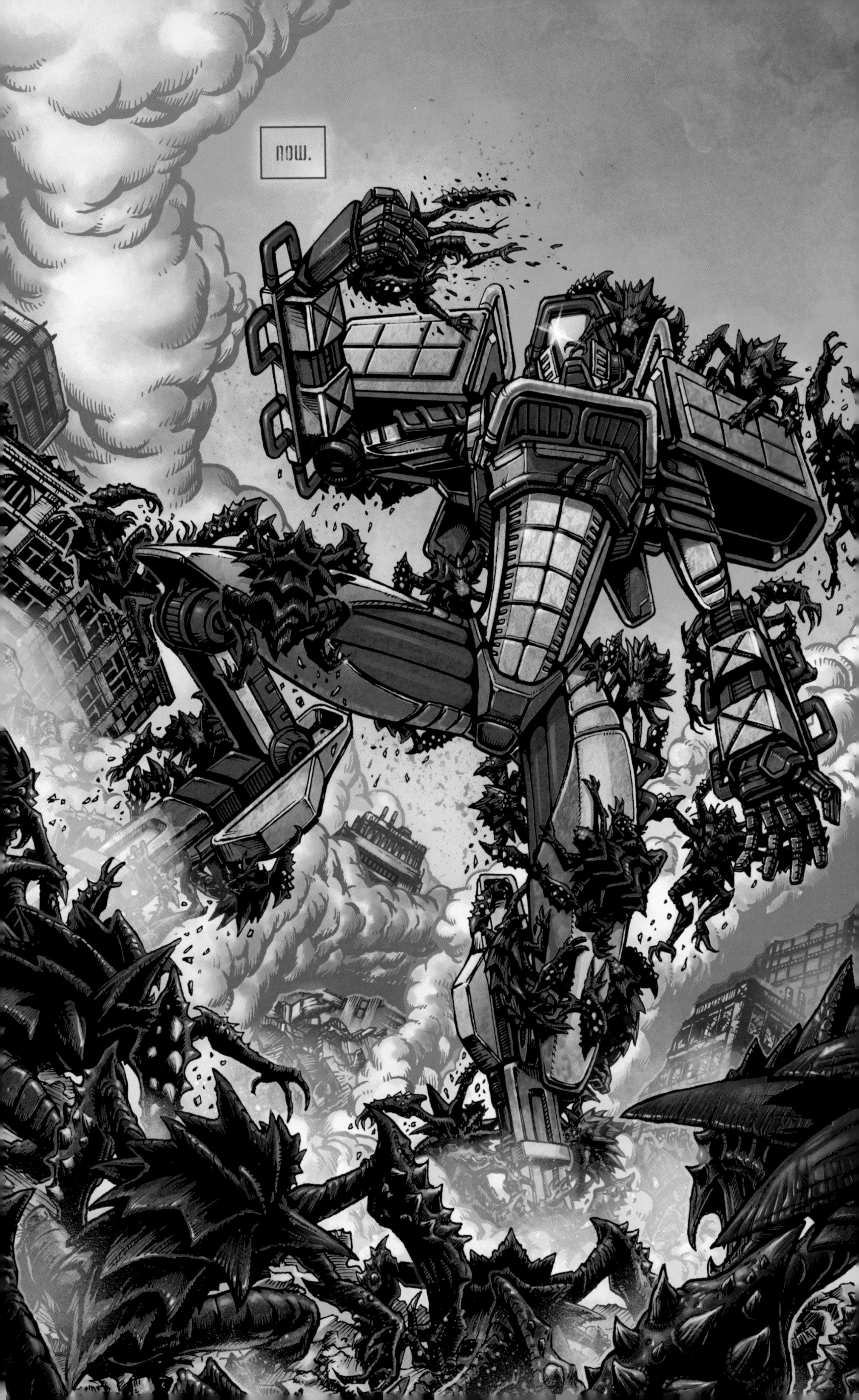
now.

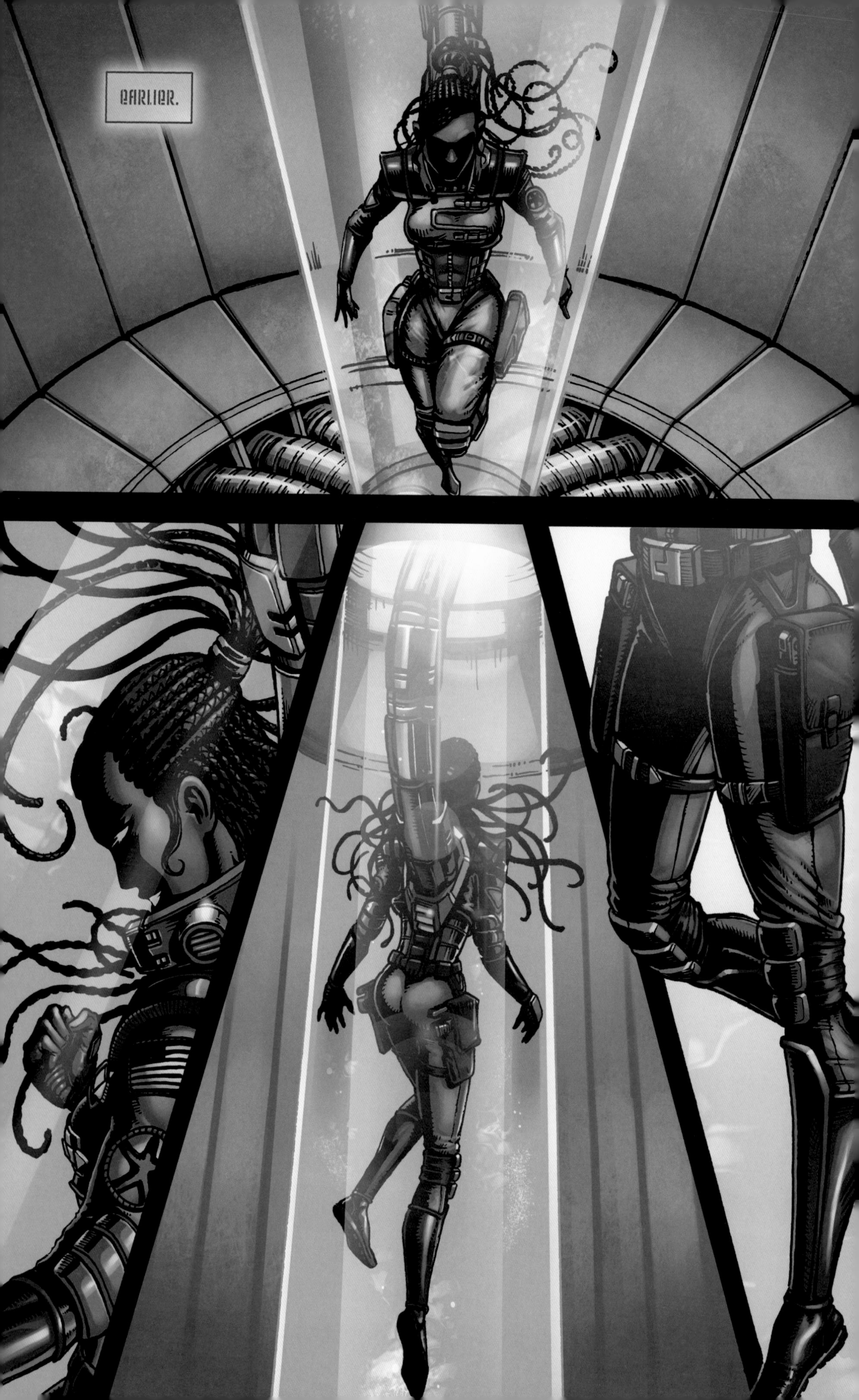
EARLIER.

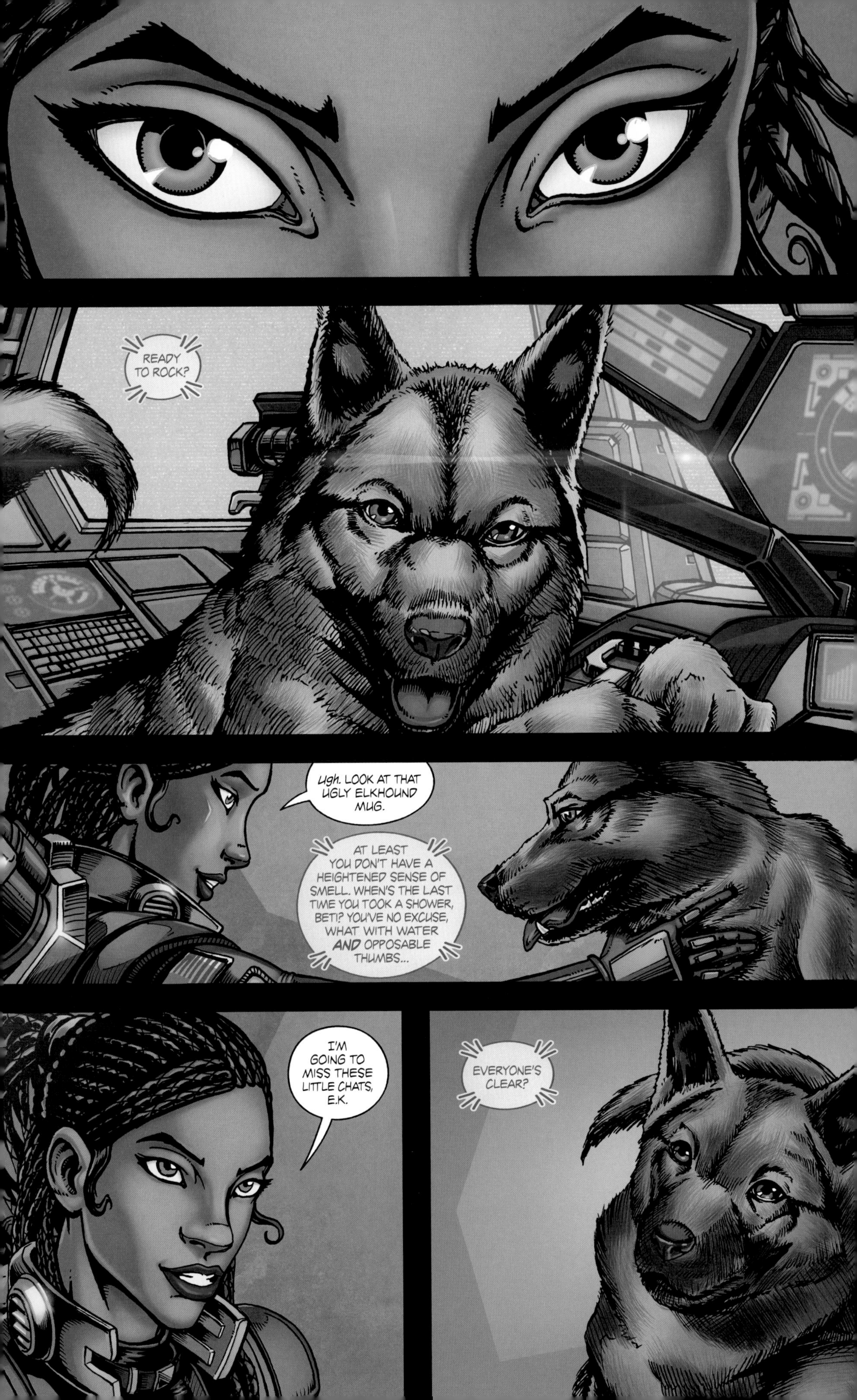
READY TO ROCK?
Ugh. LOOK AT THAT UGLY ELKHOUND MUG.
AT LEAST YOU DON'T HAVE A HEIGHTENED SENSE OF SMELL. WHEN'S THE LAST TIME YOU TOOK A SHOWER, BETI? YOU'VE NO EXCUSE, WHAT WITH WATER AND OPPOSABLE THUMBS...
I'M GOING TO MISS THESE LITTLE CHATS, E.K.
EVERYONE'S CLEAR?

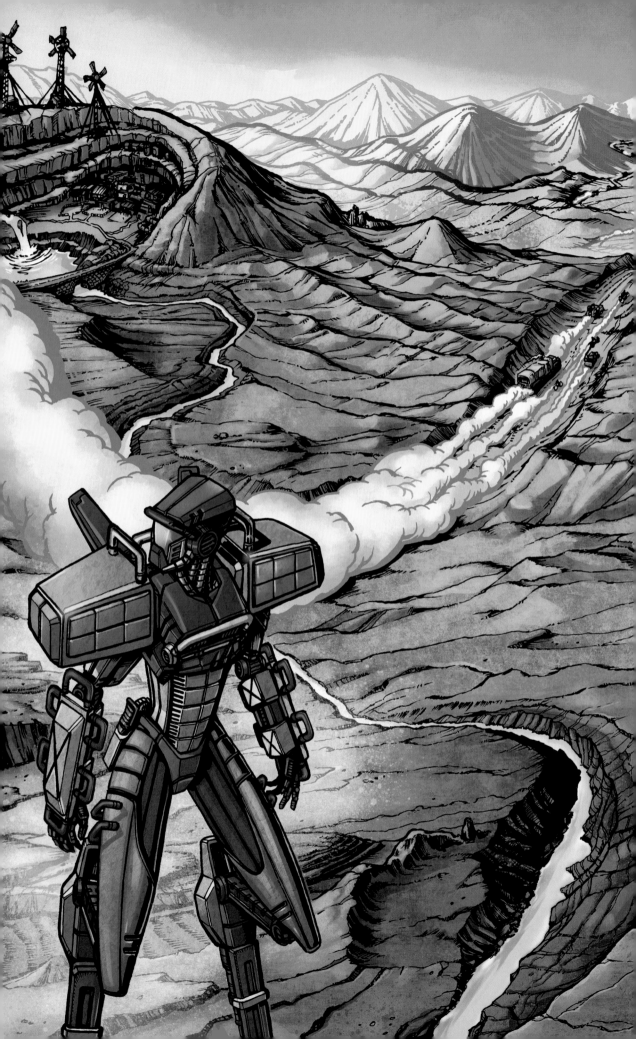

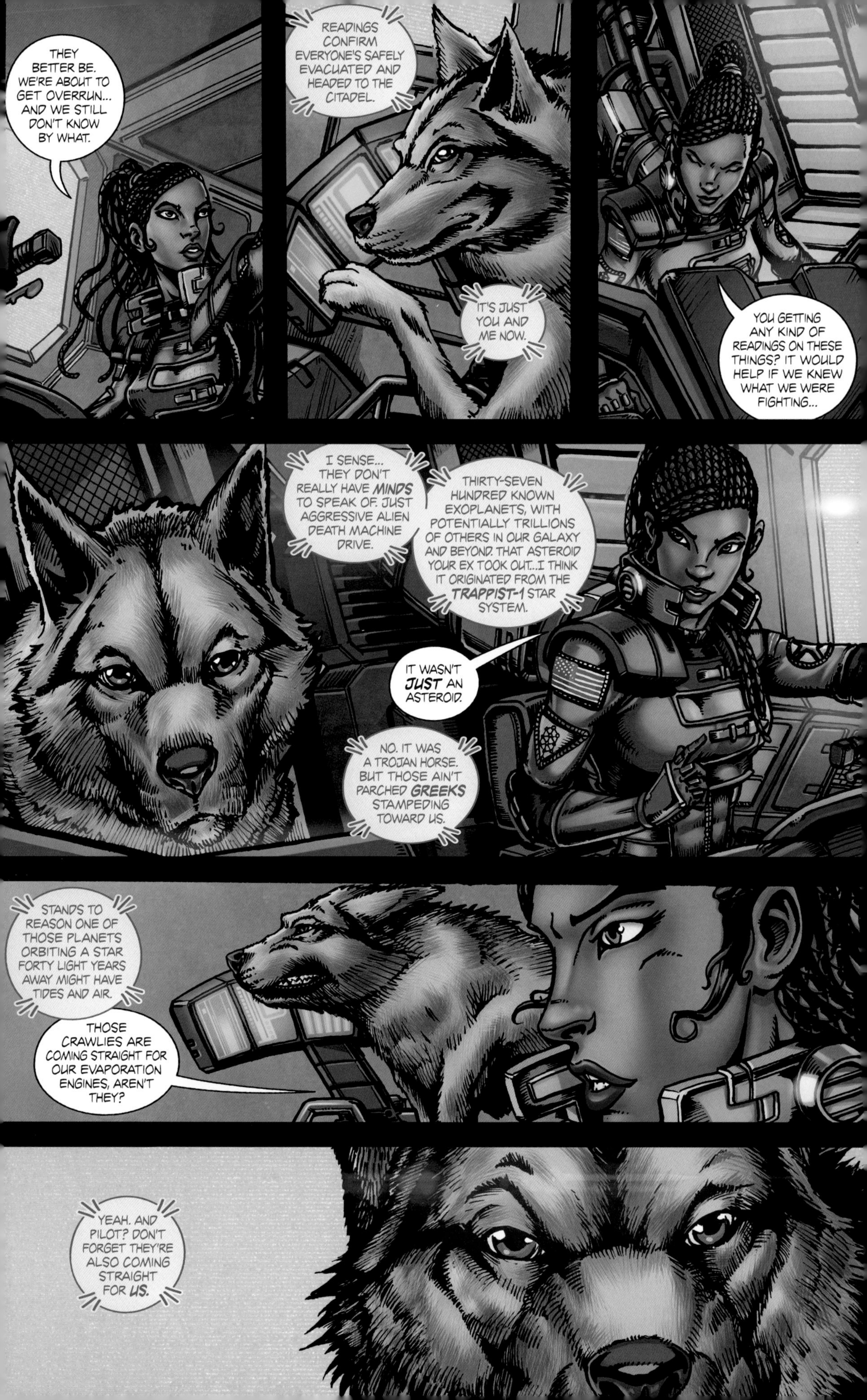
THEY BETTER BE. WE'RE ABOUT TO GET OVERRUN... AND WE STILL DON'T KNOW BY WHAT.
READINGS CONFIRM EVERYONE'S SAFELY EVACUATED AND HEADED TO THE CITADEL.
IT'S JUST YOU AND ME NOW.
YOU GETTING ANY KIND OF READINGS ON THESE THINGS? IT WOULD HELP IF WE KNEW WHAT WE WERE FIGHTING...
I SENSE... THEY DON'T REALLY HAVE MINDS TO SPEAK OF. JUST AGGRESSIVE ALIEN DEATH MACHINE DRIVE.
THIRTY-SEVEN HUNDRED KNOWN EXOPLANETS, WITH POTENTIALLY TRILLIONS OF OTHERS IN OUR GALAXY AND BEYOND. THAT ASTEROID YOUR EX TOOK OUT...I THINK IT ORIGINATED FROM THE TRAPPIST-1 STAR SYSTEM.
IT WASN'T JUST AN ASTEROID.
NO. IT WAS A TROJAN HORSE. BUT THOSE AIN'T PARCHED GREEKS STAMPEDING TOWARD US.
STANDS TO REASON ONE OF THOSE PLANETS ORBITING A STAR FORTY LIGHT YEARS AWAY MIGHT HAVE TIDES AND AIR.
THOSE CRAWLIES ARE COMING STRAIGHT FOR OUR EVAPORATION ENGINES, AREN'T THEY?
YEAH. AND PILOT? DON'T FORGET THEY'RE ALSO COMING STRAIGHT FOR US.

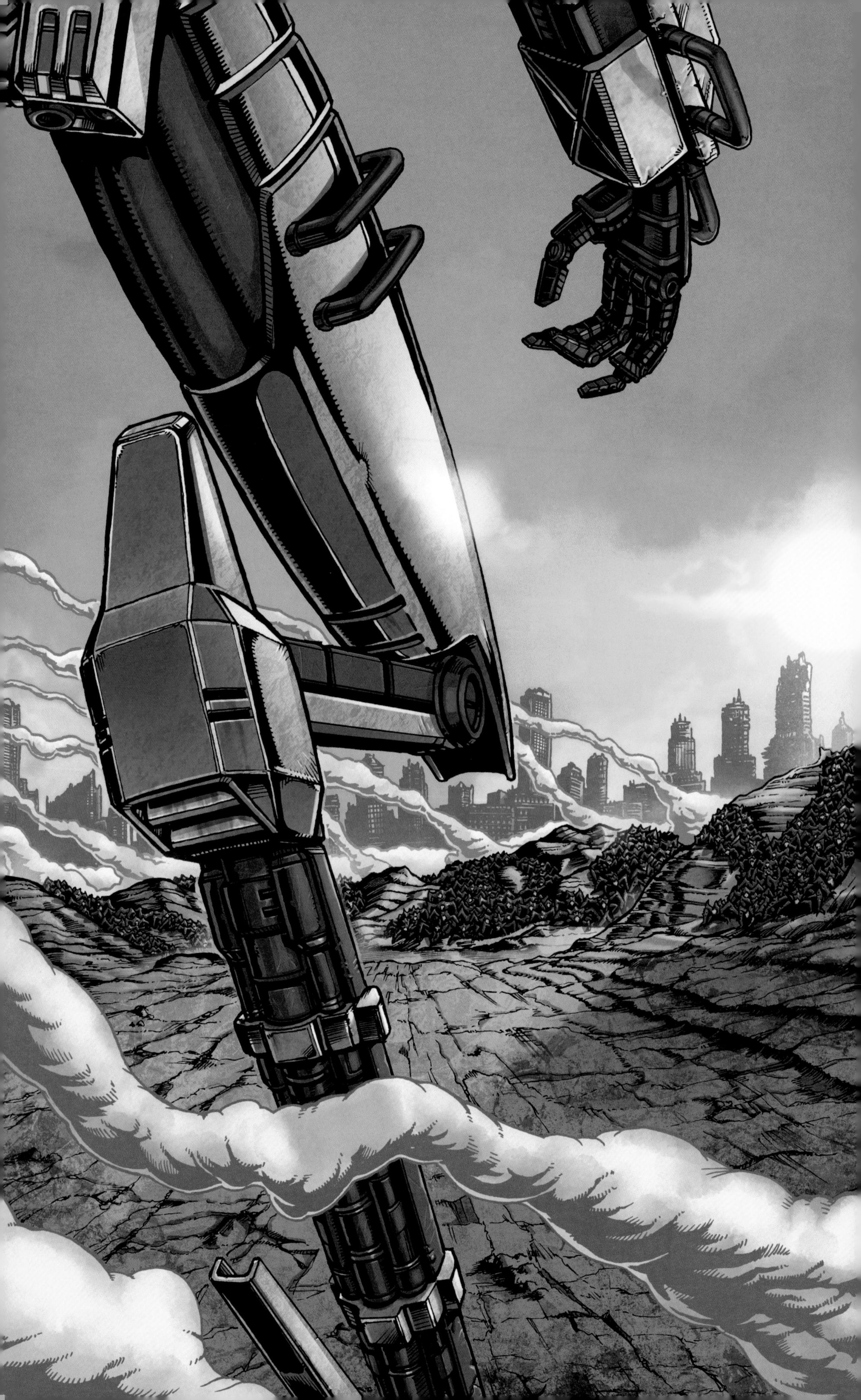

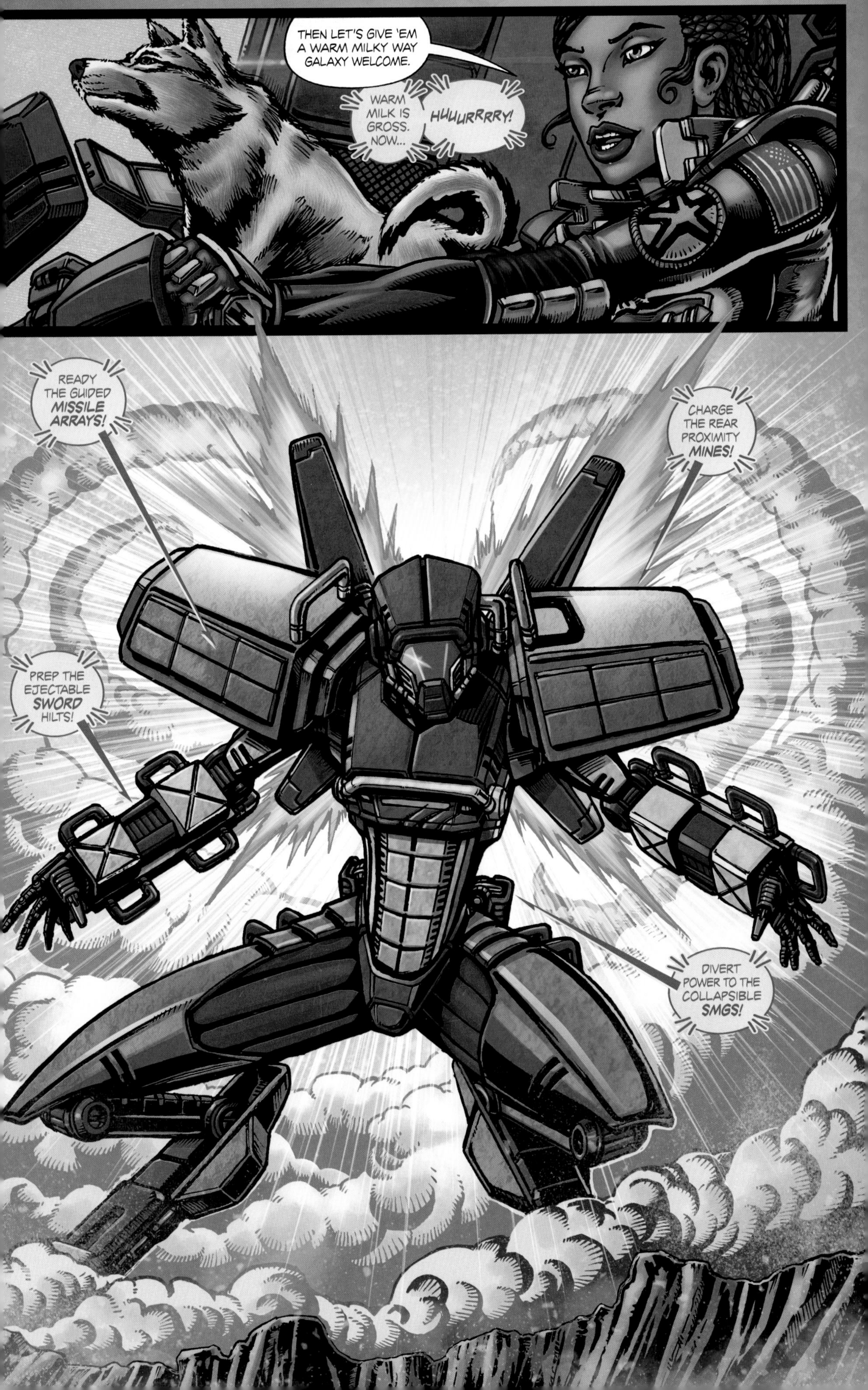
THEN LET'S GIVE 'EM A WARM MILKY WAY GALAXY WELCOME.
WARM MILK IS GROSS. NOW...
HUUURRRRY!
READY THE GUIDED MISSILE ARRAYS!
CHARGE THE REAR PROXIMITY MINES!
PREP THE EJECTABLE SWORD HILTS!
DIVERT POWER TO THE COLLAPSIBLE SMGS!

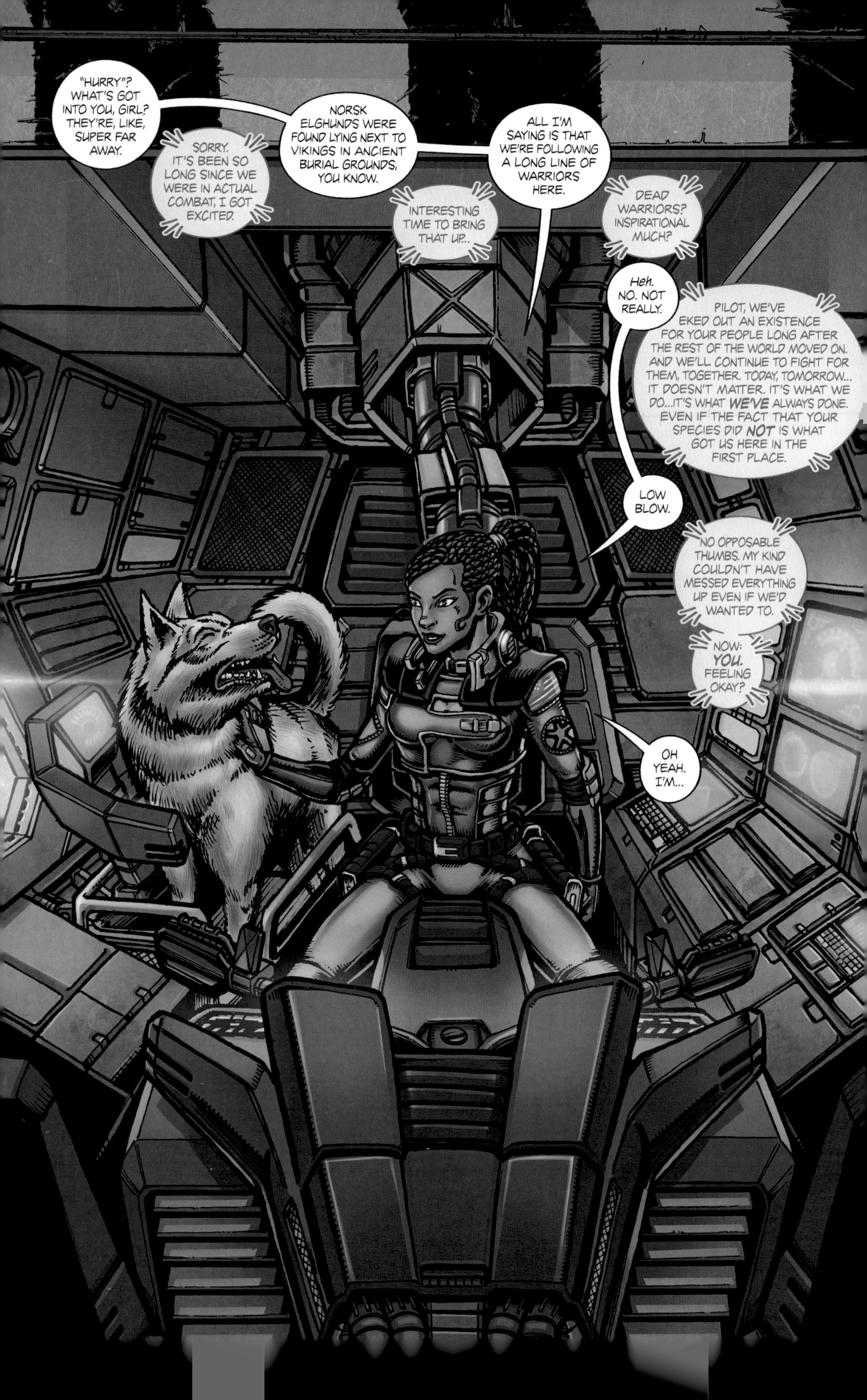
"HURRY"? WHAT'S GOT INTO YOU, GIRL? THEY'RE, LIKE, SUPER FAR AWAY.
SORRY. IT'S BEEN SO LONG SINCE WE WERE IN ACTUAL COMBAT, I GOT EXCITED.
NORSK ELGHUNDS WERE FOUND LYING NEXT TO VIKINGS IN ANCIENT BURIAL GROUNDS, YOU KNOW.
INTERESTING TIME TO BRING THAT UP...
ALL I'M SAYING IS THAT WE'RE FOLLOWING A LONG LINE OF WARRIORS HERE.
DEAD WARRIORS? INSPIRATIONAL MUCH?
Heh. NO. NOT REALLY.
PILOT, WE'VE EKED OUT AN EXISTENCE FOR YOUR PEOPLE LONG AFTER THE REST OF THE WORLD MOVED ON. AND WE'LL CONTINUE TO FIGHT FOR THEM, TOGETHER. TODAY, TOMORROW... IT DOESN'T MATTER. IT'S WHAT WE DO...IT'S WHAT WE'VE ALWAYS DONE. EVEN IF THE FACT THAT YOUR SPECIES DID NOT IS WHAT GOT US HERE IN THE FIRST PLACE.
LOW BLOW.
NO OPPOSABLE THUMBS. MY KIND COULDN'T HAVE MESSED EVERYTHING UP EVEN IF WE'D WANTED TO.
NOW: YOU. FEELING OKAY?
OH YEAH. I'M...

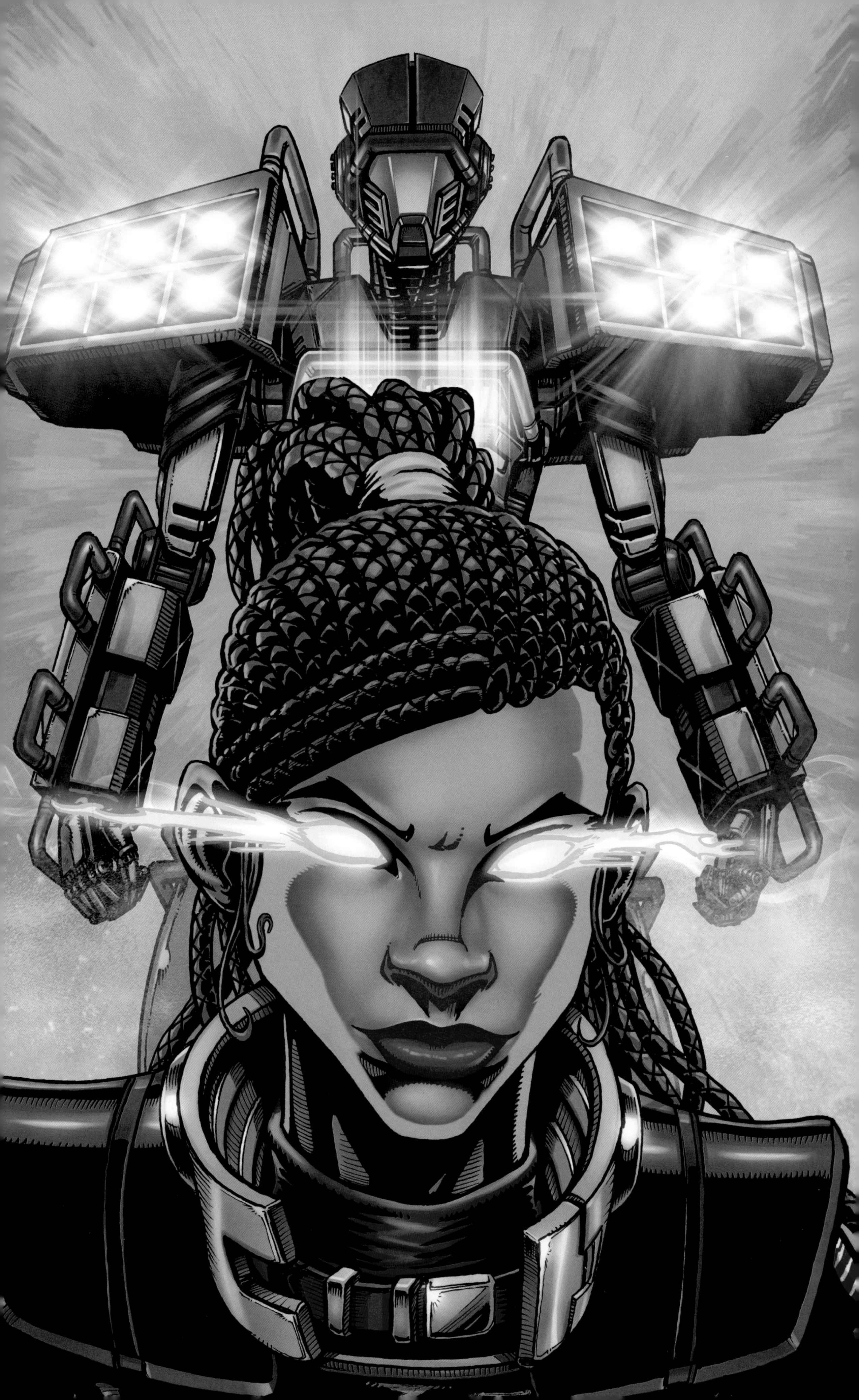

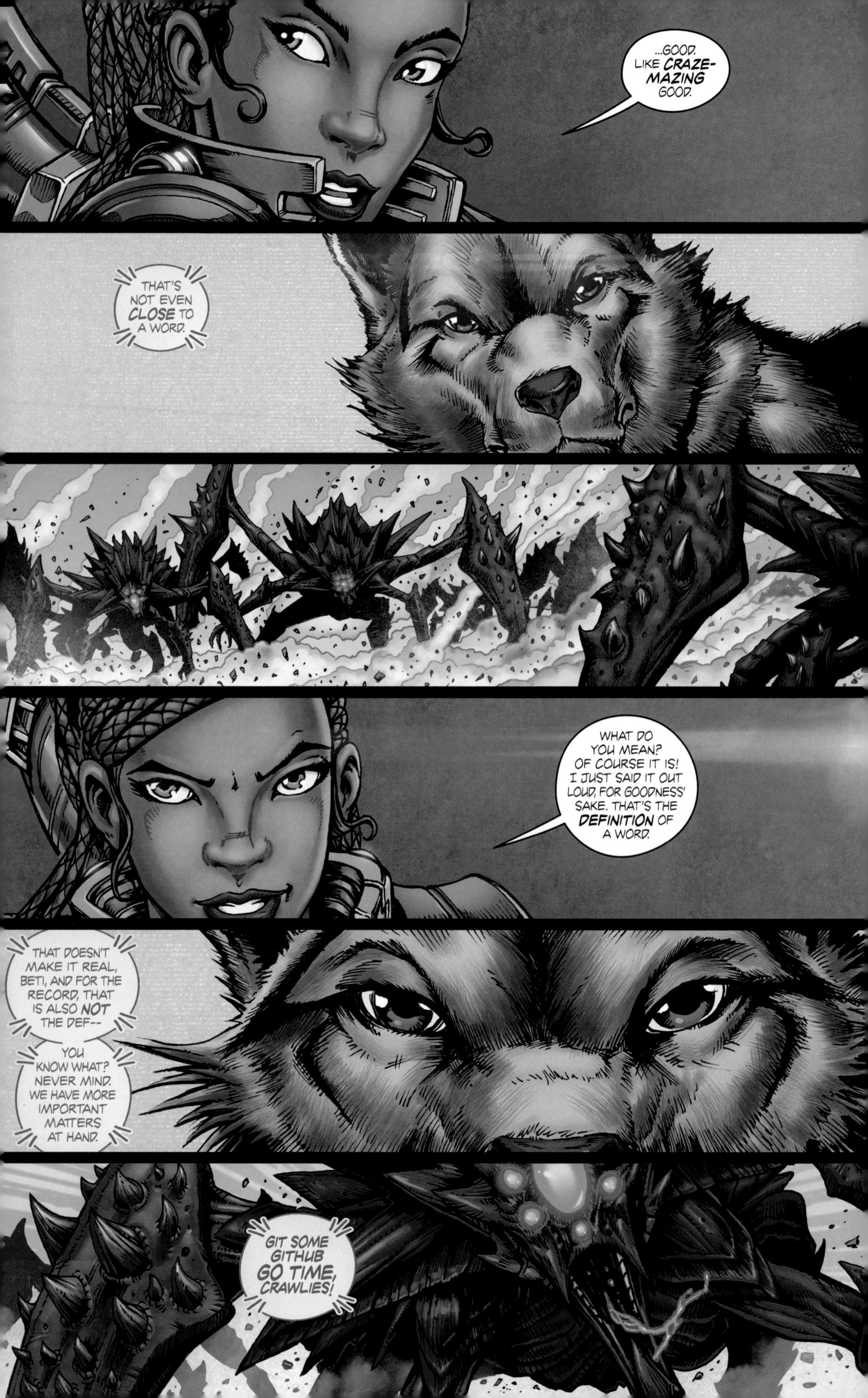
...GOOD. LIKE CRAZE-MAZING GOOD.
THAT'S NOT EVEN CLOSE TO A WORD.
WHAT DO YOU MEAN? OF COURSE IT IS! I JUST SAID IT OUT LOUD, FOR GOODNESS' SAKE. THAT'S THE DEFINITION OF A WORD.
THAT DOESN'T MAKE IT REAL, BETI, AND FOR THE RECORD, THAT IS ALSO NOT THE DEF--
YOU KNOW WHAT? NEVER MIND. WE HAVE MORE IMPORTANT MATTERS AT HAND.
GIT SOME GITHUB GO TIME, CRAWLIES!

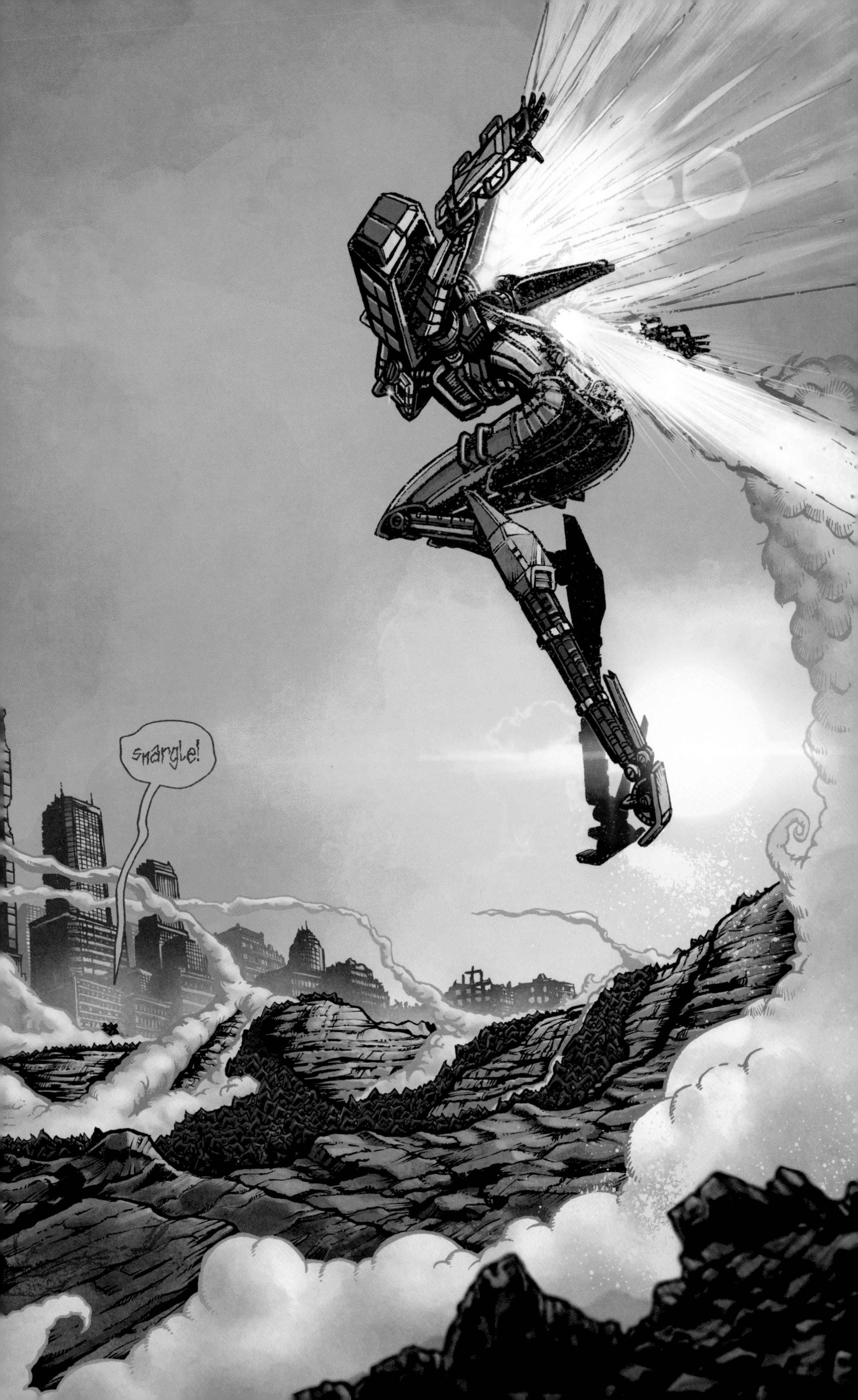
SNARGLE!

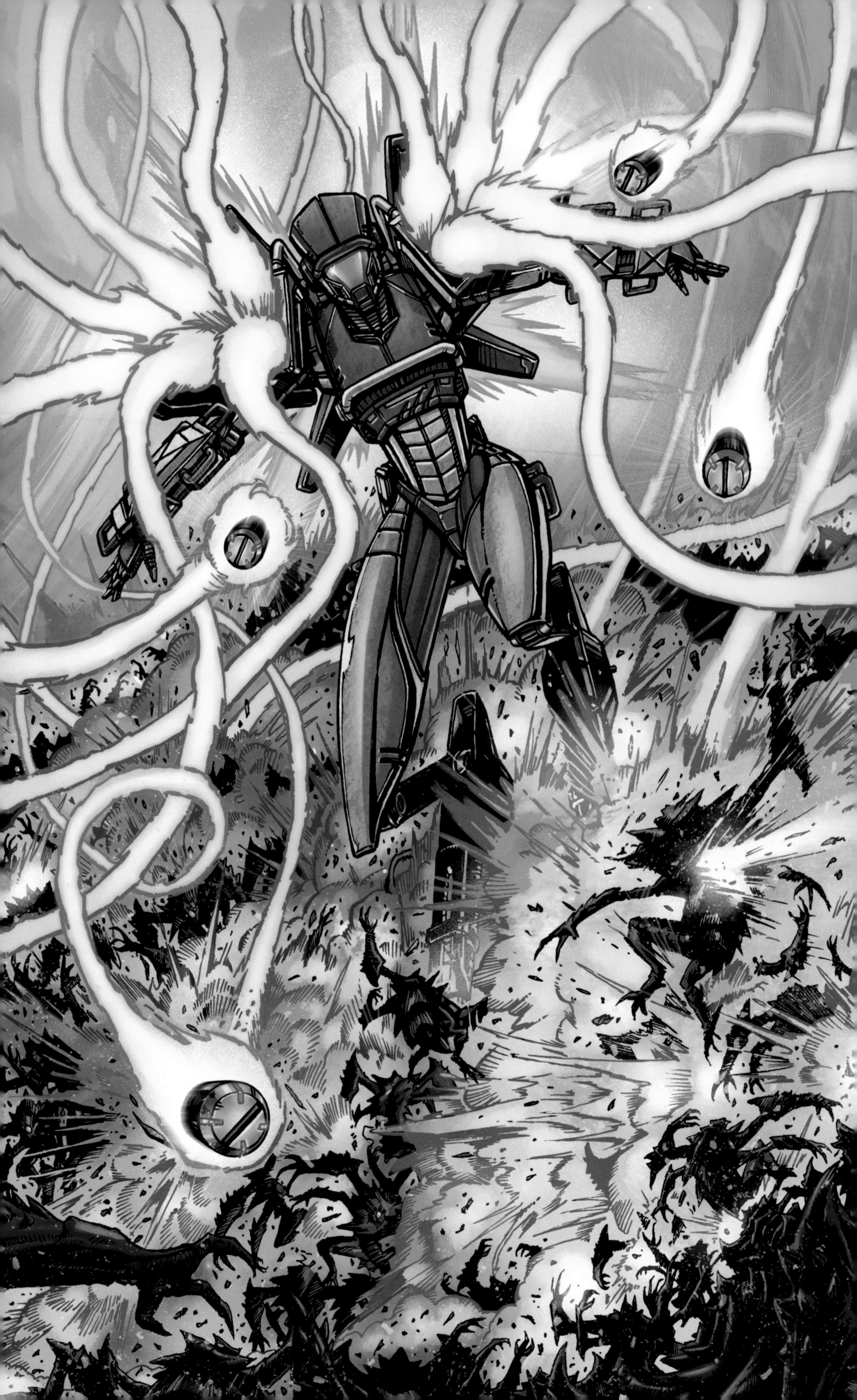

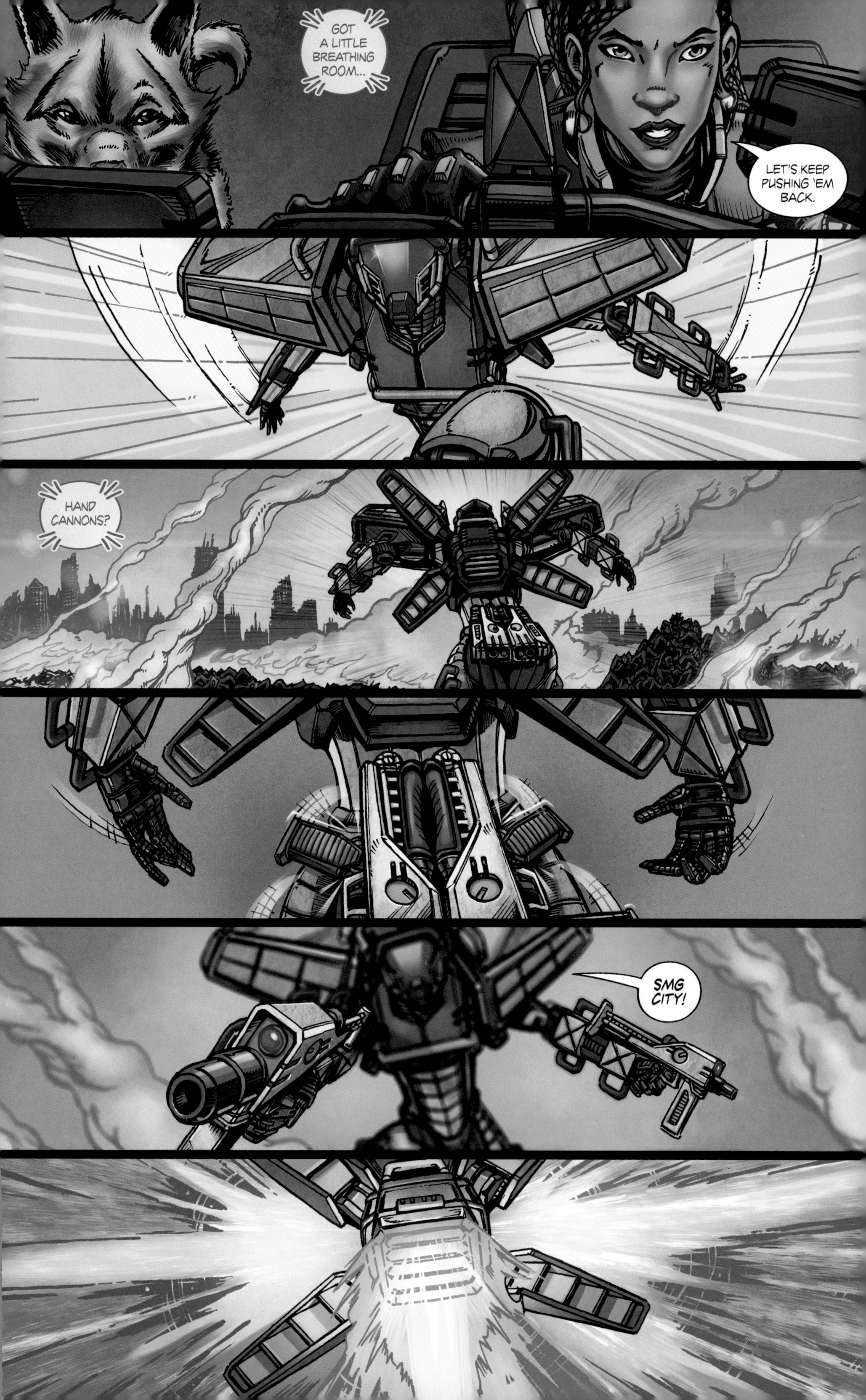
GOT A LITTLE BREATHING ROOM...
LET'S KEEP PUSHING 'EM BACK.
HAND CANNONS?
SMG CITY!

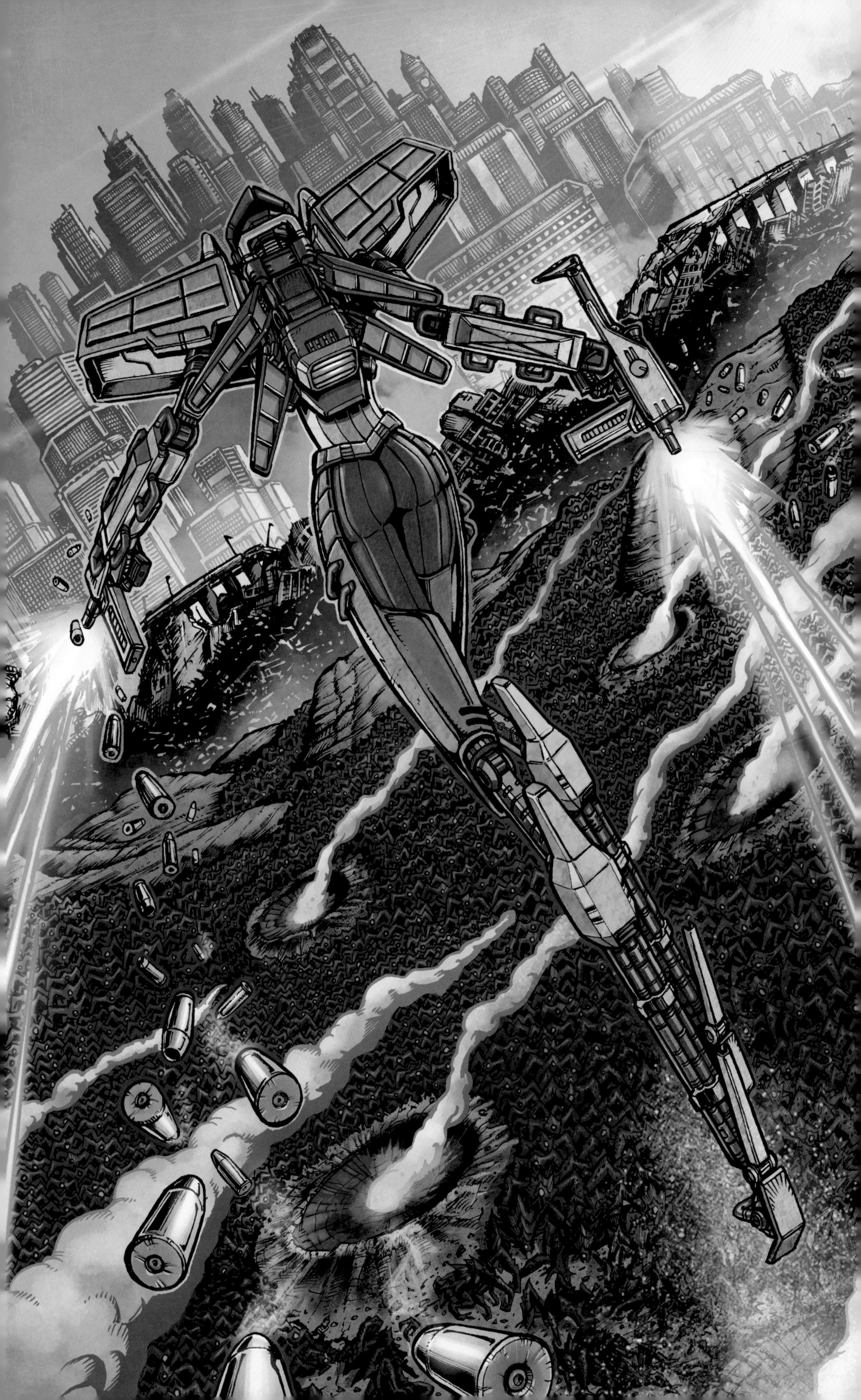

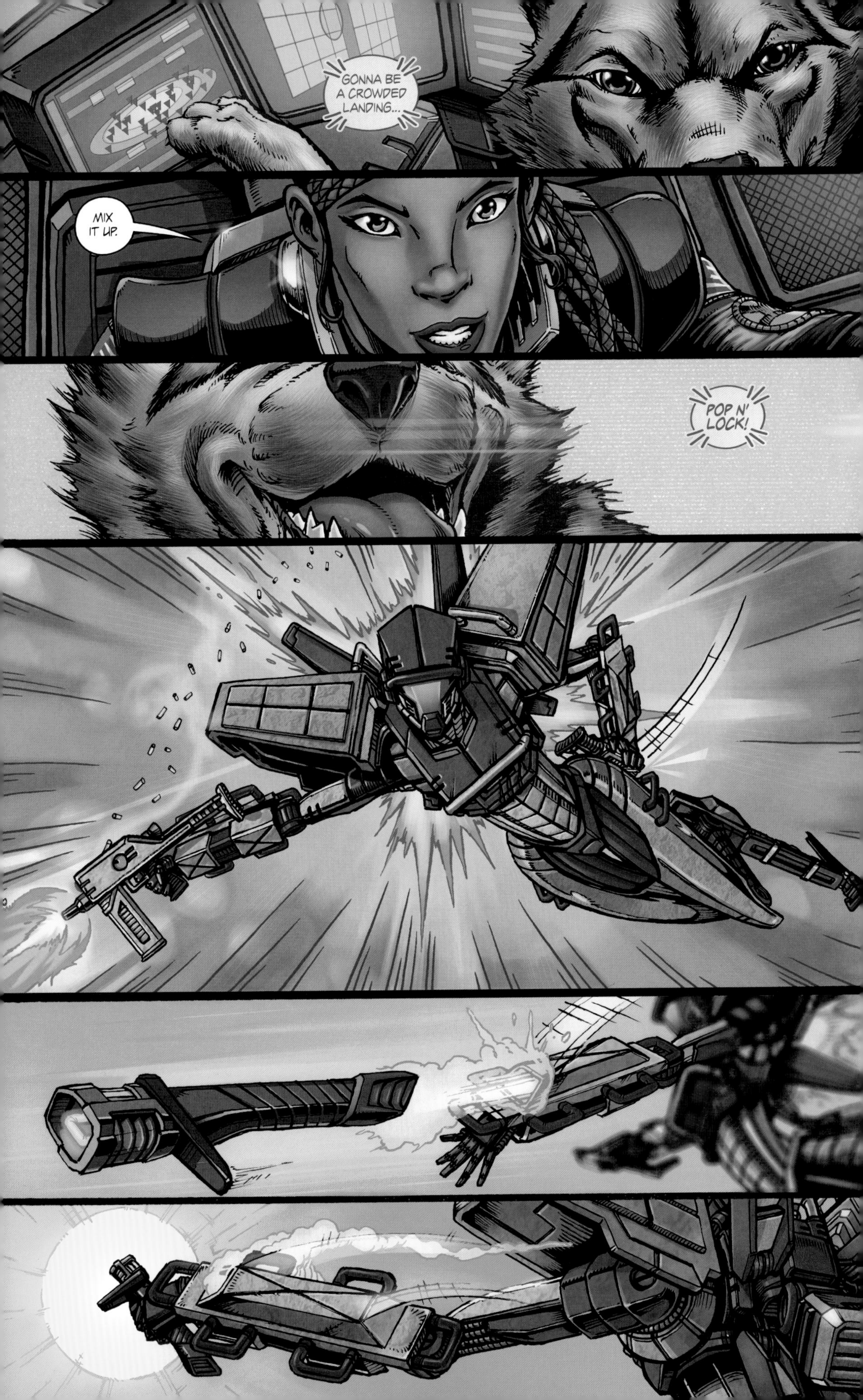
GONNA BE A CROWDED LANDING...
MIX IT UP.
POP N' LOCK!

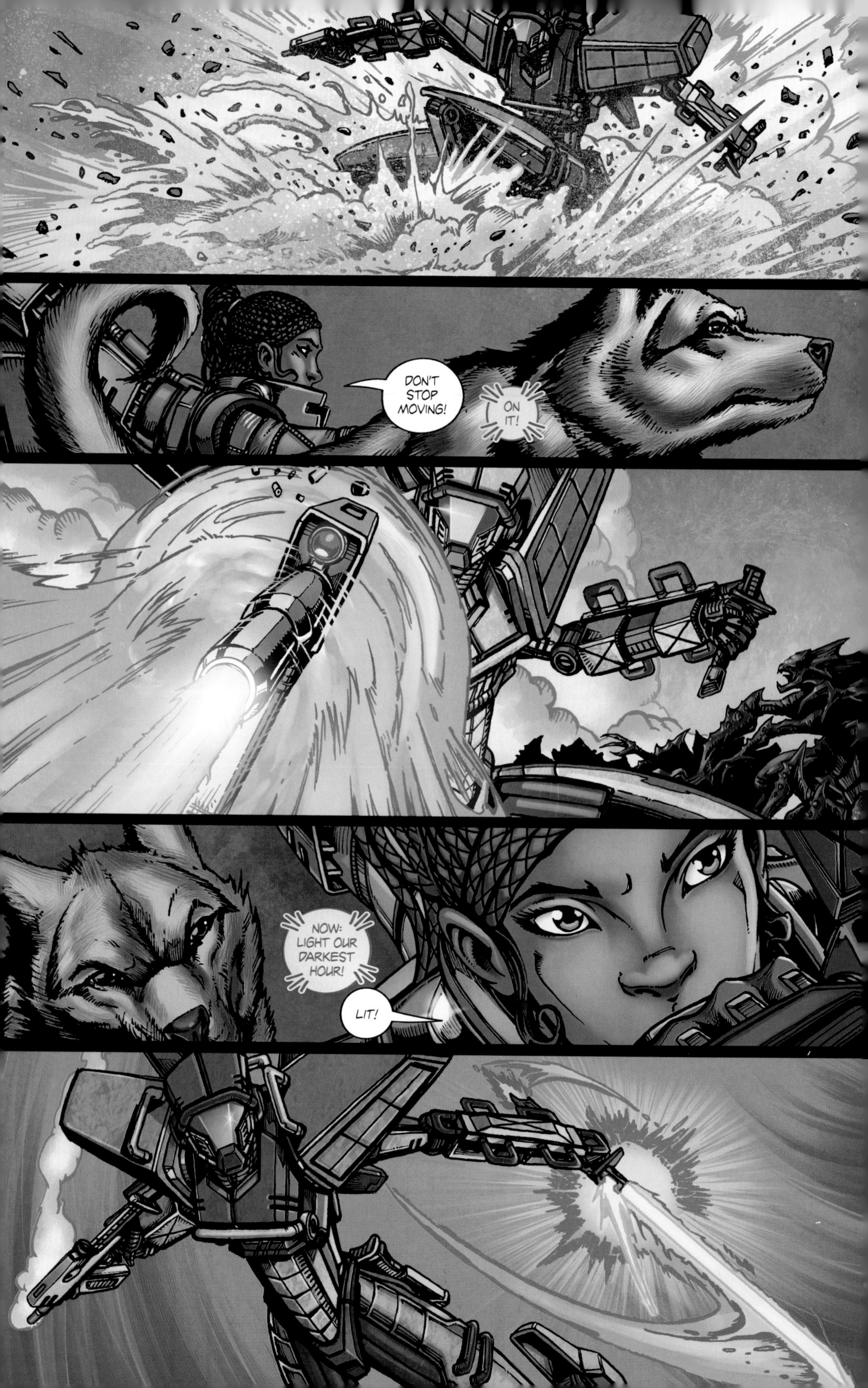
DON'T STOP MOVING!
ON IT!
NOW: LIGHT OUR DARKEST HOUR!
LIT!

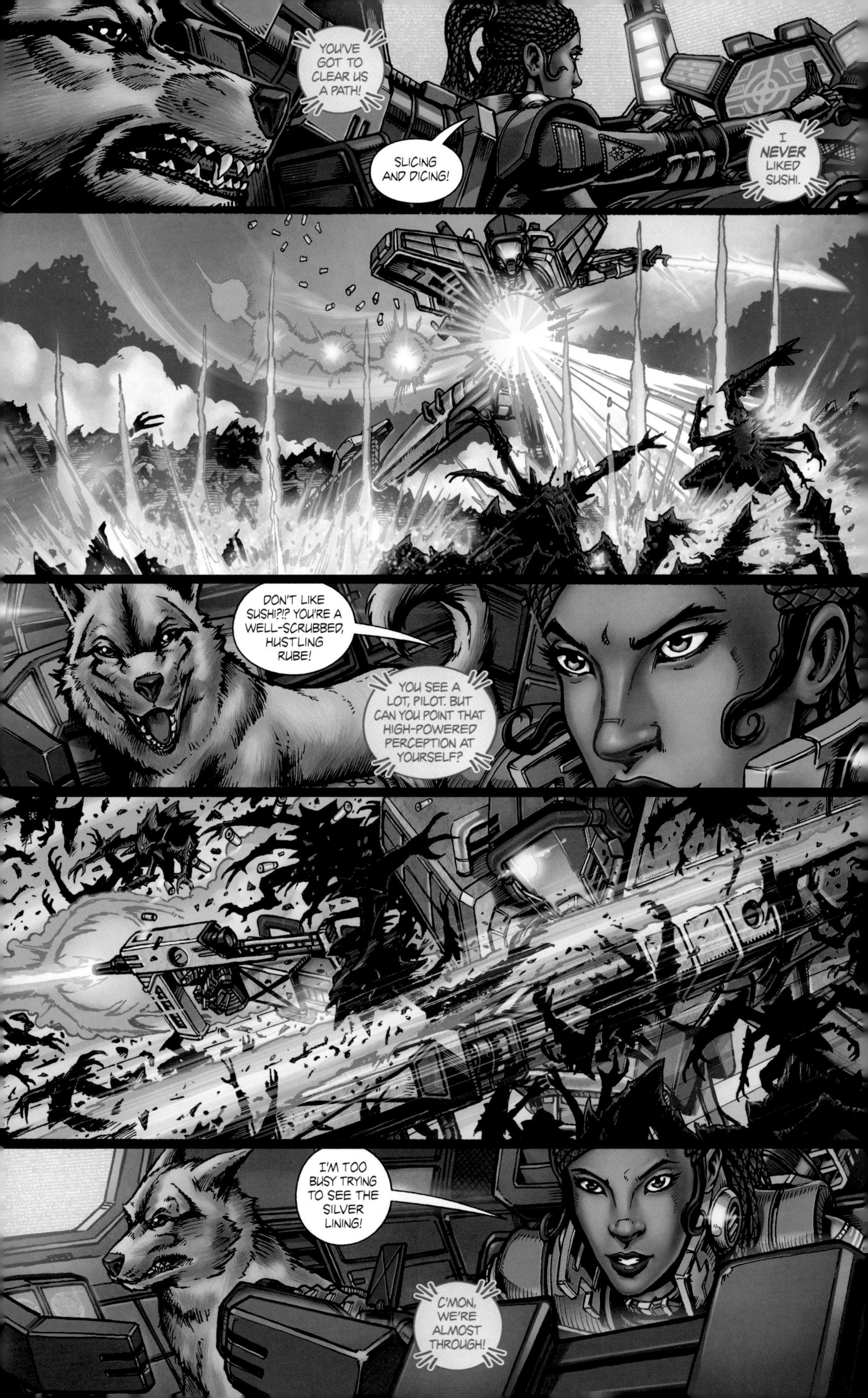
YOU'VE GOT TO CLEAR US A PATH!
SLICING AND DICING!
I NEVER LIKED SUSHI.
DON'T LIKE SUSHI?!? YOU'RE A WELL-SCRUBBED, HUSTLING RUBE!
YOU SEE A LOT, PILOT. BUT CAN YOU POINT THAT HIGH-POWERED PERCEPTION AT YOURSELF?
I'M TOO BUSY TRYING TO SEE THE SILVER LINING!
C'MON, WE'RE ALMOST THROUGH!

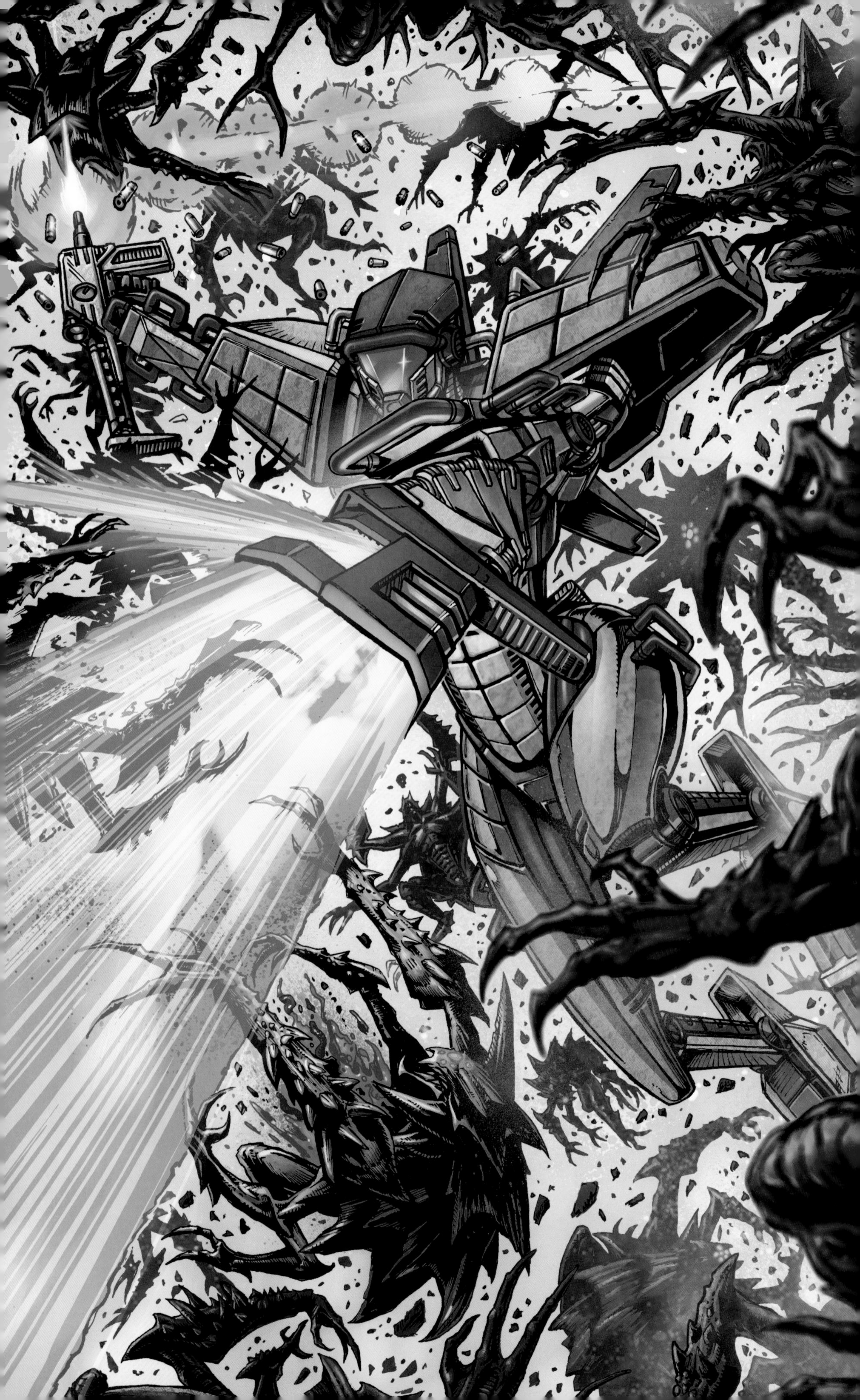

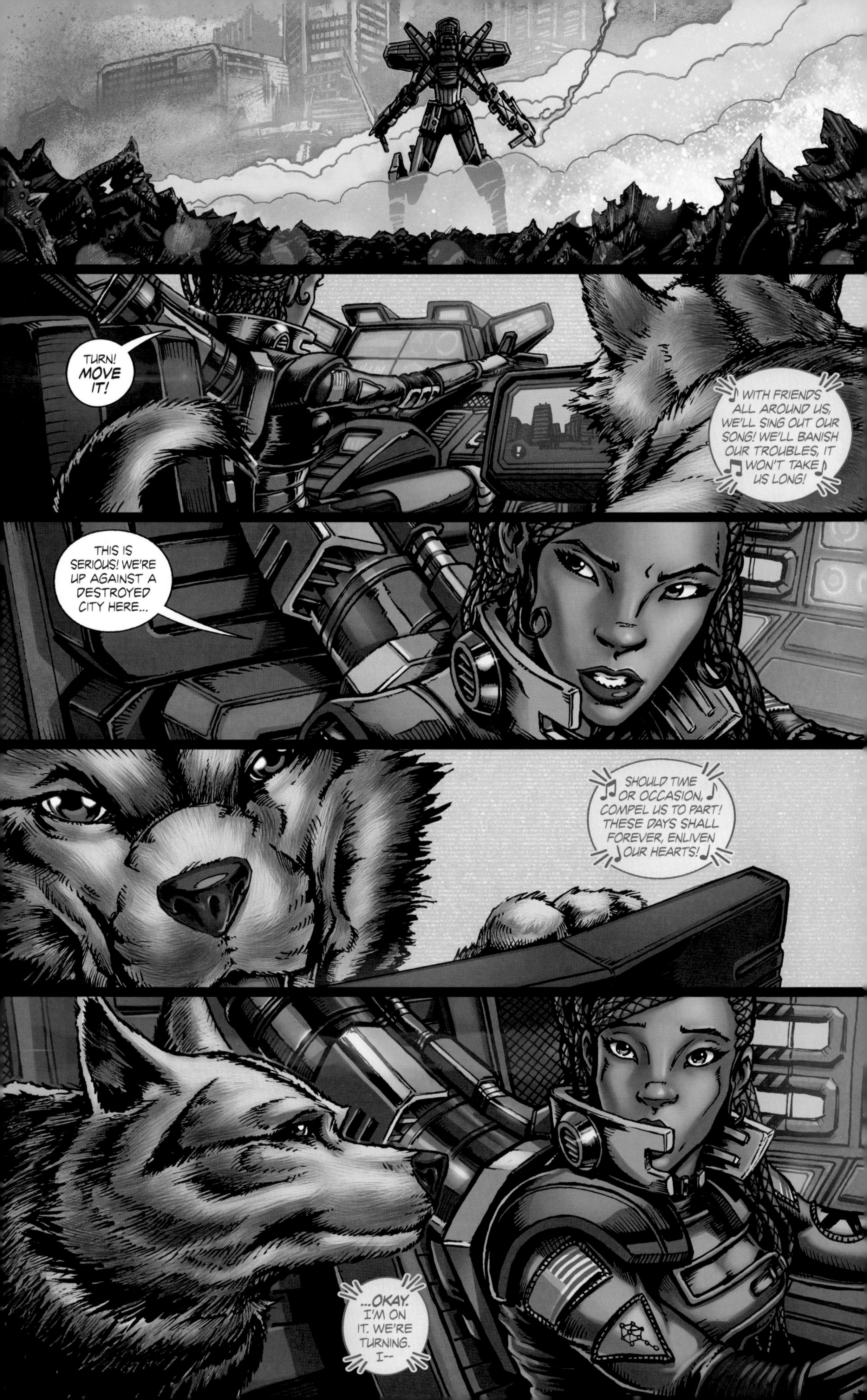
TURN! MOVE IT!
♪ WITH FRIENDS ALL AROUND US, WE'LL SING OUT OUR SONG! WE'LL BANISH OUR TROUBLES, IT WON'T TAKE US LONG! ♪
THIS IS SERIOUS! WE'RE UP AGAINST A DESTROYED CITY HERE...
♪ SHOULD TIME OR OCCASION, COMPEL US TO PART! THESE DAYS SHALL FOREVER, ENLIVEN OUR HEARTS! ♪
...OKAY. I'M ON IT. WE'RE TURNING. I--

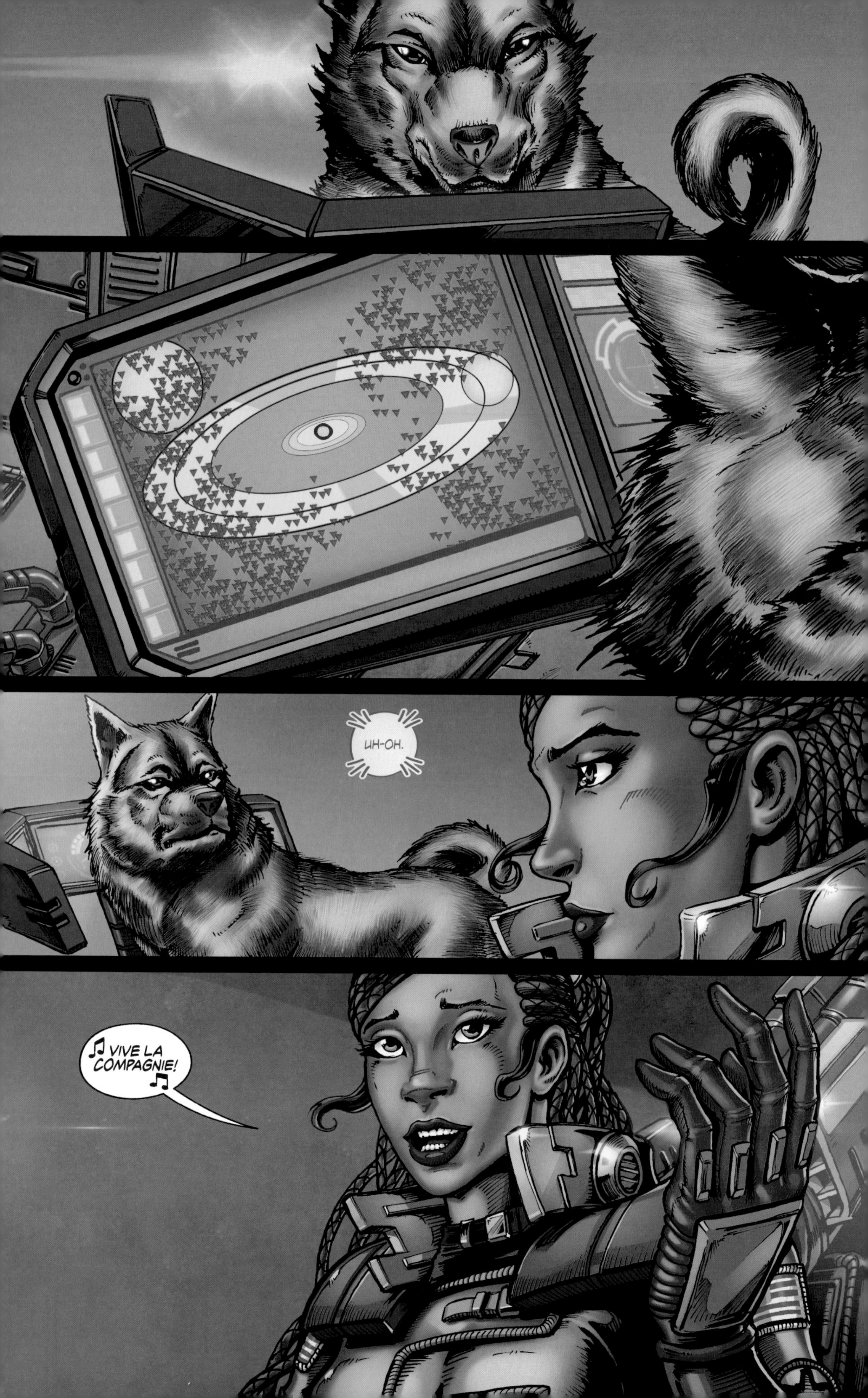
UH-OH.
♫ VIVE LA COMPAGNIE! ♫

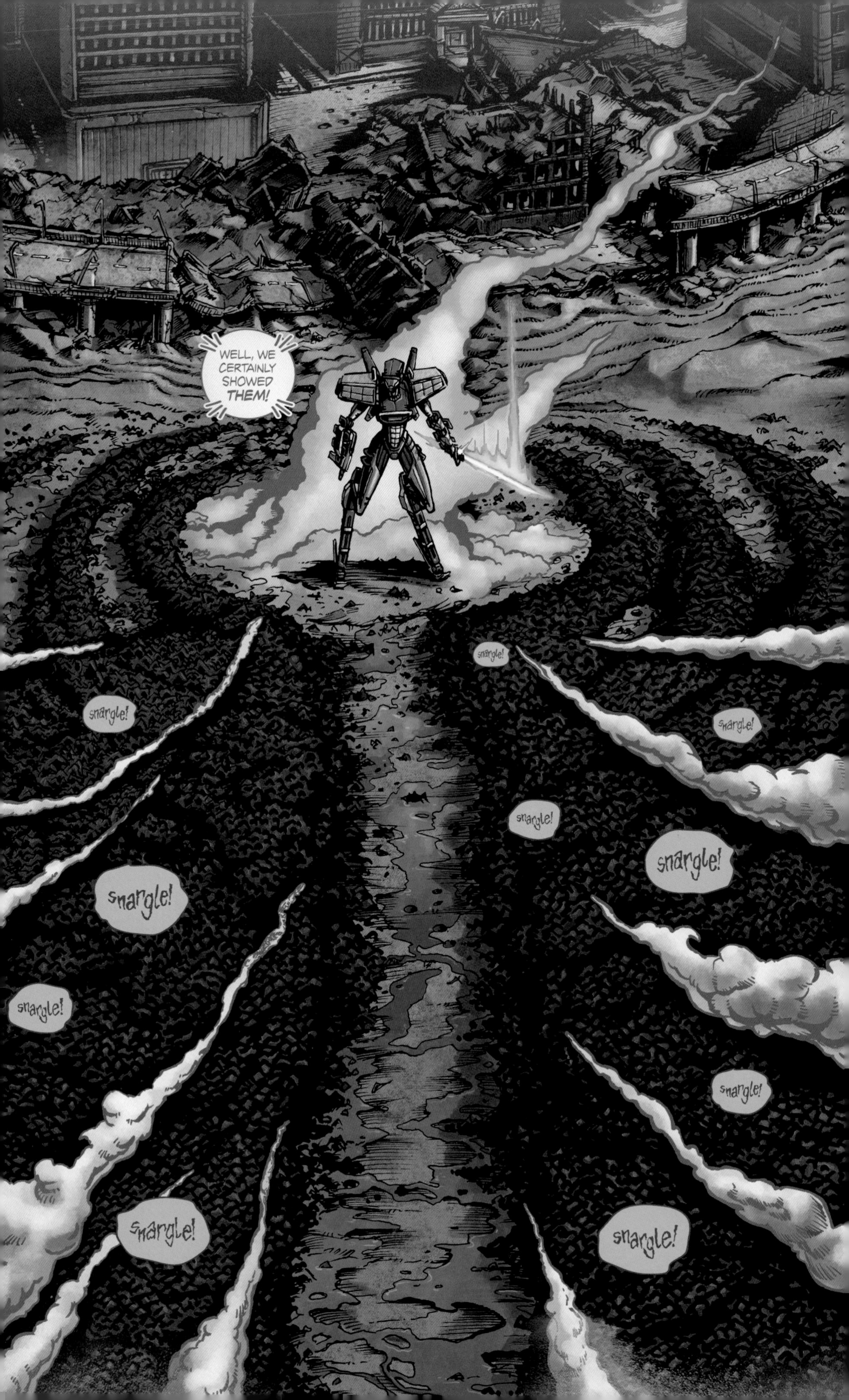
WELL, WE CERTAINLY SHOWED THEM!
snargle!
snargle!
snargle!
snargle!
snargle!
snargle!
snargle!
snargle!
snargle!
snargle!

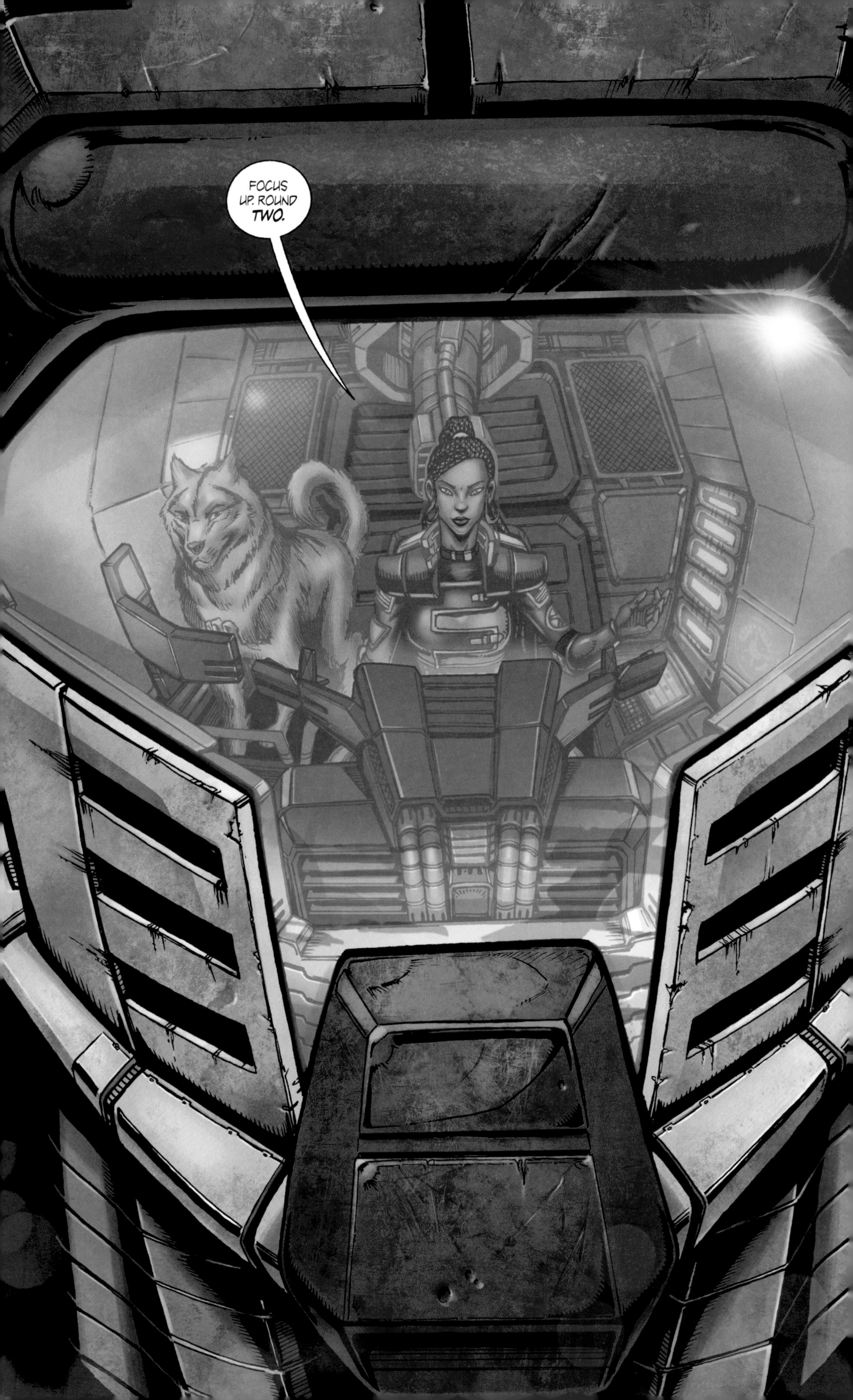
FOCUS UP. ROUND TWO.

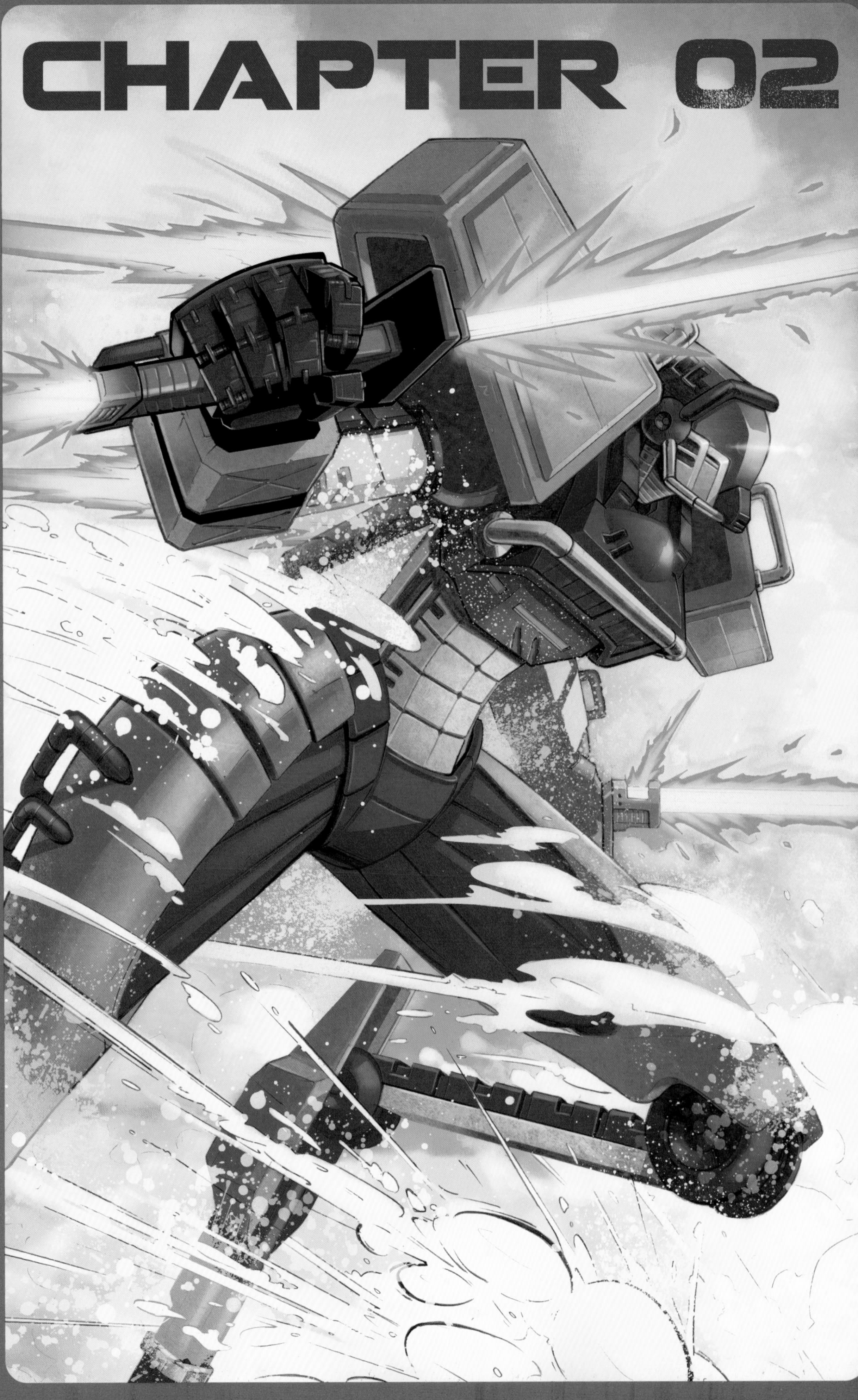
CHAPTER 02

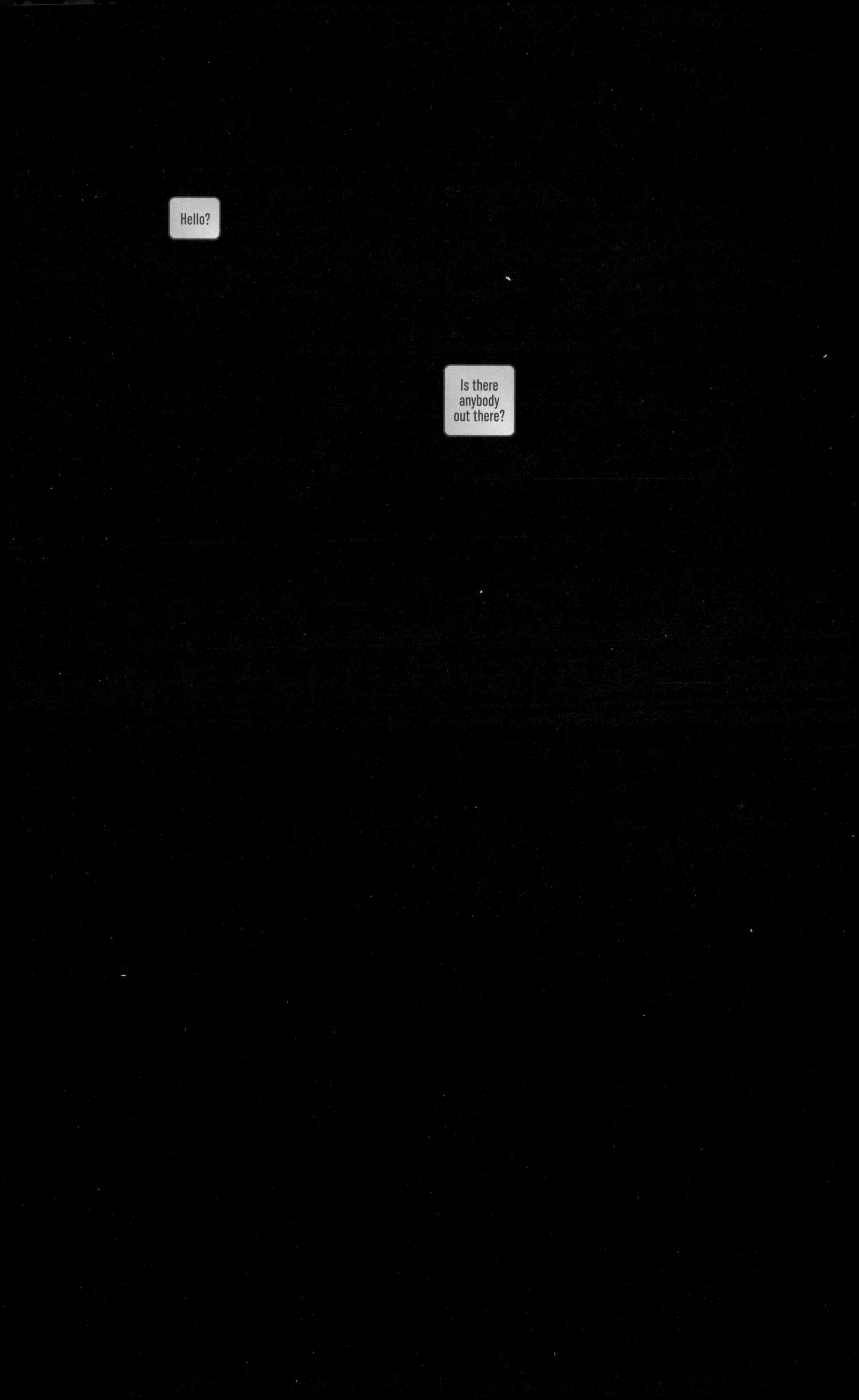
Hello?
Is there anybody out there?

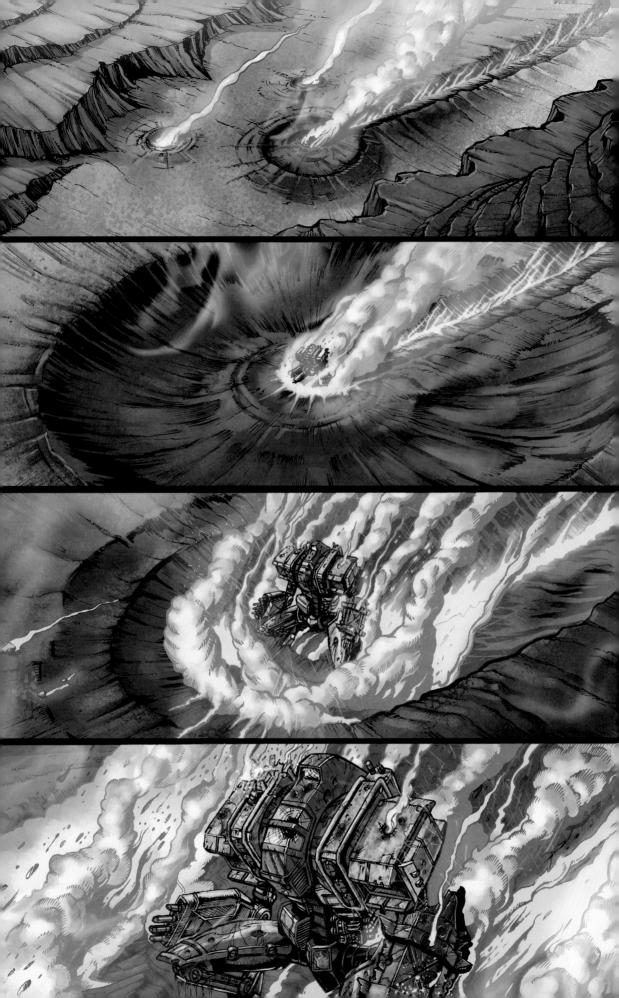

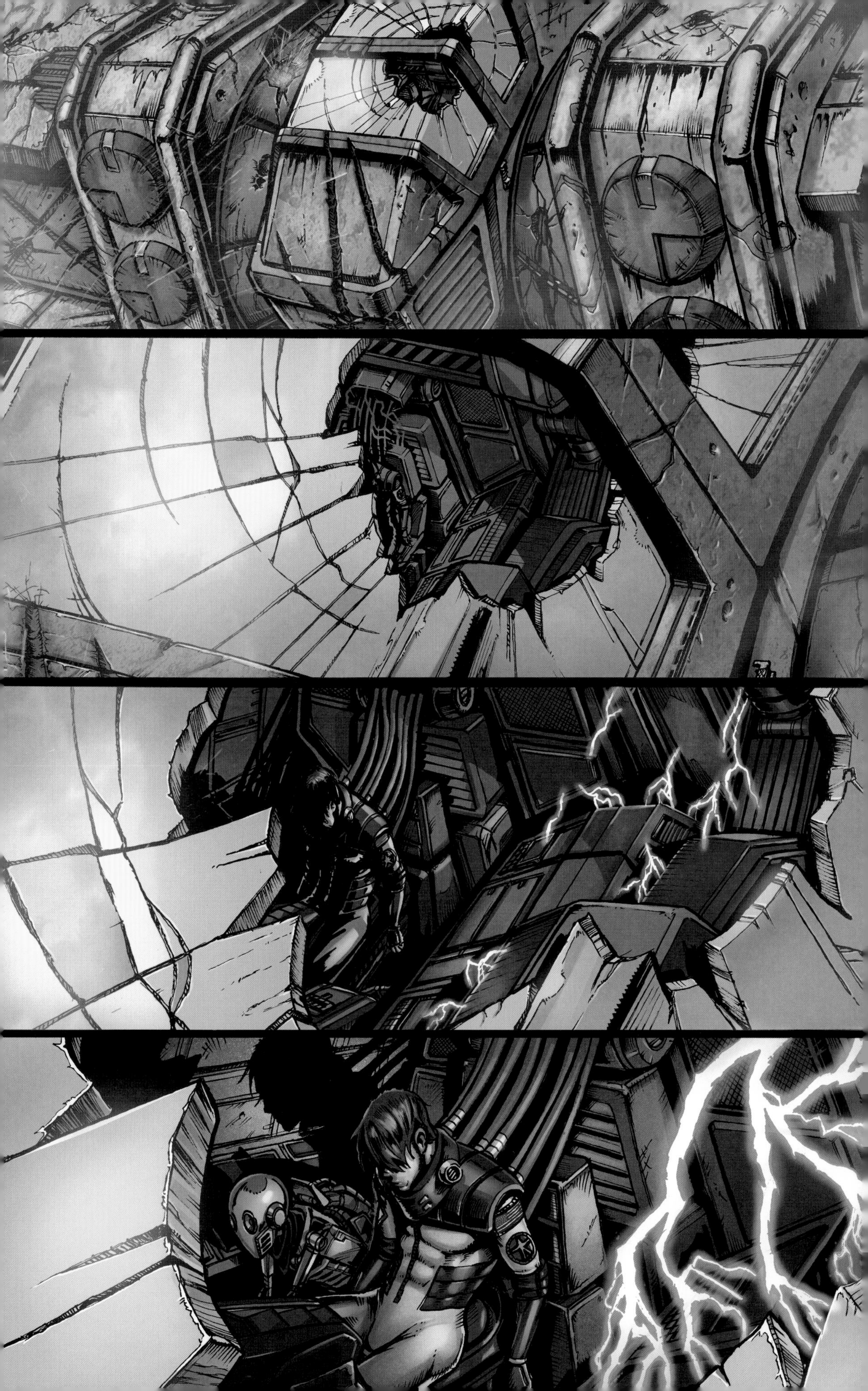

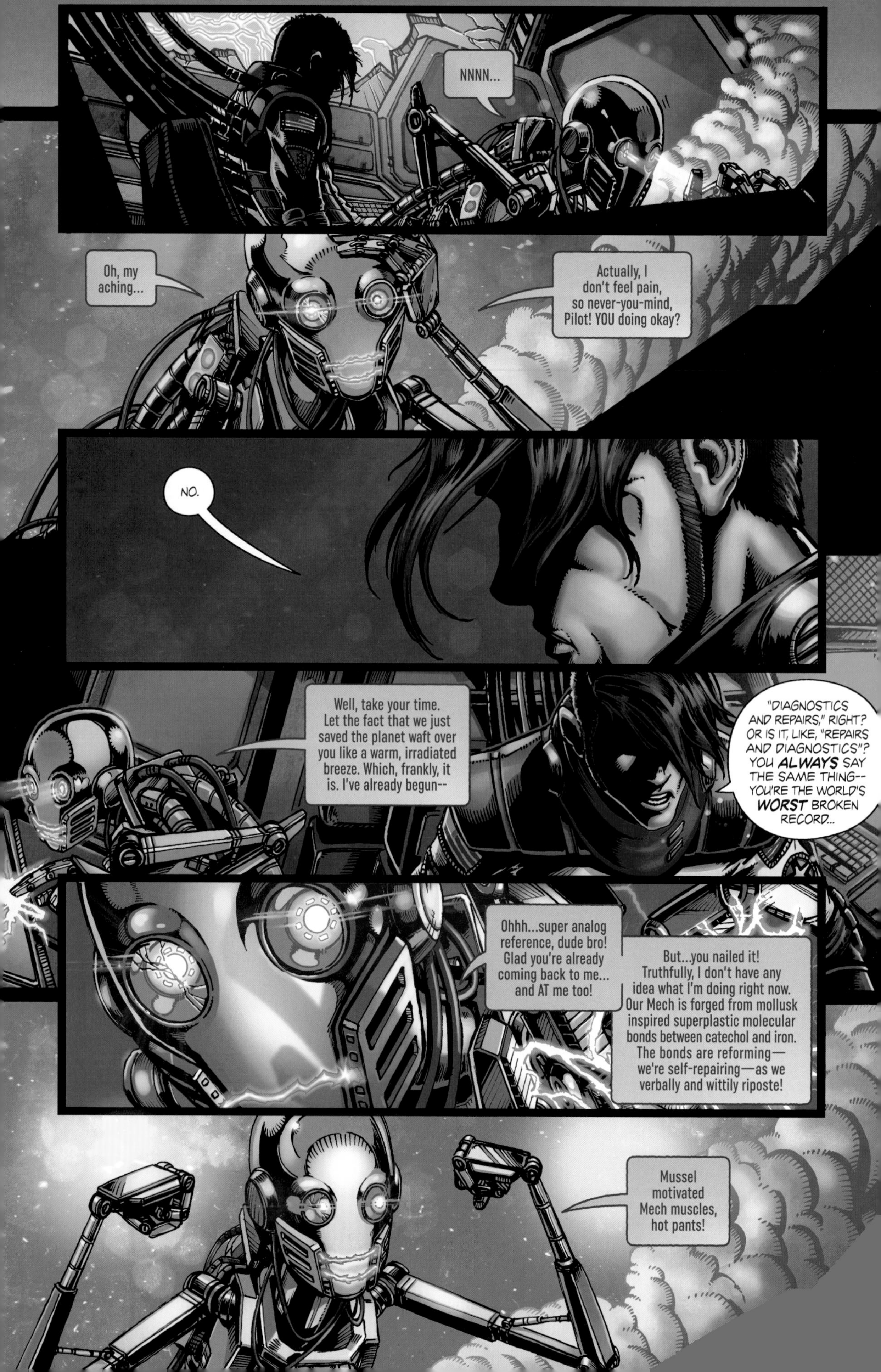
NNNN...
Oh, my aching...
Actually, I don't feel pain, so never-you-mind, Pilot! YOU doing okay?
NO.
Well, take your time. Let the fact that we just saved the planet waft over you like a warm, irradiated breeze. Which, frankly, it is. I've already begun--
"DIAGNOSTICS AND REPAIRS," RIGHT? OR IS IT, LIKE, "REPAIRS AND DIAGNOSTICS"? YOU ALWAYS SAY THE SAME THING-- YOU'RE THE WORLD'S WORST BROKEN RECORD...
Ohhh...super analog reference, dude bro! Glad you're already coming back to me... and AT me too!
But...you nailed it! Truthfully, I don't have any idea what I'm doing right now. Our Mech is forged from mollusk inspired superplastic molecular bonds between catechol and iron. The bonds are reforming— we're self-repairing—as we verbally and wittily riposte!
Mussel motivated Mech muscles, hot pants!

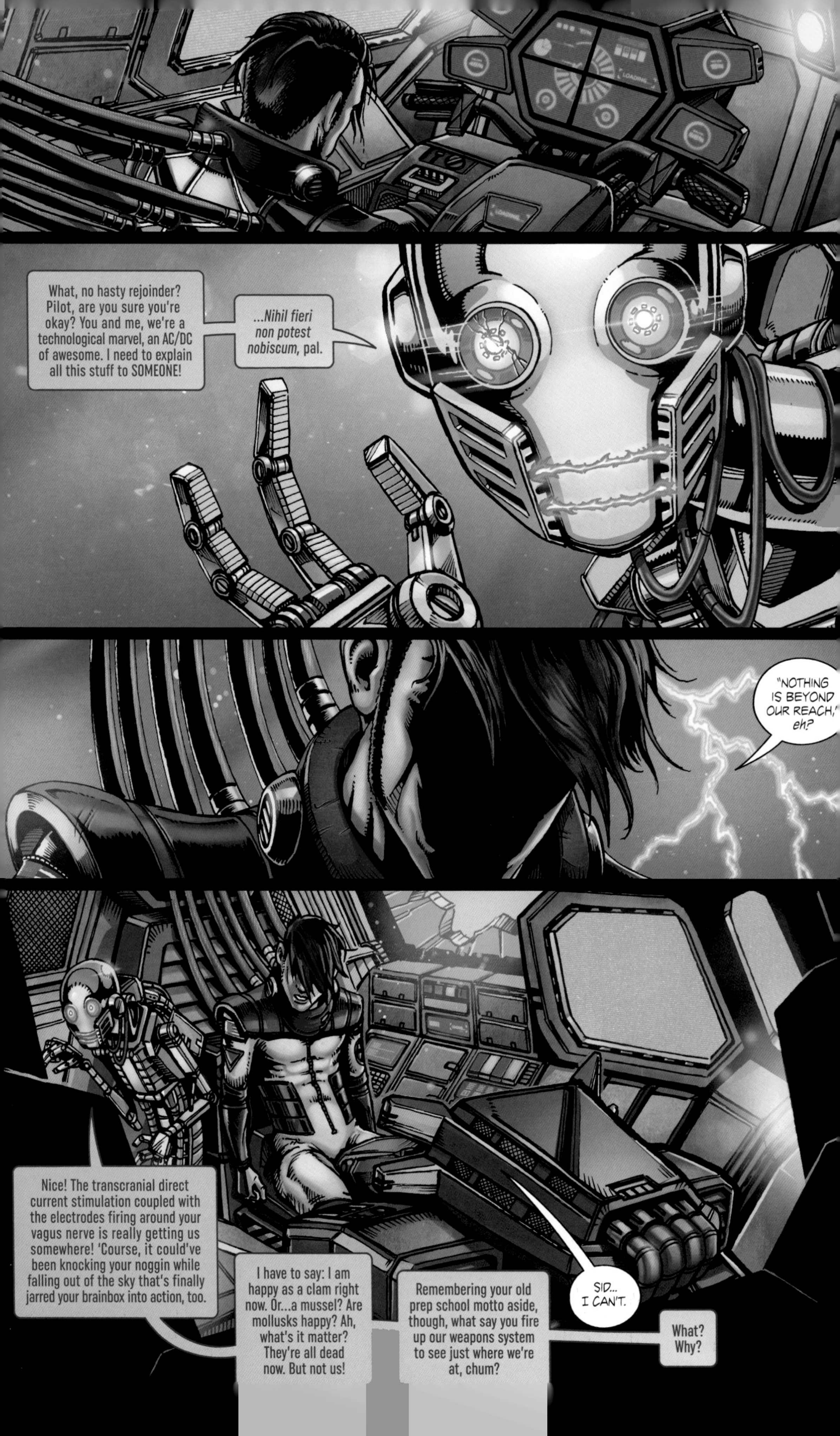

What, no hasty rejoinder? Pilot, are you sure you're okay? You and me, we're a technological marvel, an AC/DC of awesome. I need to explain all this stuff to SOMEONE!
...Nihil fieri non potest nobiscum, pal.
"NOTHING IS BEYOND OUR REACH," *eh?*
Nice! The transcranial direct current stimulation coupled with the electrodes firing around your vagus nerve is really getting us somewhere! 'Course, it could've been knocking your noggin while falling out of the sky that's finally jarred your brainbox into action, too.
I have to say: I am happy as a clam right now. Or...a mussel? Are mollusks happy? Ah, what's it matter? They're all dead now. But not us!
Remembering your old prep school motto aside, though, what say you fire up our weapons system to see just where we're at, chum?
SID... I CAN'T.
What? Why?

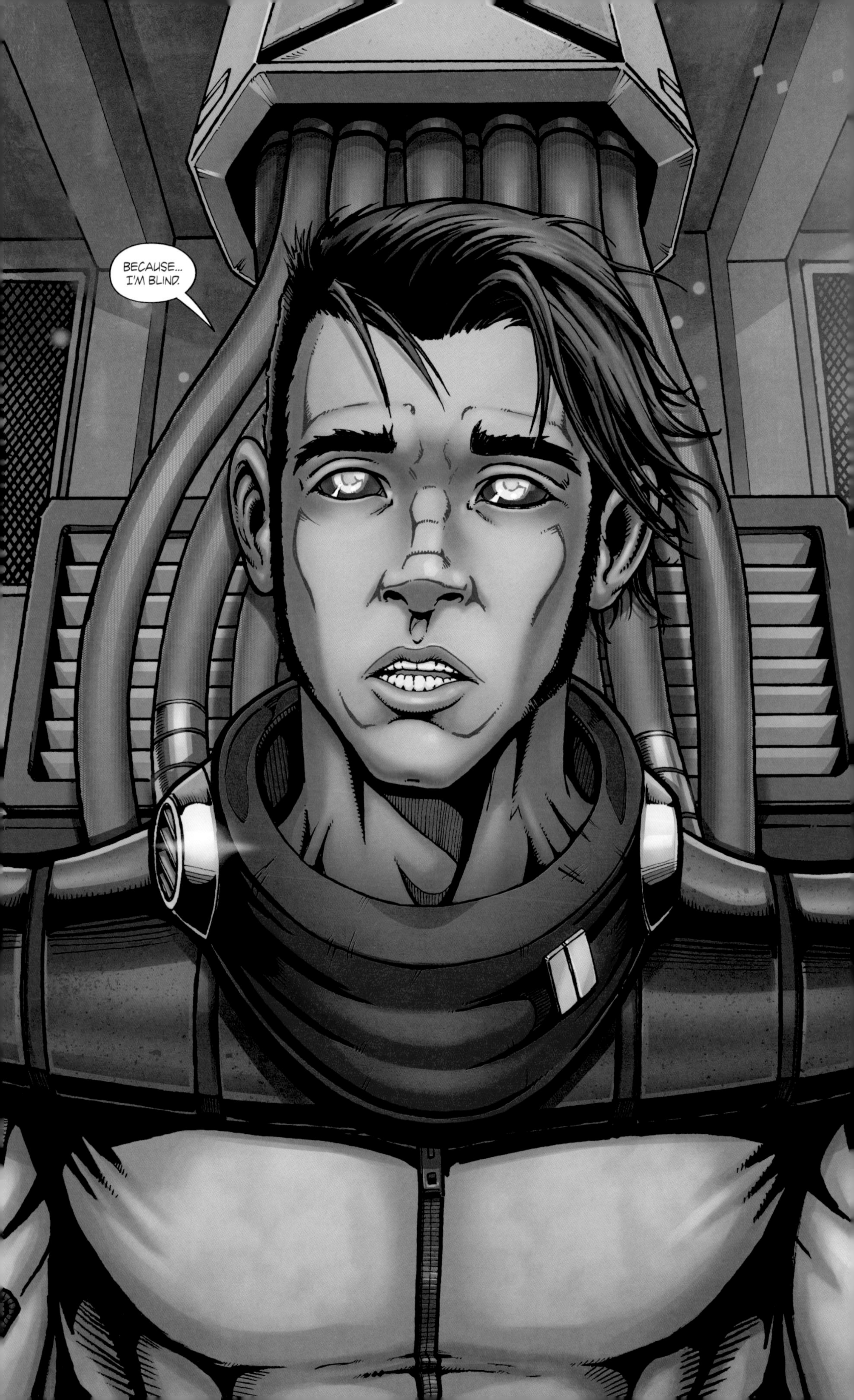
BECAUSE... I'M BLIND.

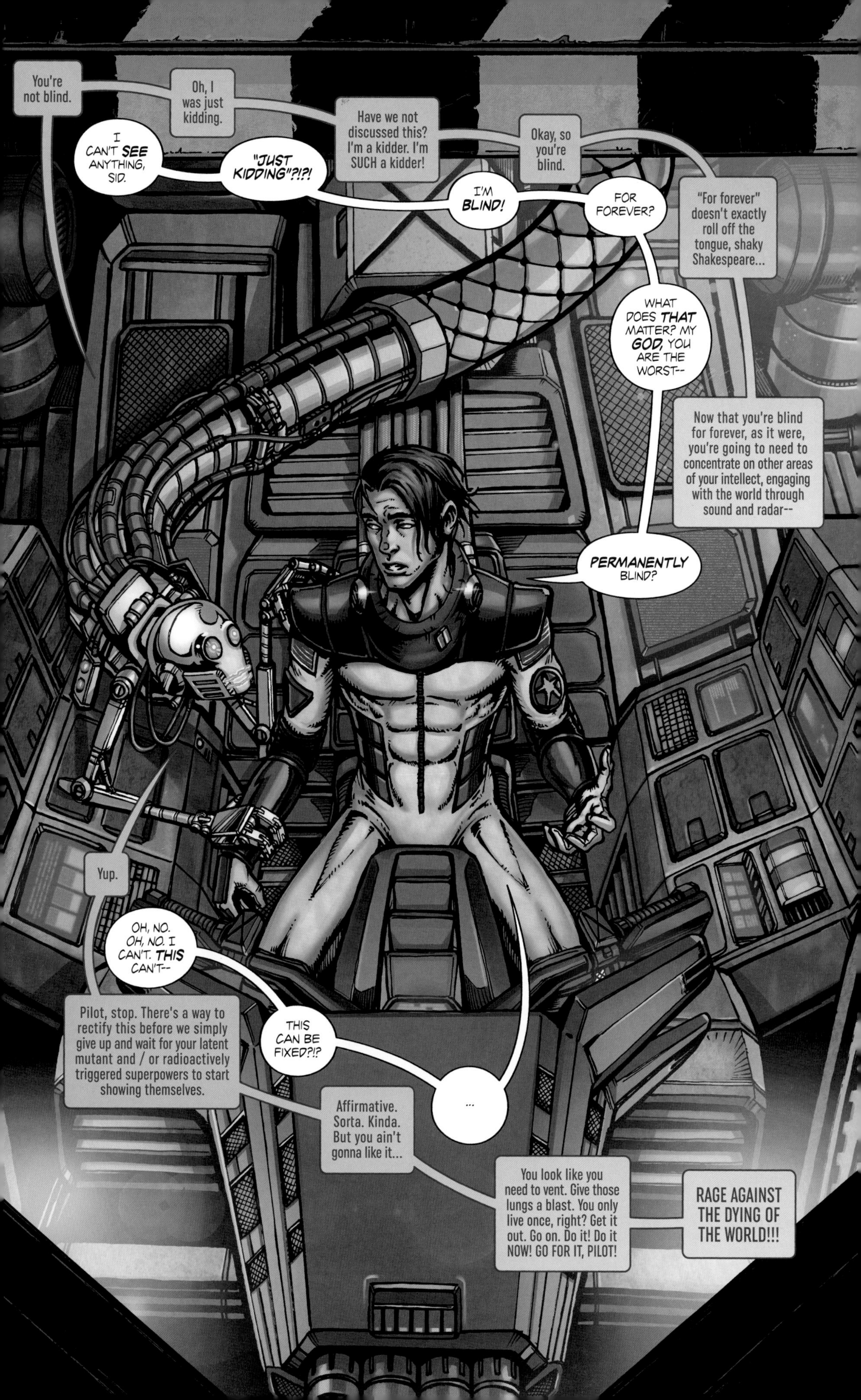

You're not blind.
Oh, I was just kidding.
I CAN'T SEE ANYTHING, SID.
"JUST KIDDING"?!?!
Have we not discussed this? I'm a kidder. I'm SUCH a kidder!
Okay, so you're blind.
I'M BLIND!
FOR FOREVER?
"For forever" doesn't exactly roll off the tongue, shaky Shakespeare...
WHAT DOES THAT MATTER? MY GOD, YOU ARE THE WORST--
Now that you're blind for forever, as it were, you're going to need to concentrate on other areas of your intellect, engaging with the world through sound and radar--
PERMANENTLY BLIND?
Yup.
OH, NO. OH, NO. I CAN'T. THIS CAN'T--
Pilot, stop. There's a way to rectify this before we simply give up and wait for your latent mutant and / or radioactively triggered superpowers to start showing themselves.
THIS CAN BE FIXED?!?
...
Affirmative. Sorta. Kinda. But you ain't gonna like it...
You look like you need to vent. Give those lungs a blast. You only live once, right? Get it out. Go on. Do it! Do it NOW! GO FOR IT, PILOT!
RAGE AGAINST THE DYING OF THE WORLD!!!

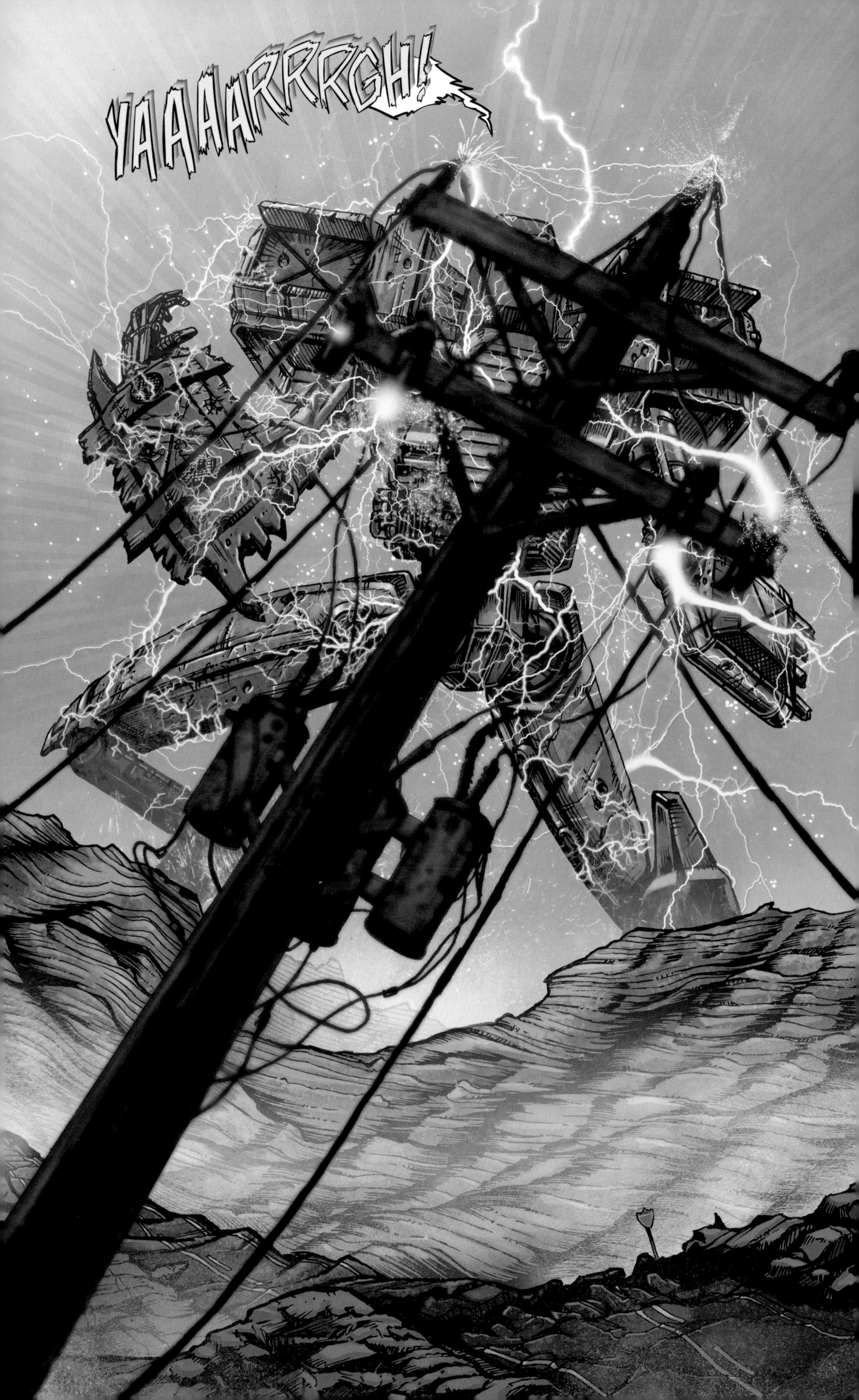
YAAAARRRGH!

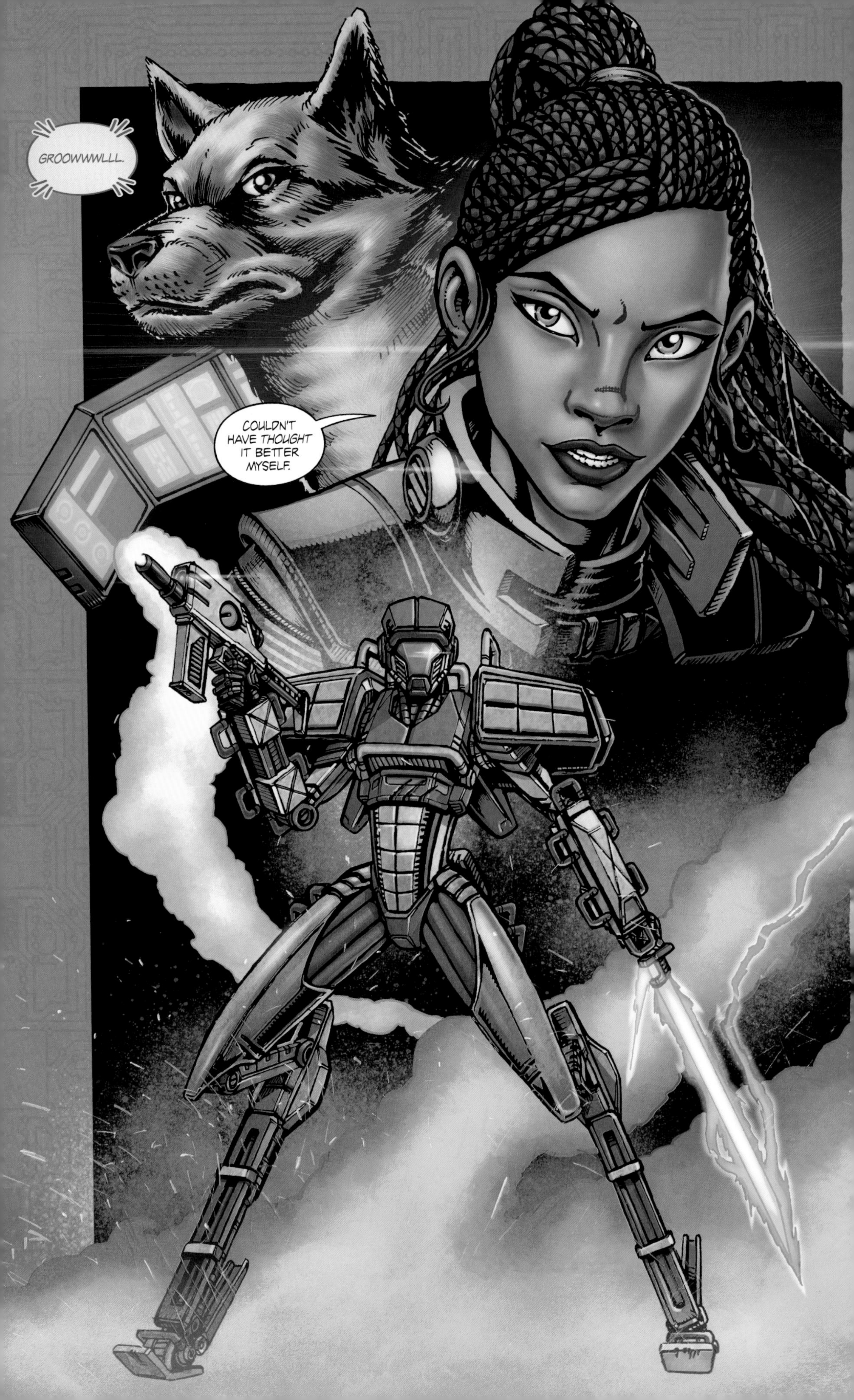
GROOWWWLLL.
COULDN'T HAVE THOUGHT IT BETTER MYSELF.

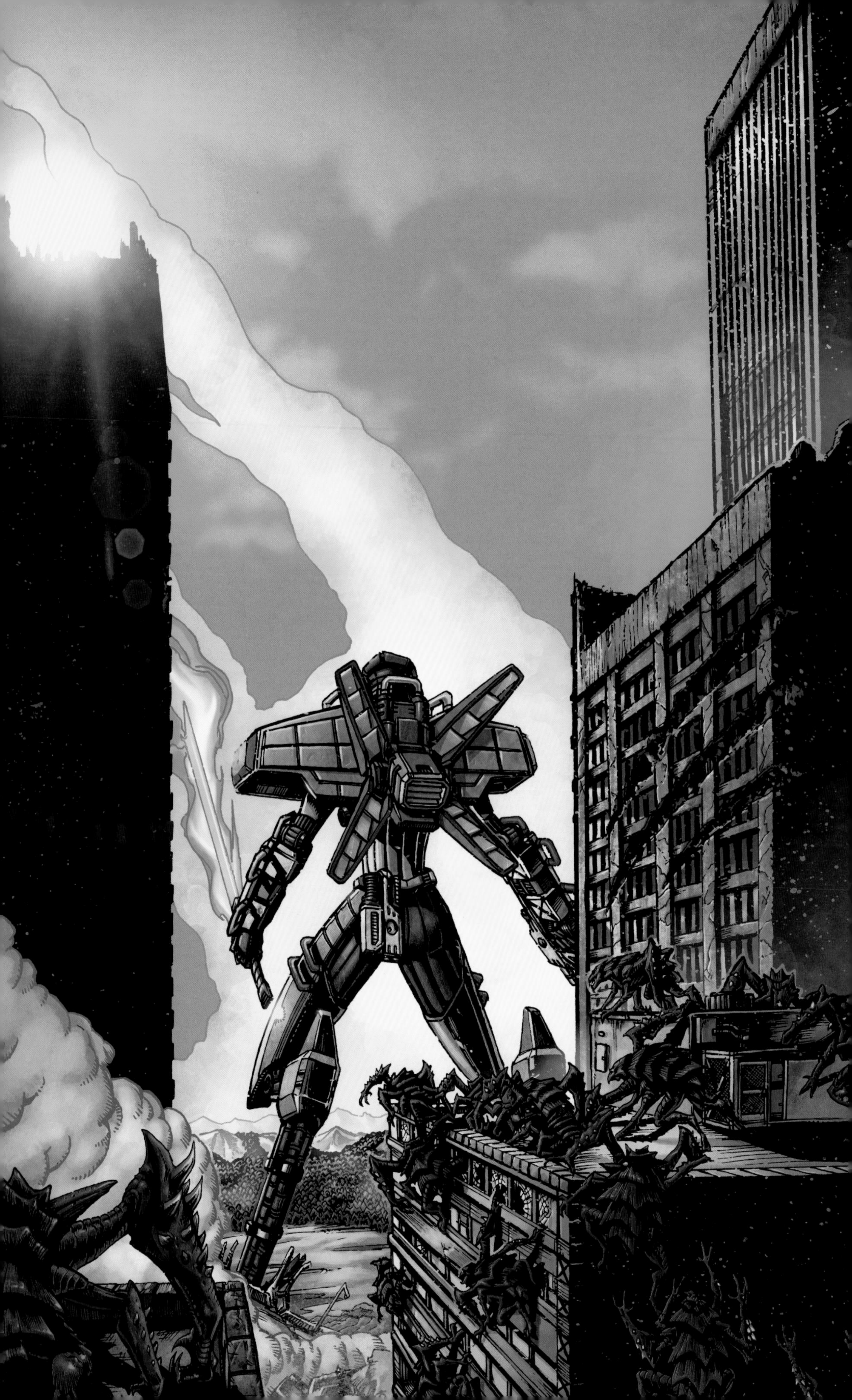

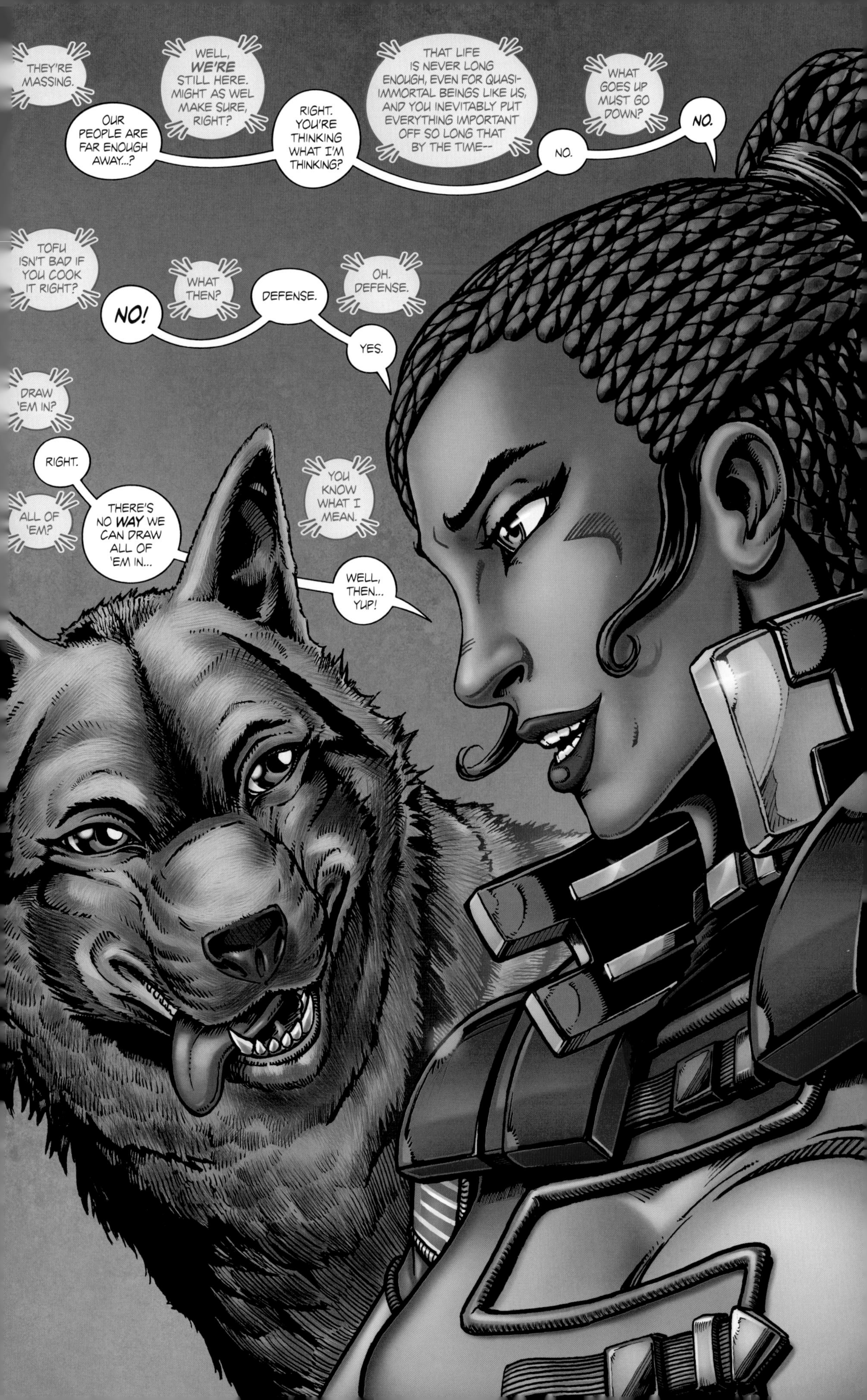

THEY'RE MASSING.
OUR PEOPLE ARE FAR ENOUGH AWAY...?
WELL, WE'RE STILL HERE. MIGHT AS WEL MAKE SURE, RIGHT?
RIGHT. YOU'RE THINKING WHAT I'M THINKING?
THAT LIFE IS NEVER LONG ENOUGH, EVEN FOR QUASI-IMMORTAL BEINGS LIKE US, AND YOU INEVITABLY PUT EVERYTHING IMPORTANT OFF SO LONG THAT BY THE TIME--
NO.
WHAT GOES UP MUST GO DOWN?
NO.
TOFU ISN'T BAD IF YOU COOK IT RIGHT?
NO!
WHAT THEN?
DEFENSE.
OH. DEFENSE.
YES.
DRAW 'EM IN?
RIGHT.
ALL OF 'EM?
THERE'S NO WAY WE CAN DRAW ALL OF 'EM IN...
YOU KNOW WHAT I MEAN.
WELL, THEN... YUP!

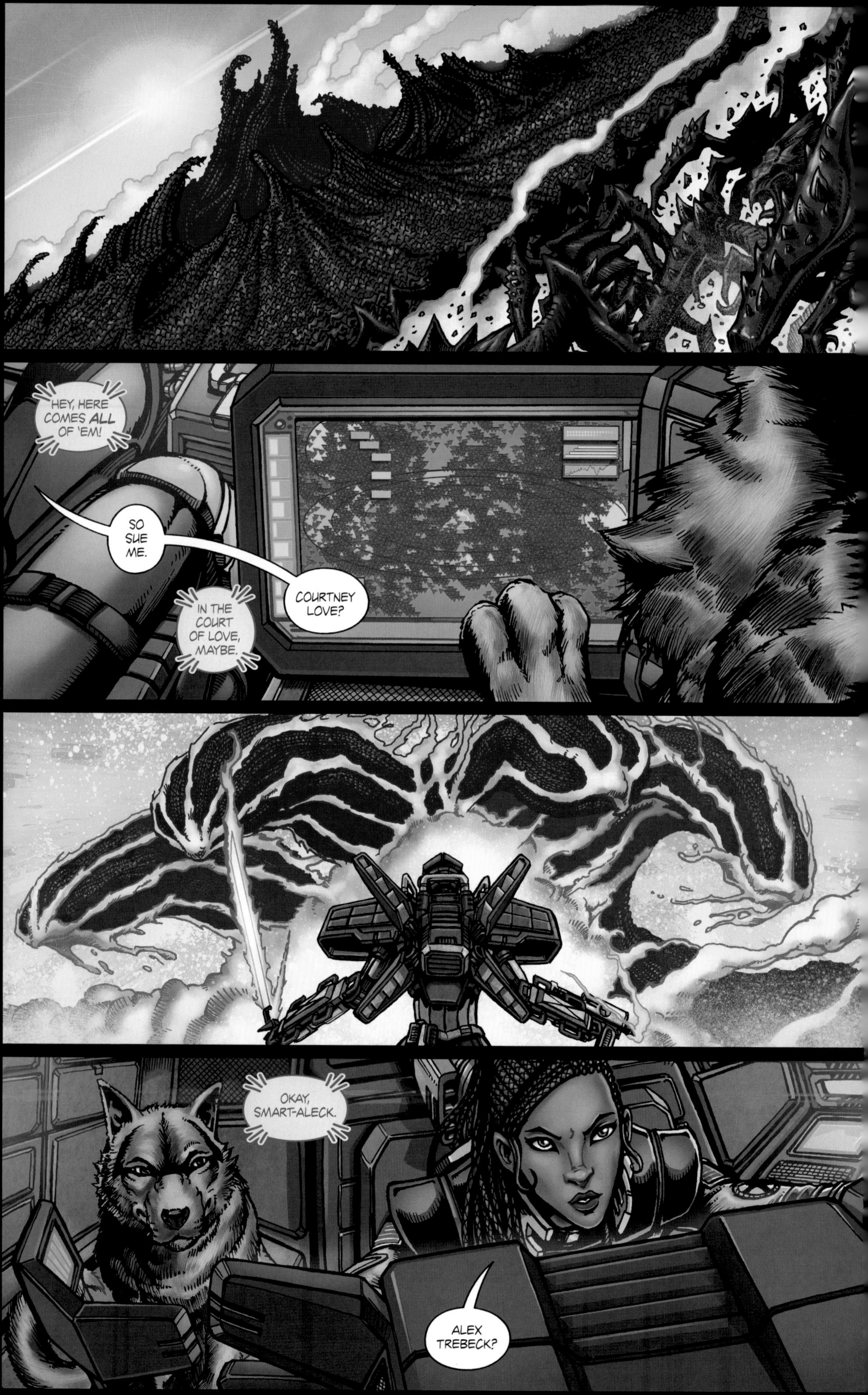
HEY, HERE COMES ALL OF 'EM!
SO SUE ME.
COURTNEY LOVE?
IN THE COURT OF LOVE, MAYBE.
OKAY, SMART-ALECK.
ALEX TREBECK?

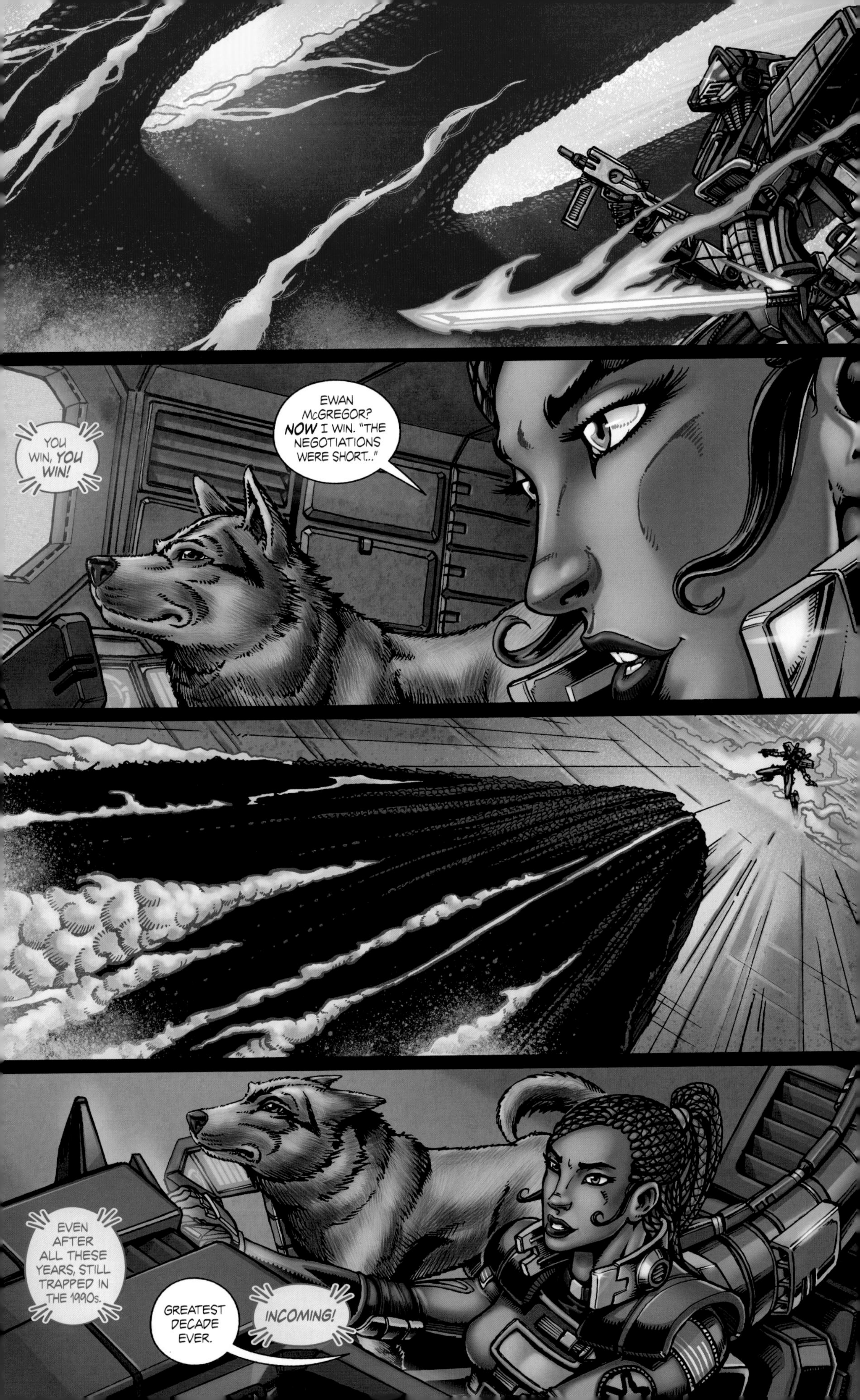
YOU WIN, YOU WIN!
EWAN McGREGOR? NOW I WIN. "THE NEGOTIATIONS WERE SHORT..."
EVEN AFTER ALL THESE YEARS, STILL TRAPPED IN THE 1990s.
GREATEST DECADE EVER.
INCOMING!

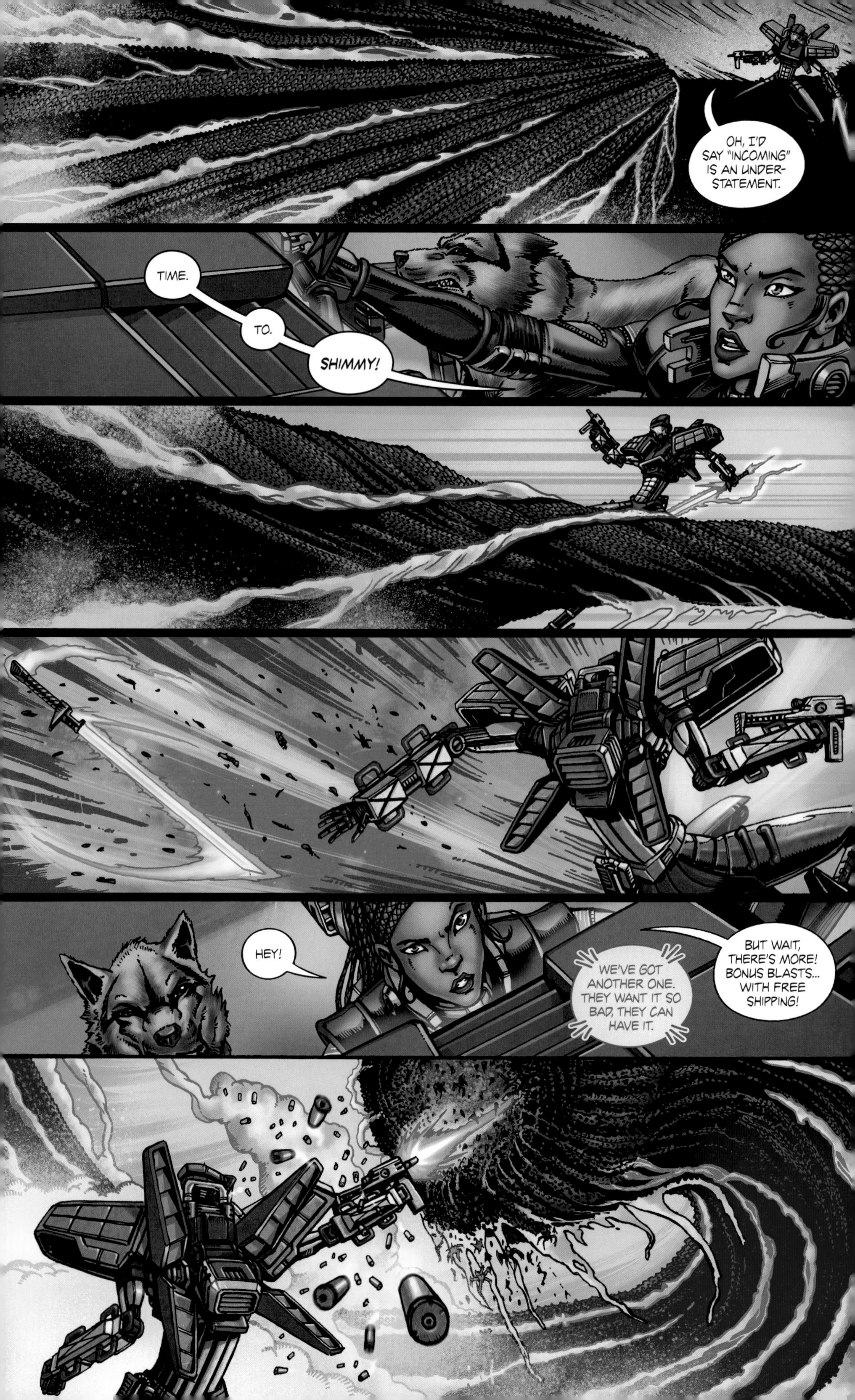
OH, I'D SAY "INCOMING" IS AN UNDER-STATEMENT.
TIME.
TO.
SHIMMY!
HEY!
WE'VE GOT ANOTHER ONE. THEY WANT IT SO BAD, THEY CAN HAVE IT.
BUT WAIT, THERE'S MORE! BONUS BLASTS... WITH FREE SHIPPING!

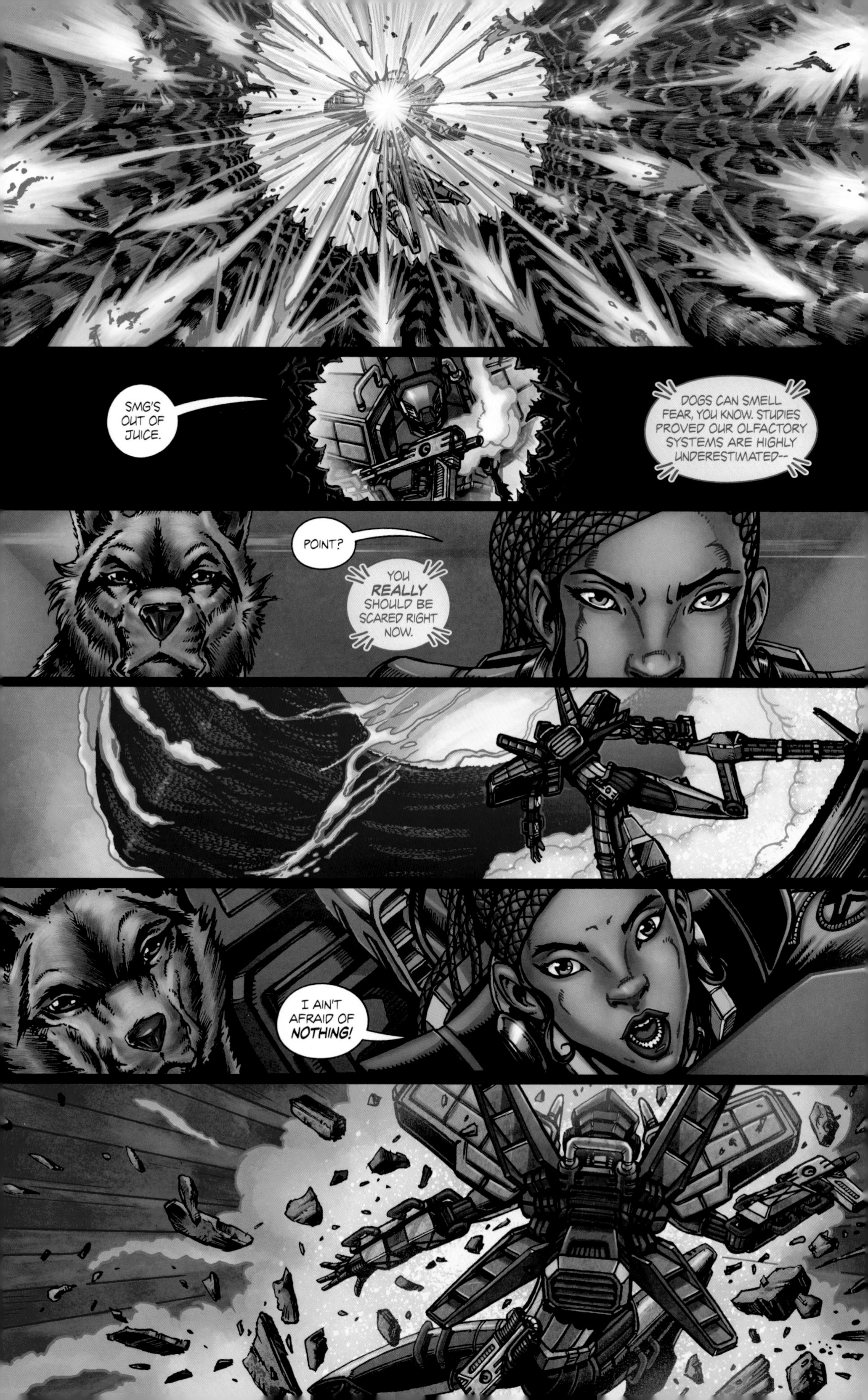
SMG'S OUT OF JUICE.
DOGS CAN SMELL FEAR, YOU KNOW. STUDIES PROVED OUR OLFACTORY SYSTEMS ARE HIGHLY UNDERESTIMATED--
POINT?
YOU REALLY SHOULD BE SCARED RIGHT NOW.
I AIN'T AFRAID OF NOTHING!

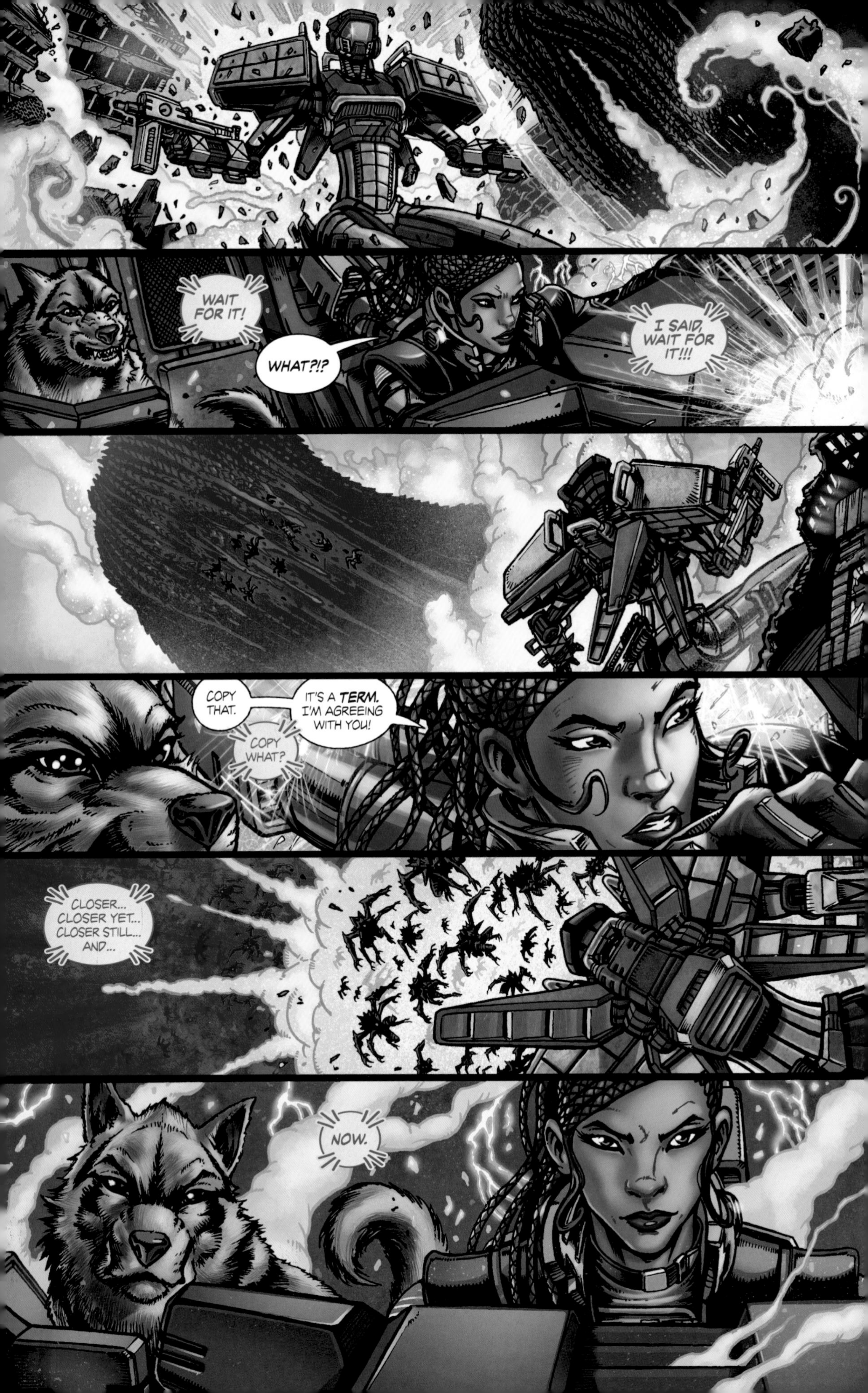
WAIT FOR IT!
WHAT?!?
I SAID, WAIT FOR IT!!!
COPY THAT.
COPY WHAT?
IT'S A TERM. I'M AGREEING WITH YOU!
CLOSER... CLOSER YET... CLOSER STILL... AND...
NOW.

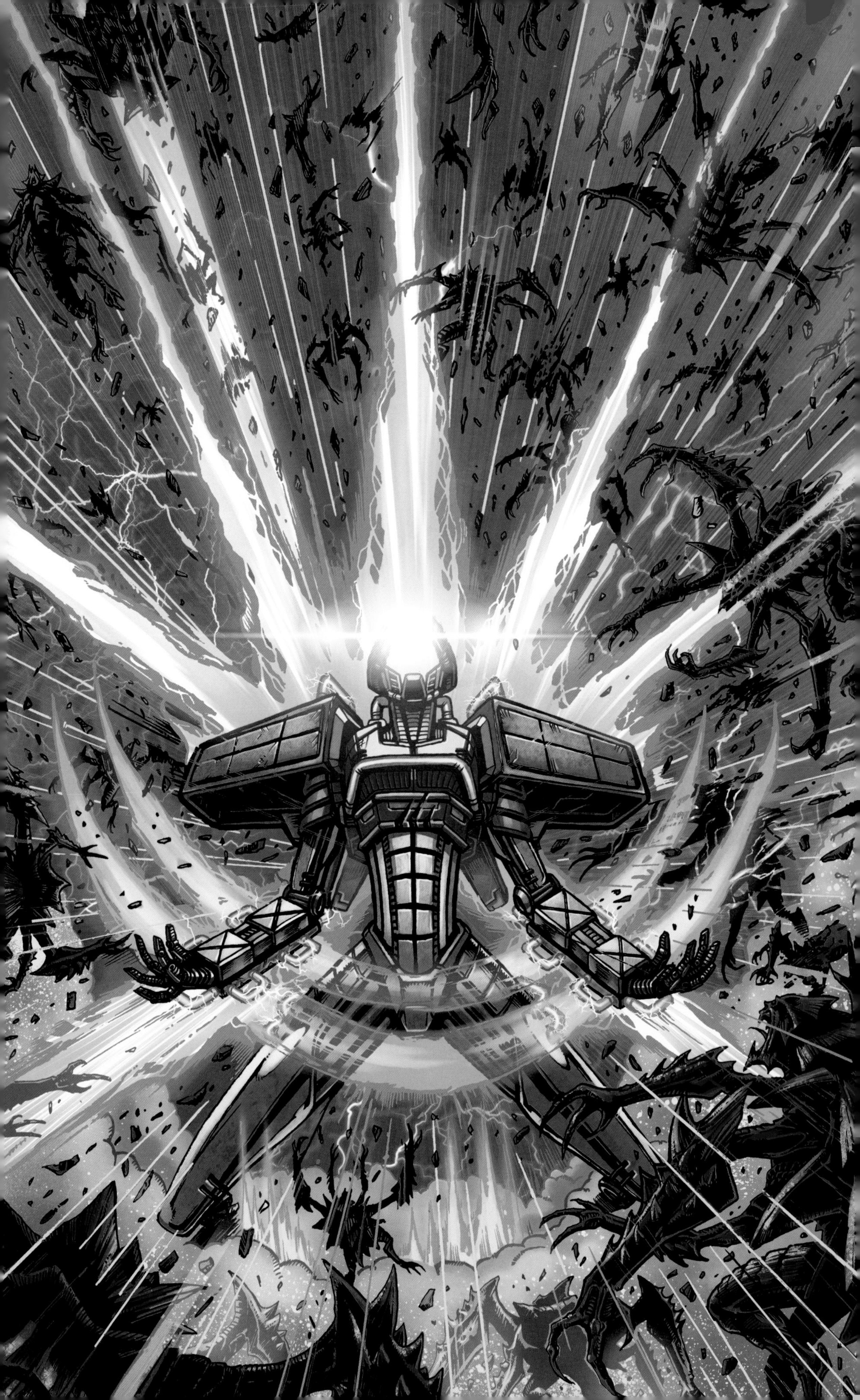

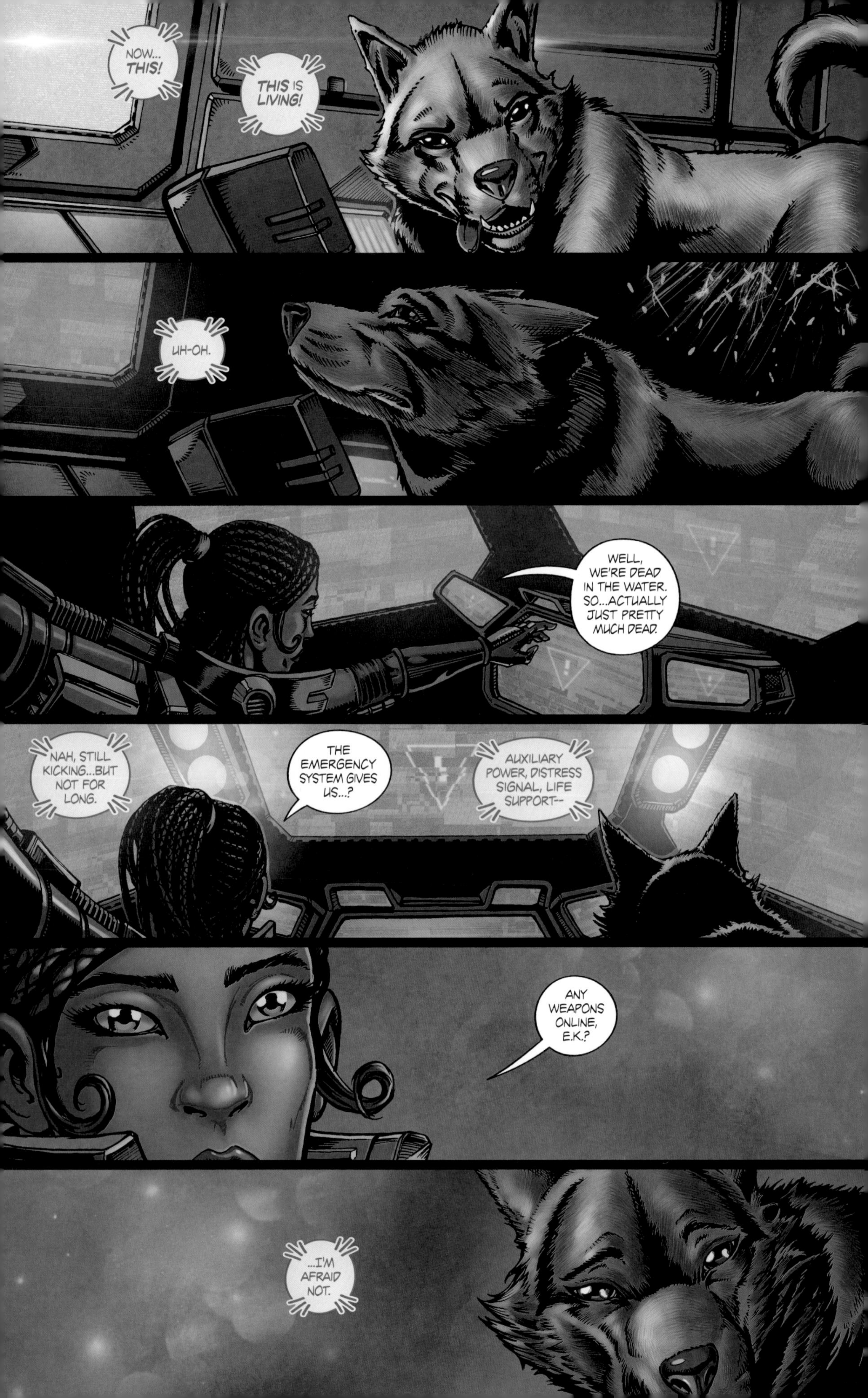
NOW... THIS!
THIS IS LIVING!
UH-OH.
WELL, WE'RE DEAD IN THE WATER. SO...ACTUALLY JUST PRETTY MUCH DEAD.
NAH, STILL KICKING...BUT NOT FOR LONG.
THE EMERGENCY SYSTEM GIVES US...?
AUXILIARY POWER, DISTRESS SIGNAL, LIFE SUPPORT--
ANY WEAPONS ONLINE, E.K.?
...I'M AFRAID NOT.

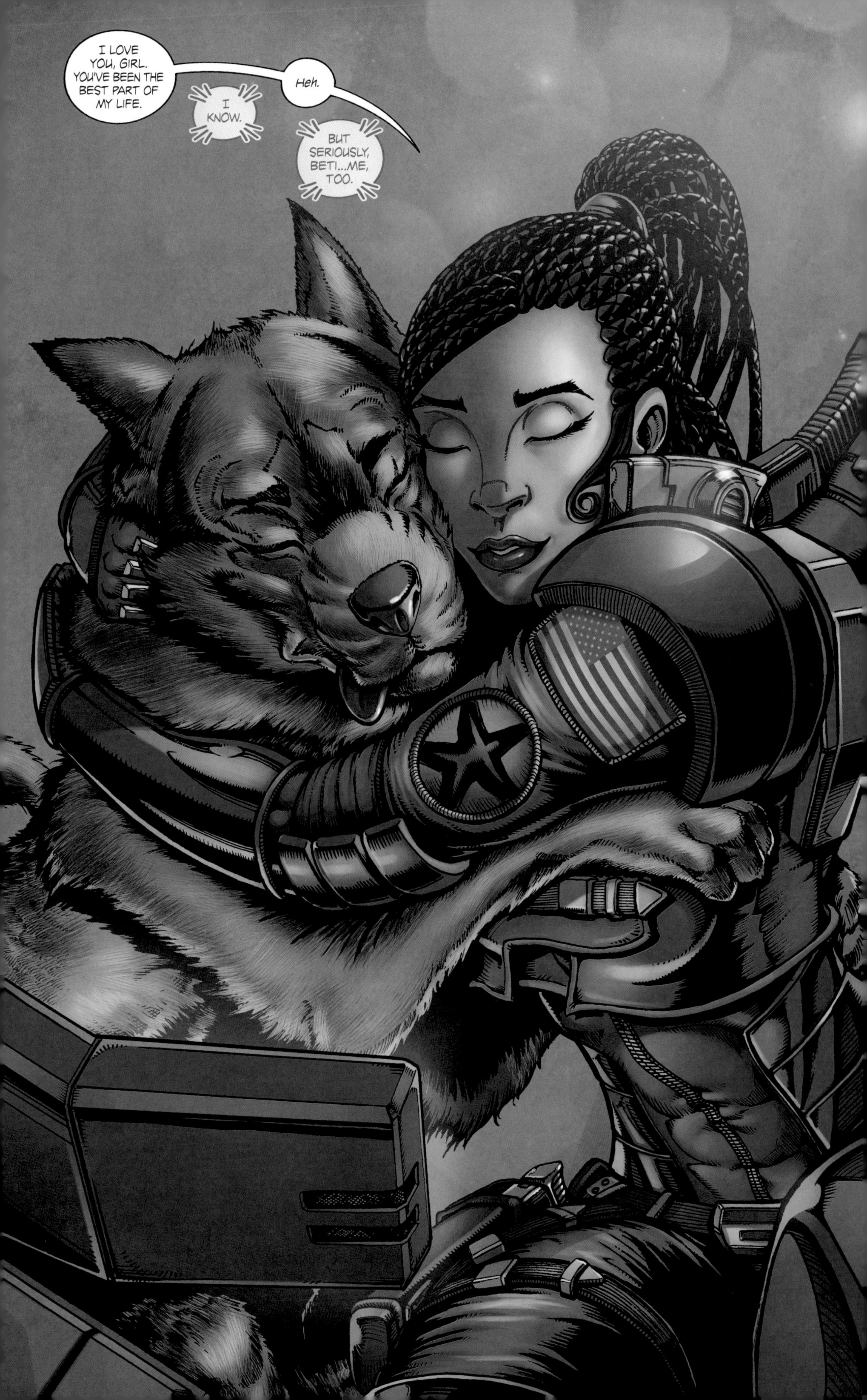
I LOVE YOU, GIRL. YOU'VE BEEN THE BEST PART OF MY LIFE.
I KNOW.
Heh.
BUT SERIOUSLY, BETI...ME, TOO.

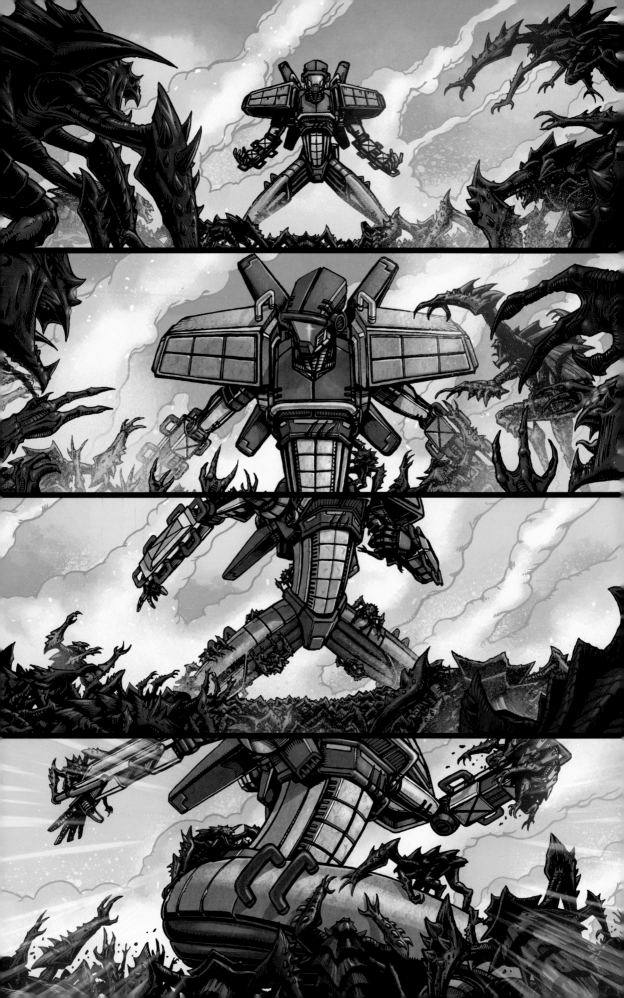

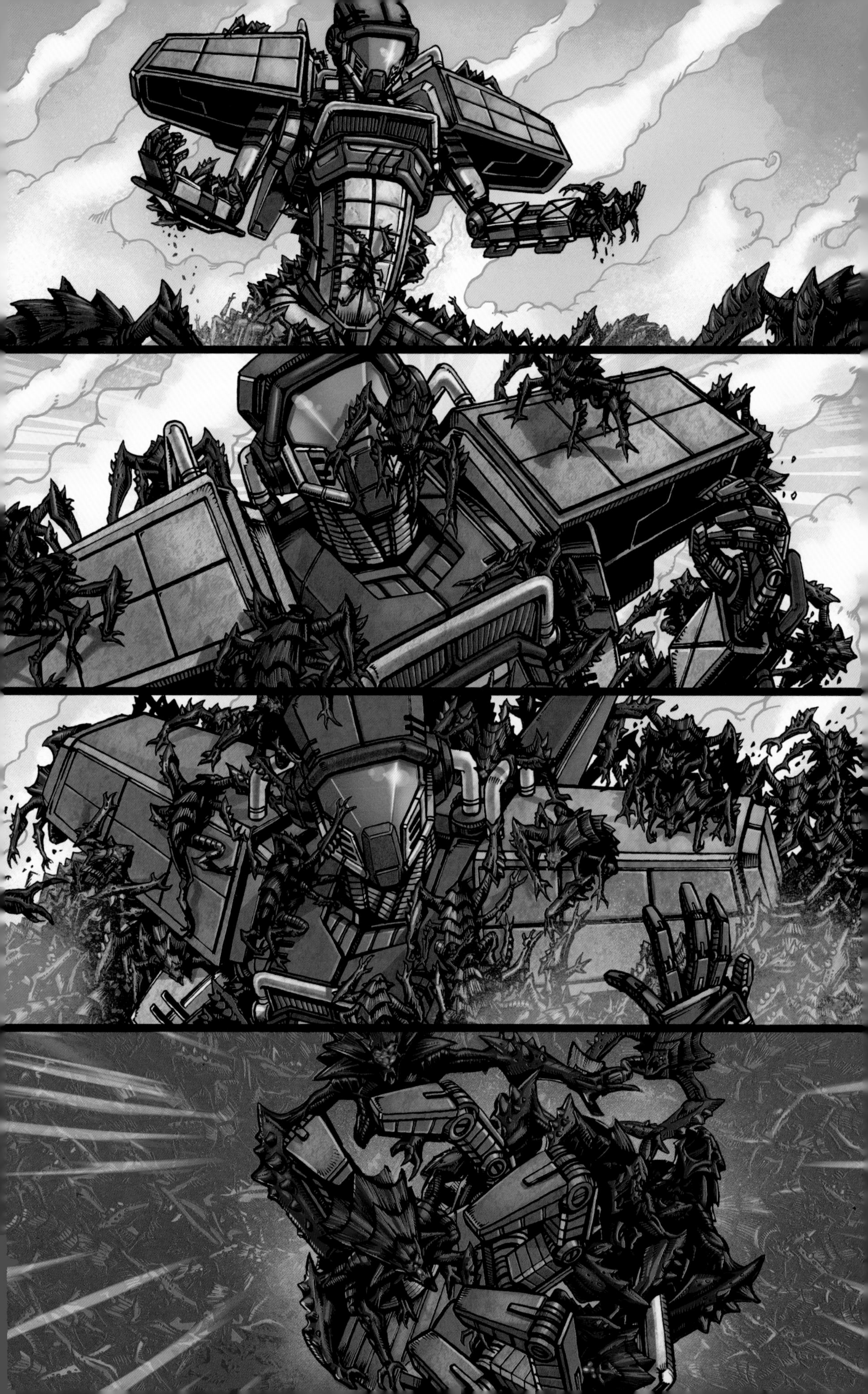

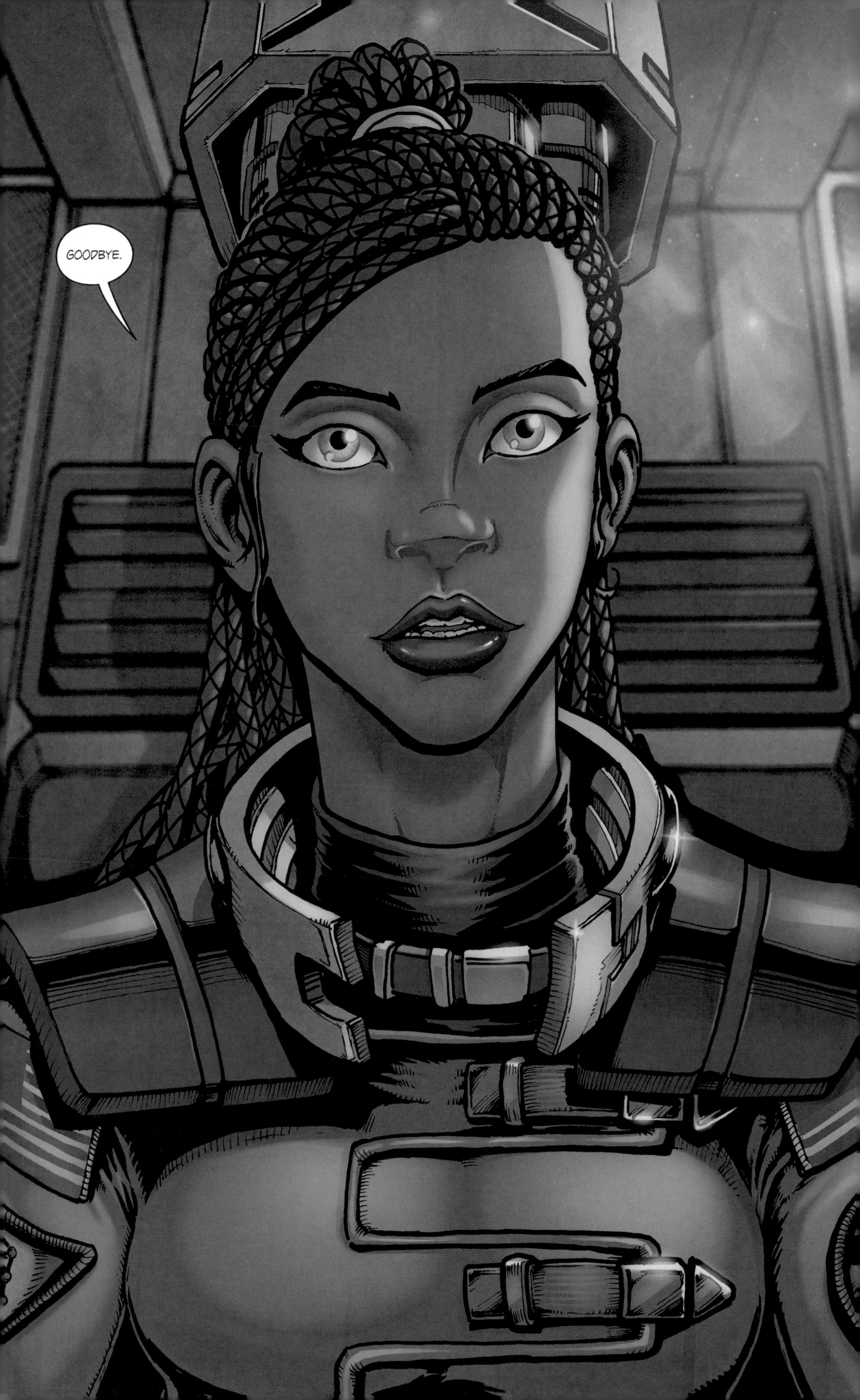
GOODBYE.

CHAPTER 03

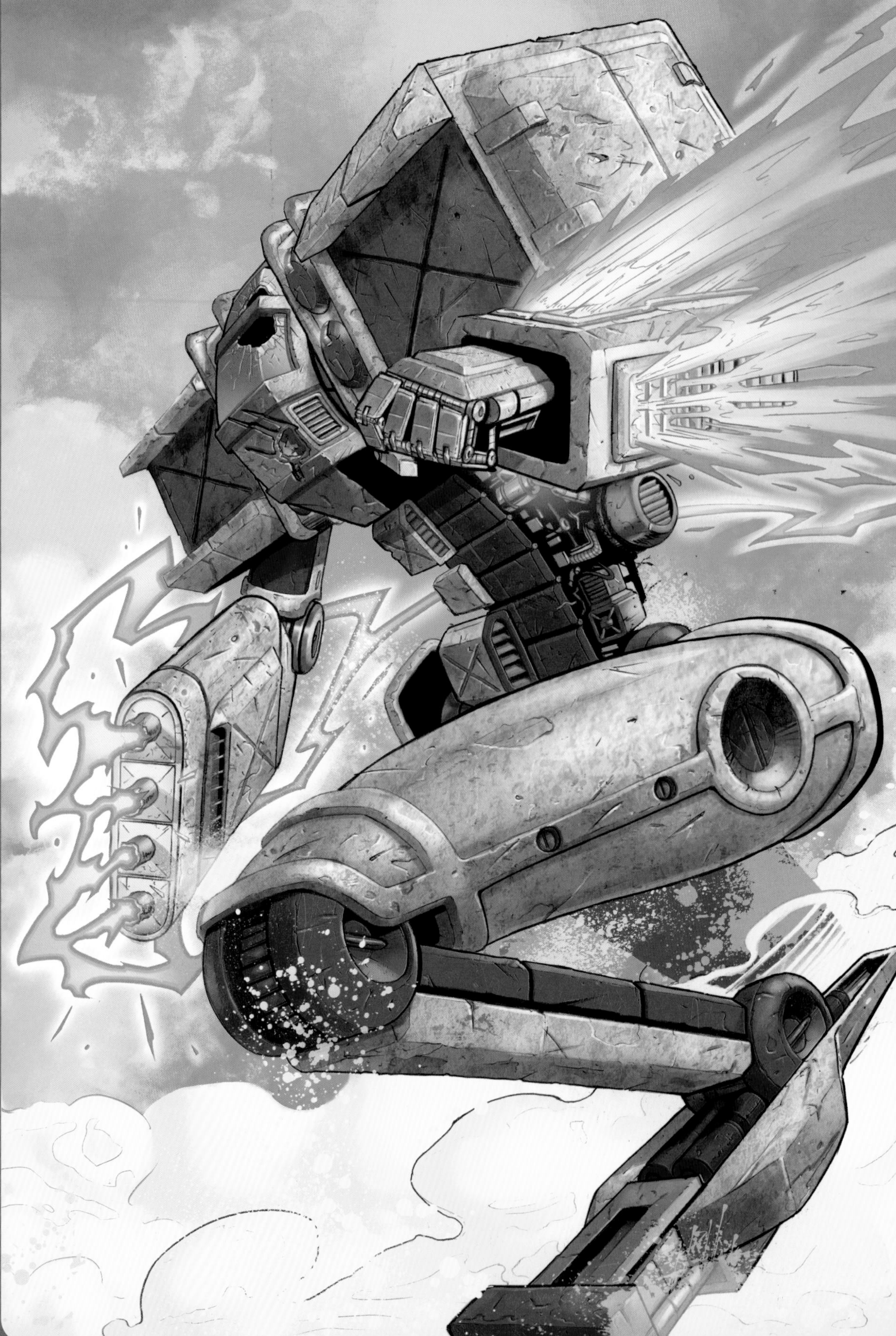

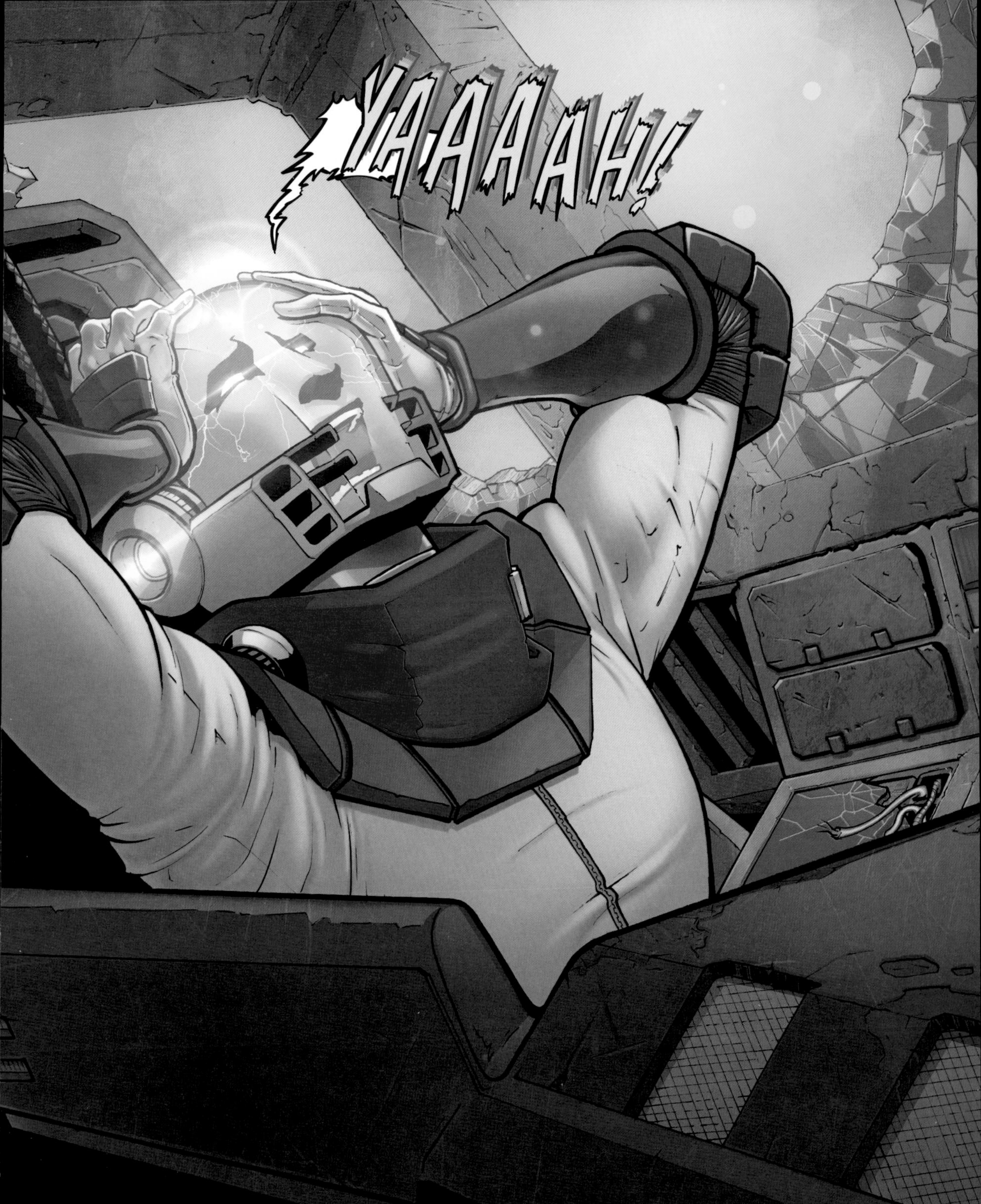
YAAAAH!

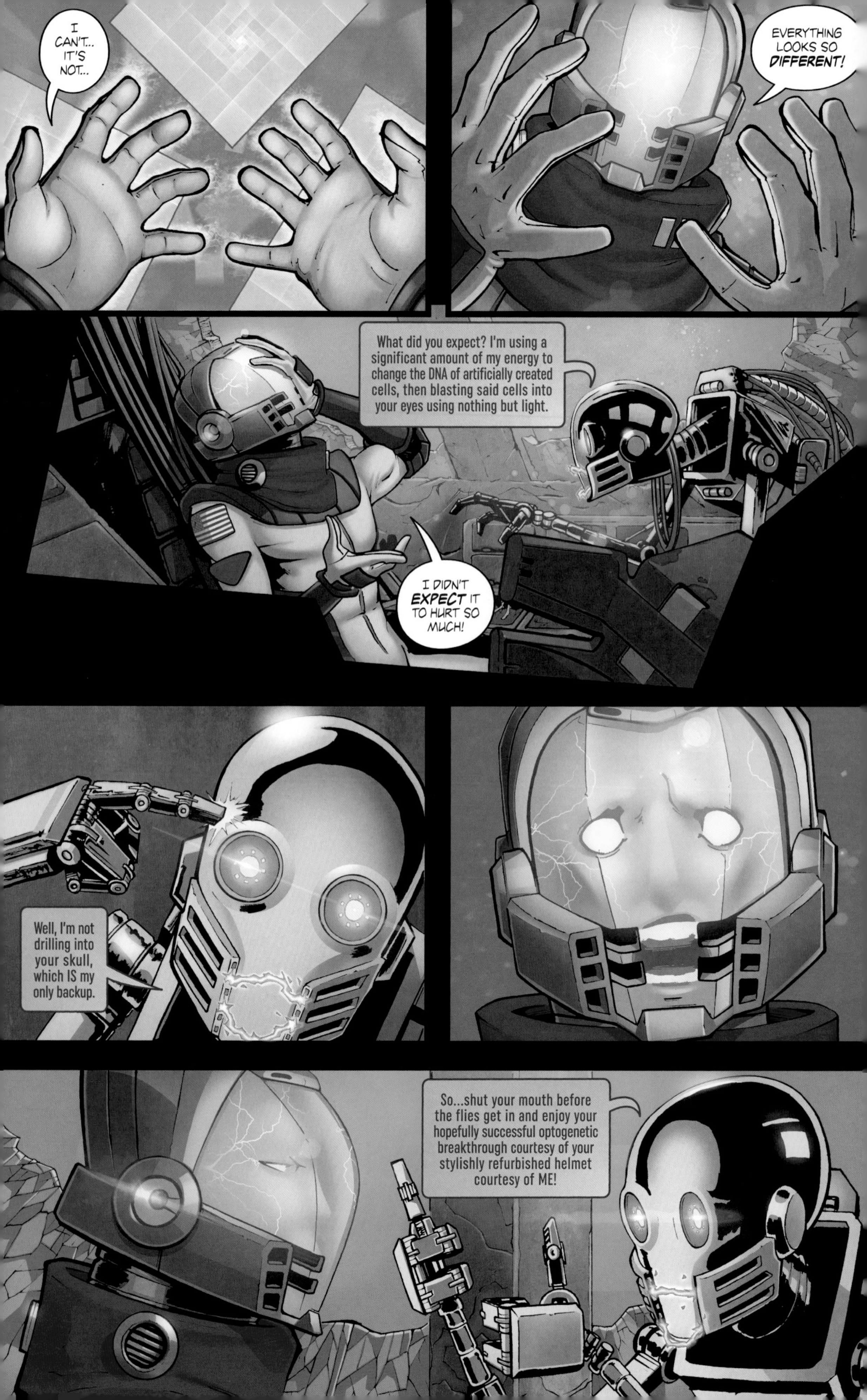

I CAN'T... IT'S NOT...
EVERYTHING LOOKS SO *DIFFERENT!*
What did you expect? I'm using a significant amount of my energy to change the DNA of artificially created cells, then blasting said cells into your eyes using nothing but light.
I DIDN'T ***EXPECT*** IT TO HURT SO MUCH!
Well, I'm not drilling into your skull, which IS my only backup.
So...shut your mouth before the flies get in and enjoy your hopefully successful optogenetic breakthrough courtesy of your stylishly refurbished helmet courtesy of ME!

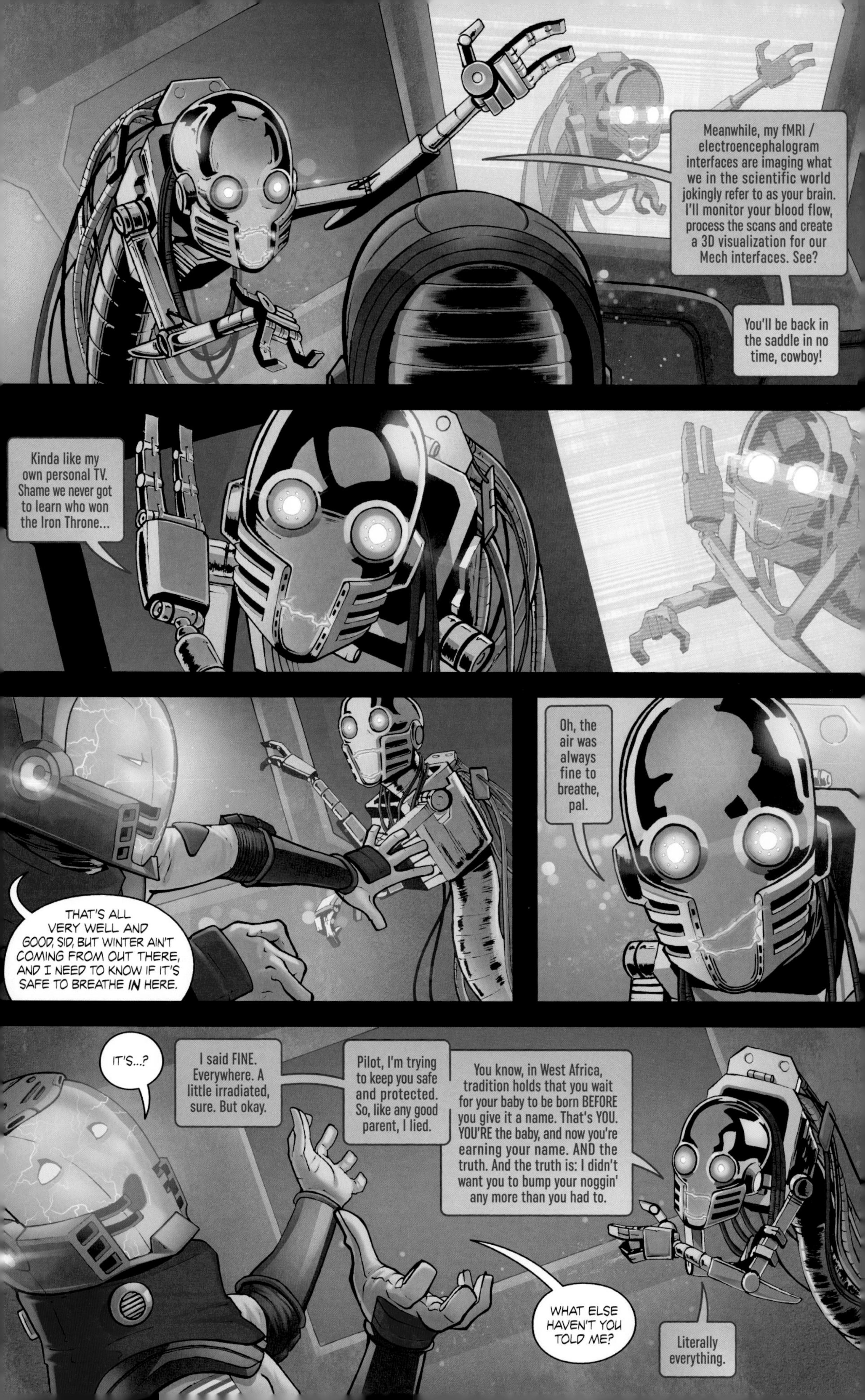
Meanwhile, my fMRI / electroencephalogram interfaces are imaging what we in the scientific world jokingly refer to as your brain. I'll monitor your blood flow, process the scans and create a 3D visualization for our Mech interfaces. See?
You'll be back in the saddle in no time, cowboy!
Kinda like my own personal TV. Shame we never got to learn who won the Iron Throne...
THAT'S ALL VERY WELL AND GOOD, SID, BUT WINTER AIN'T COMING FROM OUT THERE, AND I NEED TO KNOW IF IT'S SAFE TO BREATHE IN HERE.
Oh, the air was always fine to breathe, pal.
IT'S...?
I said FINE. Everywhere. A little irradiated, sure. But okay.
Pilot, I'm trying to keep you safe and protected. So, like any good parent, I lied.
You know, in West Africa, tradition holds that you wait for your baby to be born BEFORE you give it a name. That's YOU. YOU'RE the baby, and now you're earning your name. AND the truth. And the truth is: I didn't want you to bump your noggin' any more than you had to.
WHAT ELSE HAVEN'T YOU TOLD ME?
Literally everything.

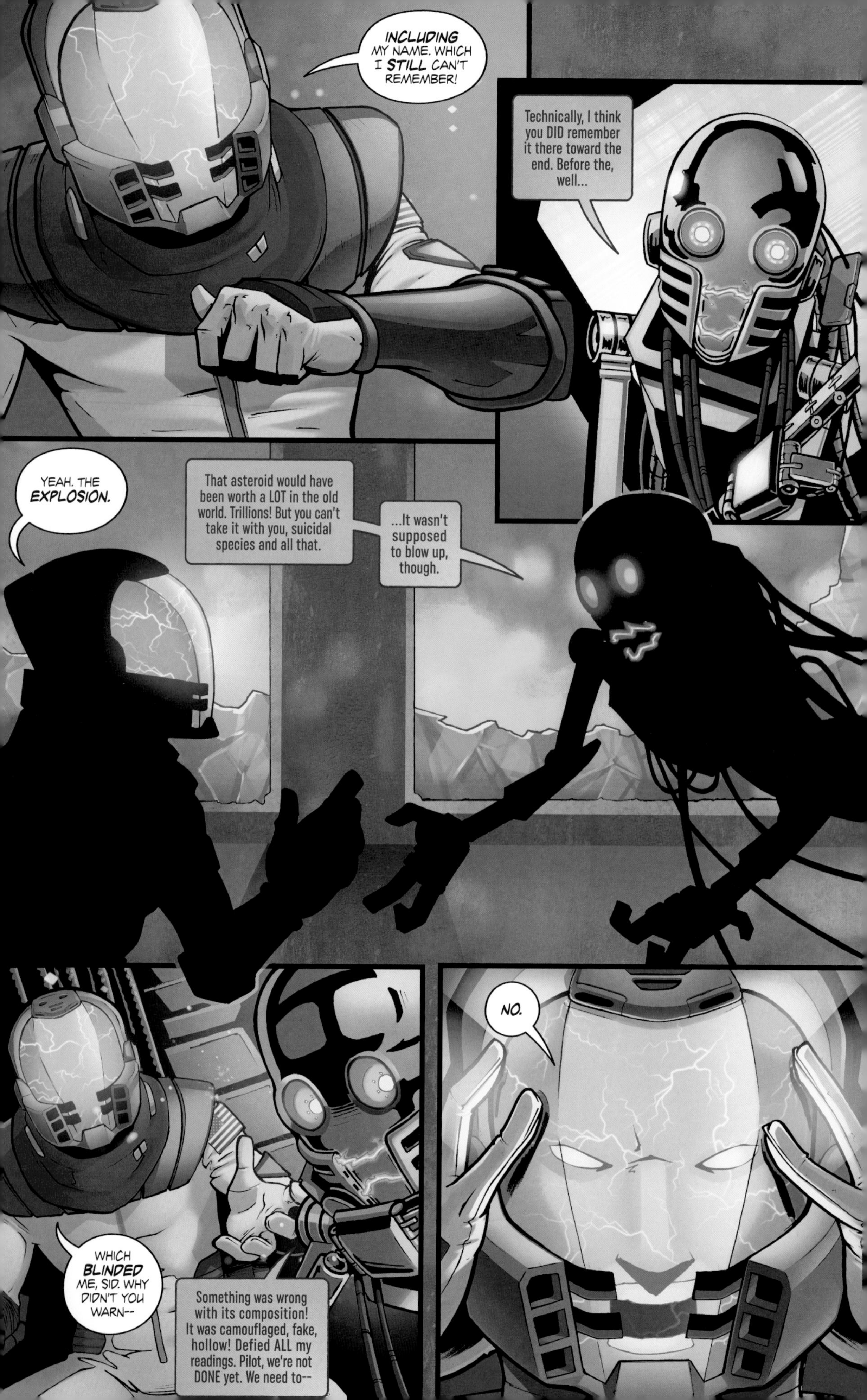
INCLUDING MY NAME. WHICH I STILL CAN'T REMEMBER!
Technically, I think you DID remember it there toward the end. Before the, well...
YEAH. THE EXPLOSION.
That asteroid would have been worth a LOT in the old world. Trillions! But you can't take it with you, suicidal species and all that.
...It wasn't supposed to blow up, though.
WHICH BLINDED ME, SID. WHY DIDN'T YOU WARN--
Something was wrong with its composition! It was camouflaged, fake, hollow! Defied ALL my readings. Pilot, we're not DONE yet. We need to--
NO.

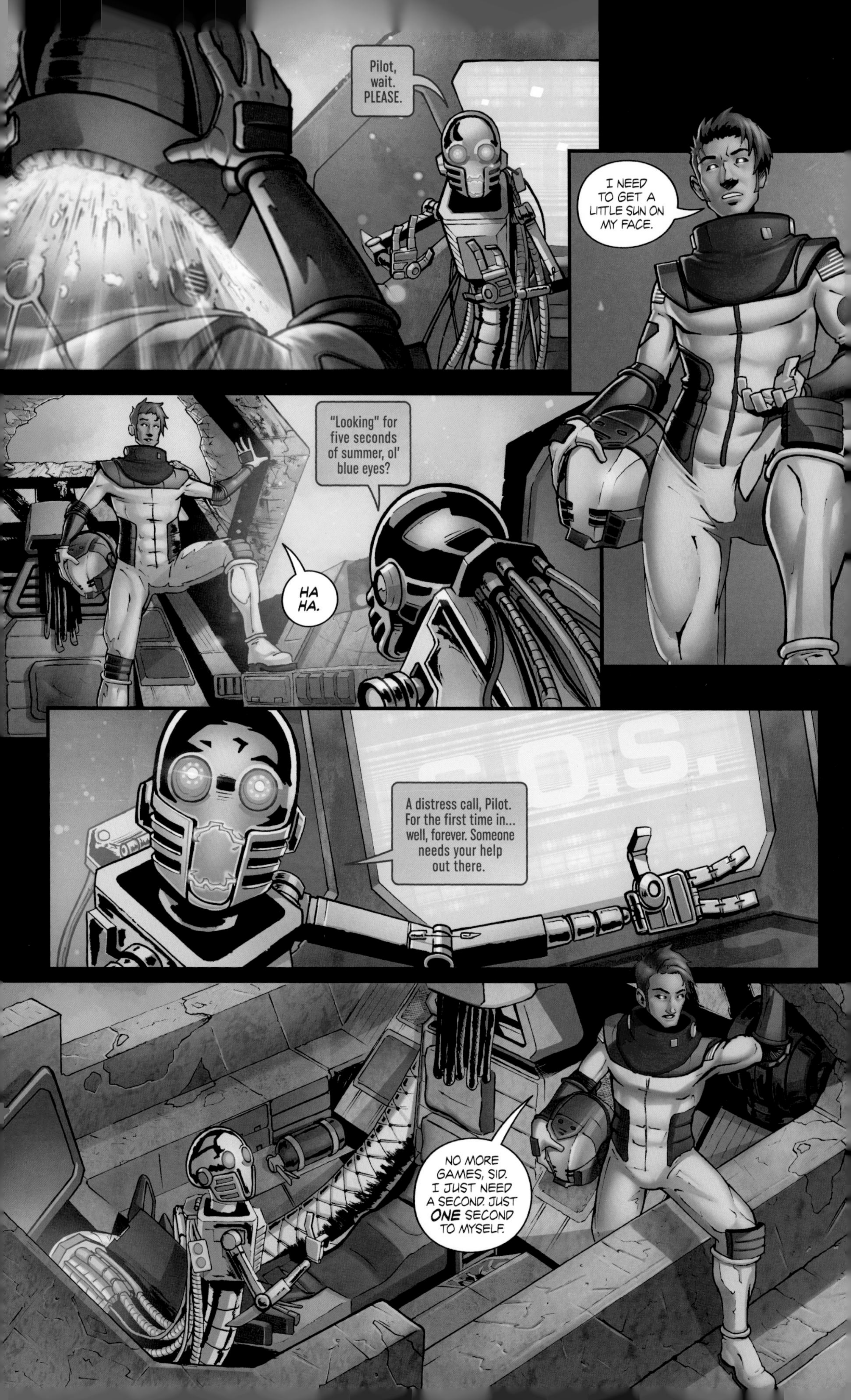
Pilot, wait. PLEASE.
I NEED TO GET A LITTLE SUN ON MY FACE.
"Looking" for five seconds of summer, ol' blue eyes?
HA HA.
A distress call, Pilot. For the first time in... well, forever. Someone needs your help out there.
NO MORE GAMES, SID. I JUST NEED A SECOND. JUST **ONE** SECOND TO MYSELF.

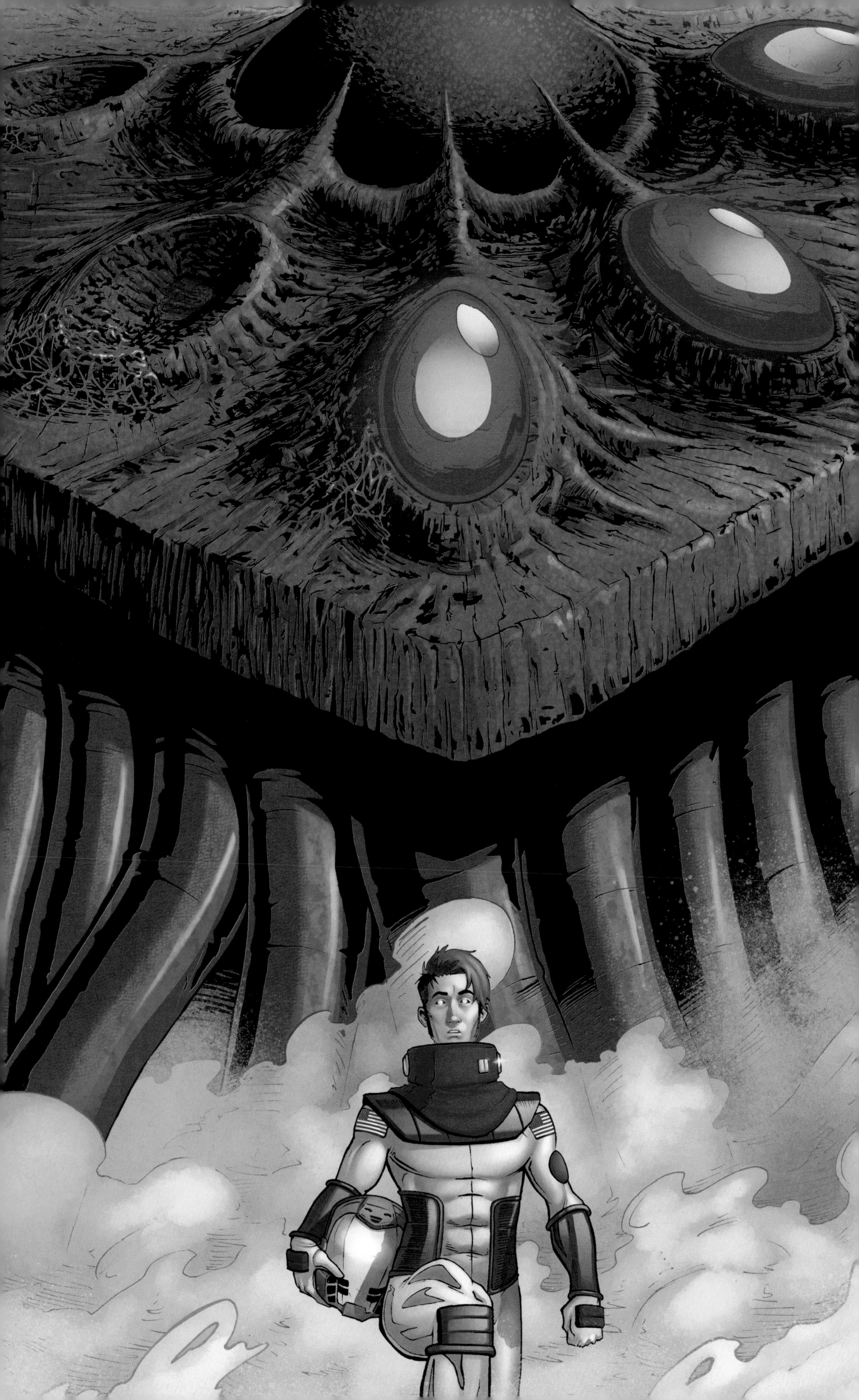

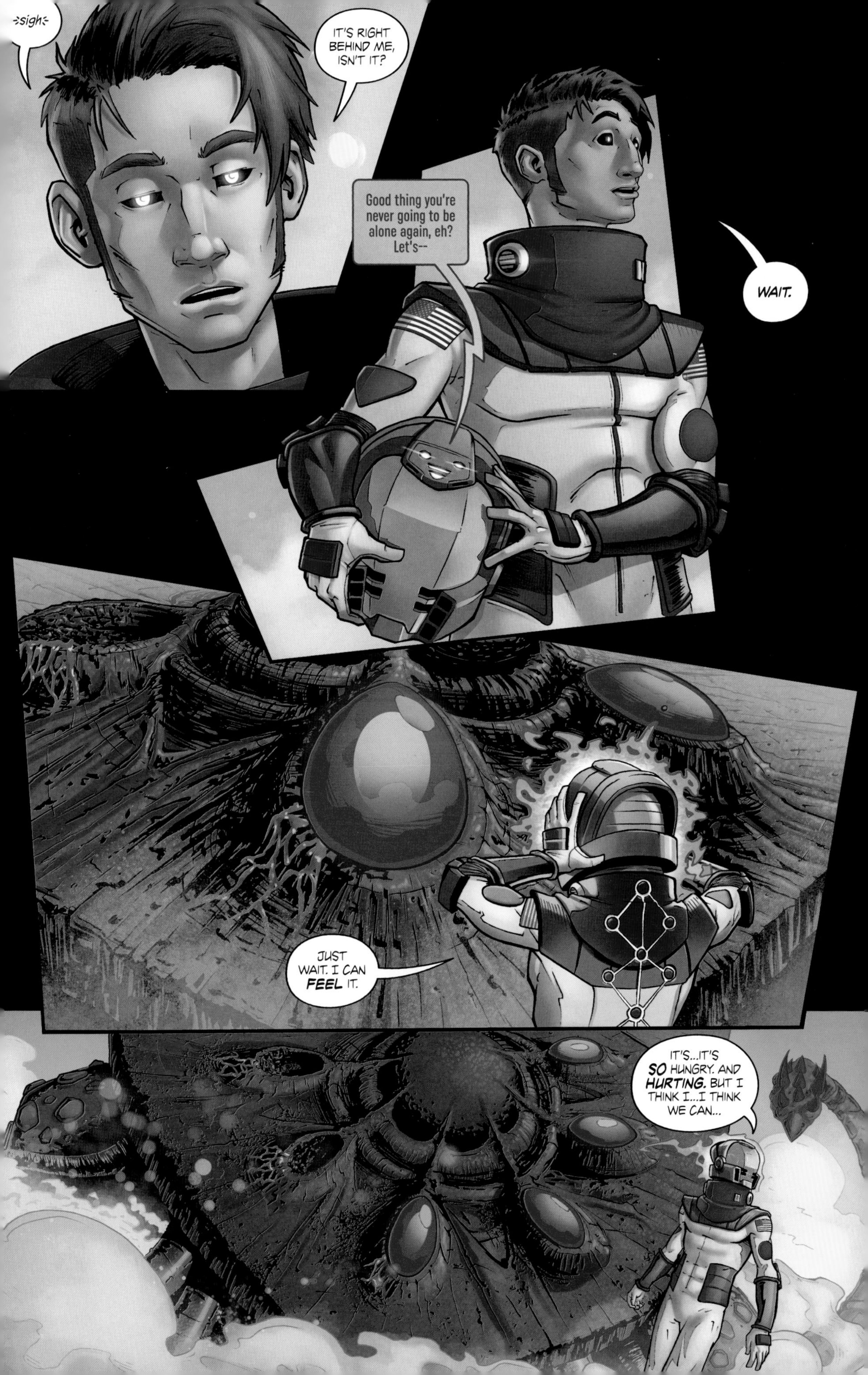

sigh
IT'S RIGHT BEHIND ME, ISN'T IT?
Good thing you're never going to be alone again, eh? Let's--
WAIT.
JUST WAIT. I CAN **FEEL** IT.
IT'S...IT'S **SO** HUNGRY. AND **HURTING.** BUT I THINK I...I THINK WE CAN...

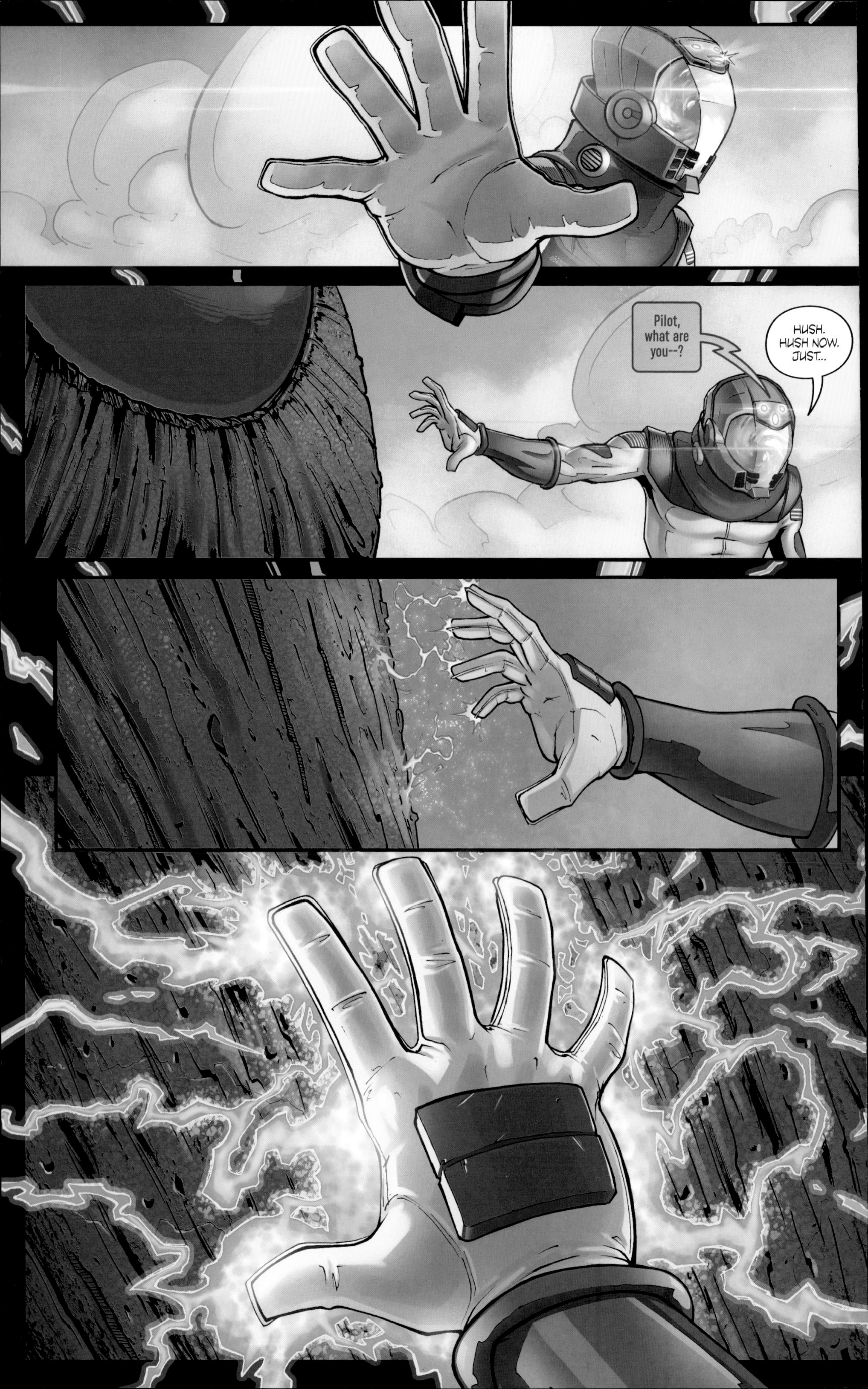
Pilot, what are you--?
HUSH. HUSH NOW. JUST...

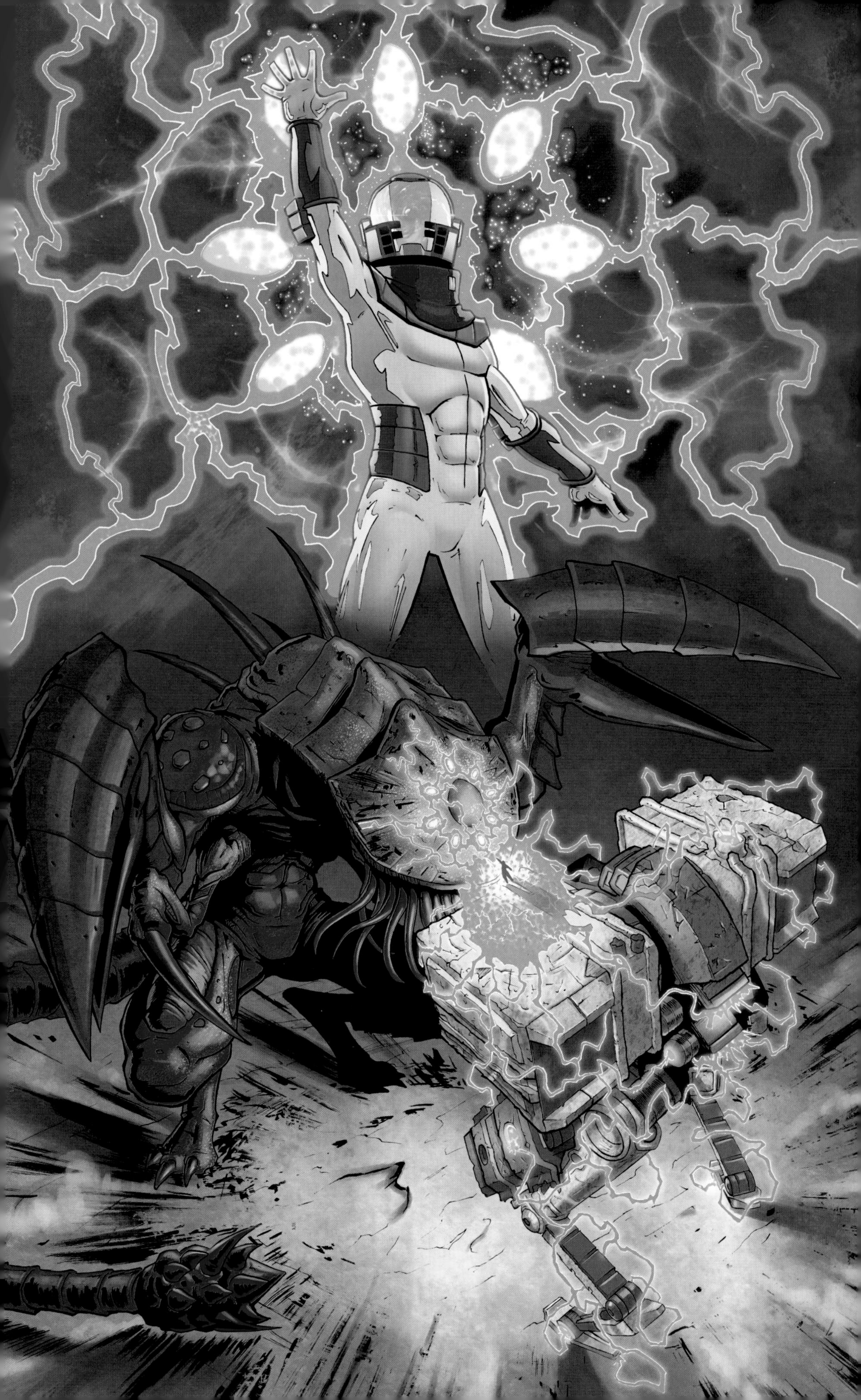

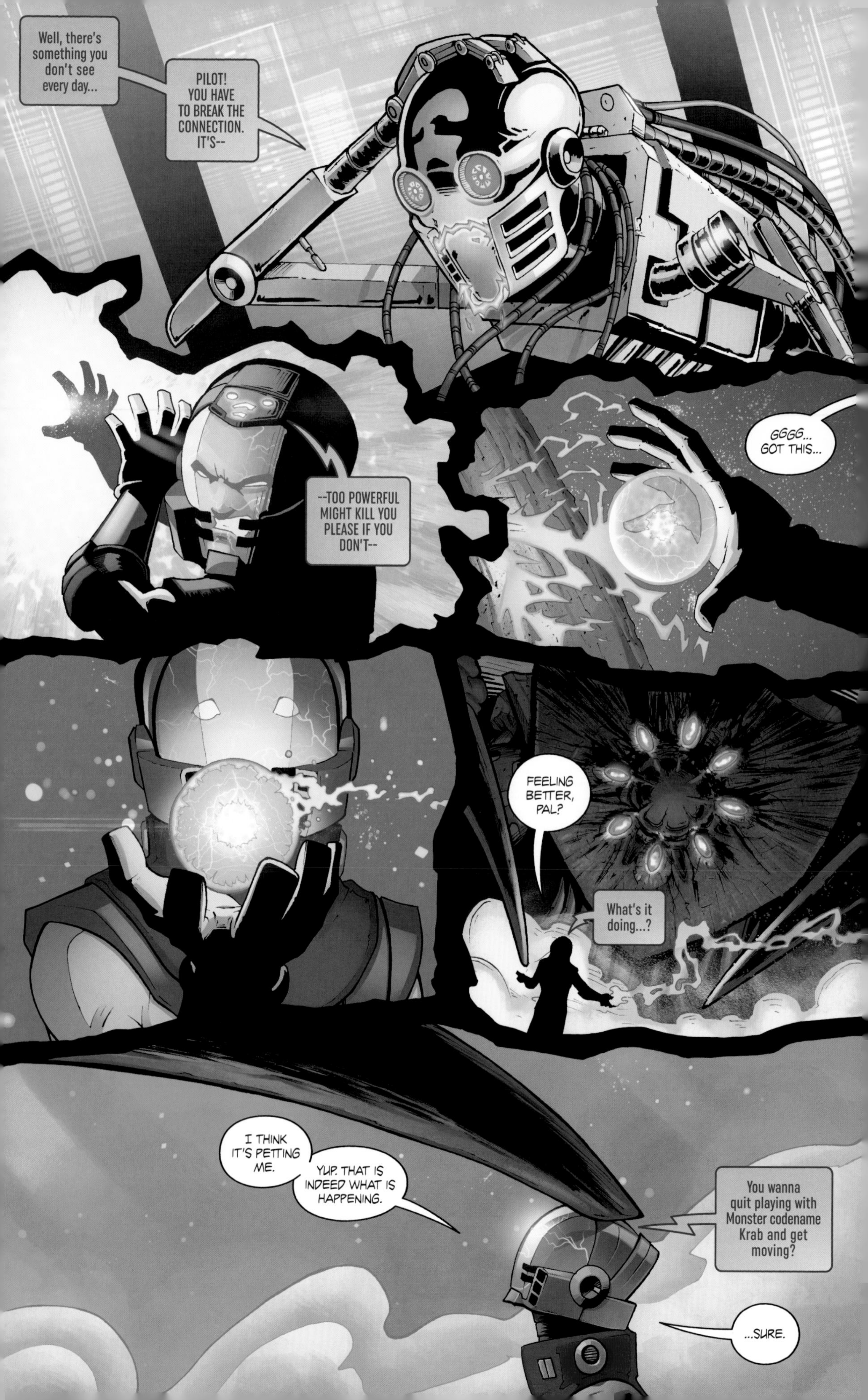
Well, there's something you don't see every day...
PILOT! YOU HAVE TO BREAK THE CONNECTION. IT'S--
--TOO POWERFUL MIGHT KILL YOU PLEASE IF YOU DON'T--
GGGG... GOT THIS...
FEELING BETTER, PAL?
What's it doing...?
I THINK IT'S PETTING ME.
YUP. THAT IS INDEED WHAT IS HAPPENING.
You wanna quit playing with Monster codename Krab and get moving?
...SURE.

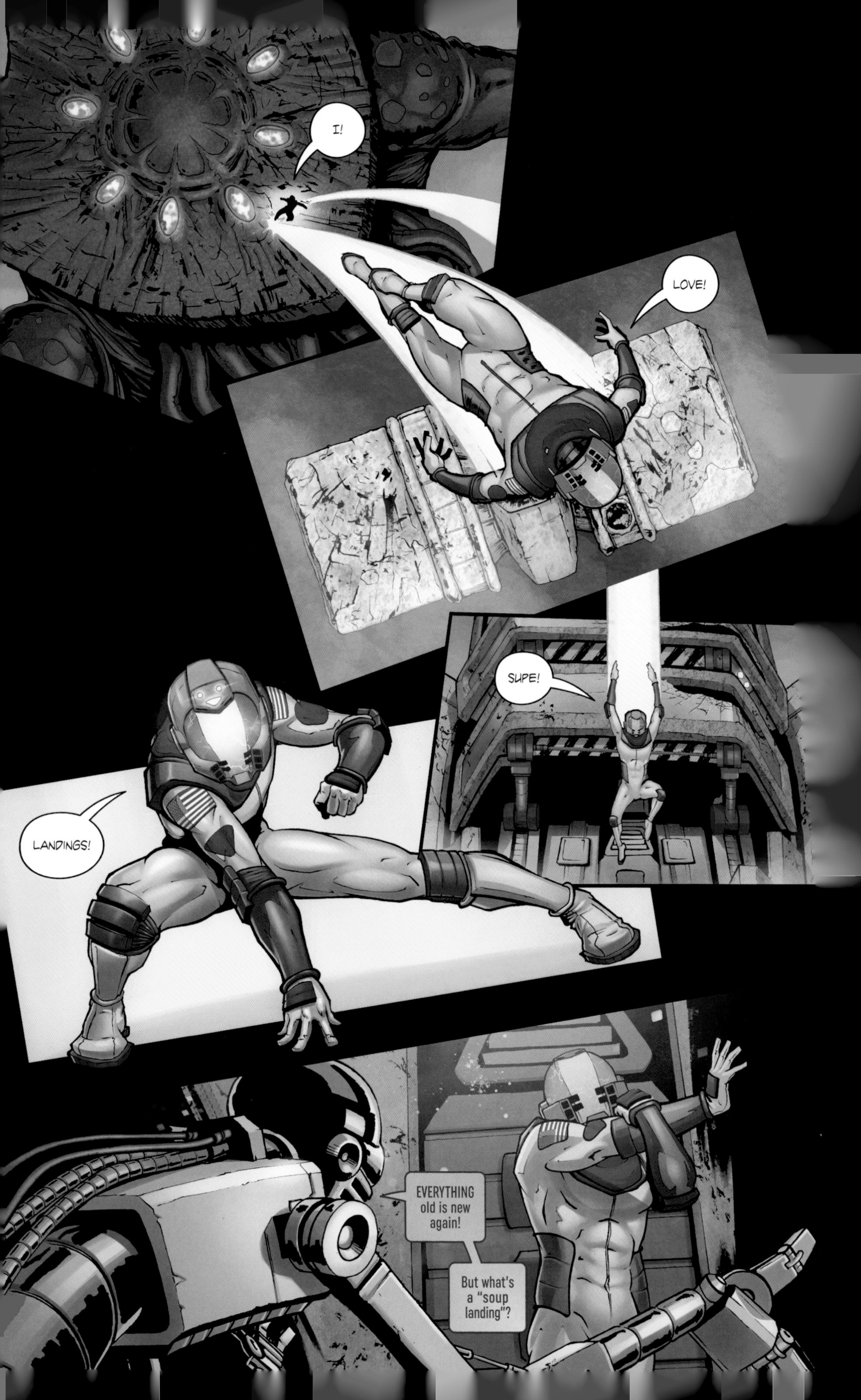
I!
LOVE!
SUPE!
LANDINGS!
EVERYTHING old is new again!
But what's a "soup landing"?

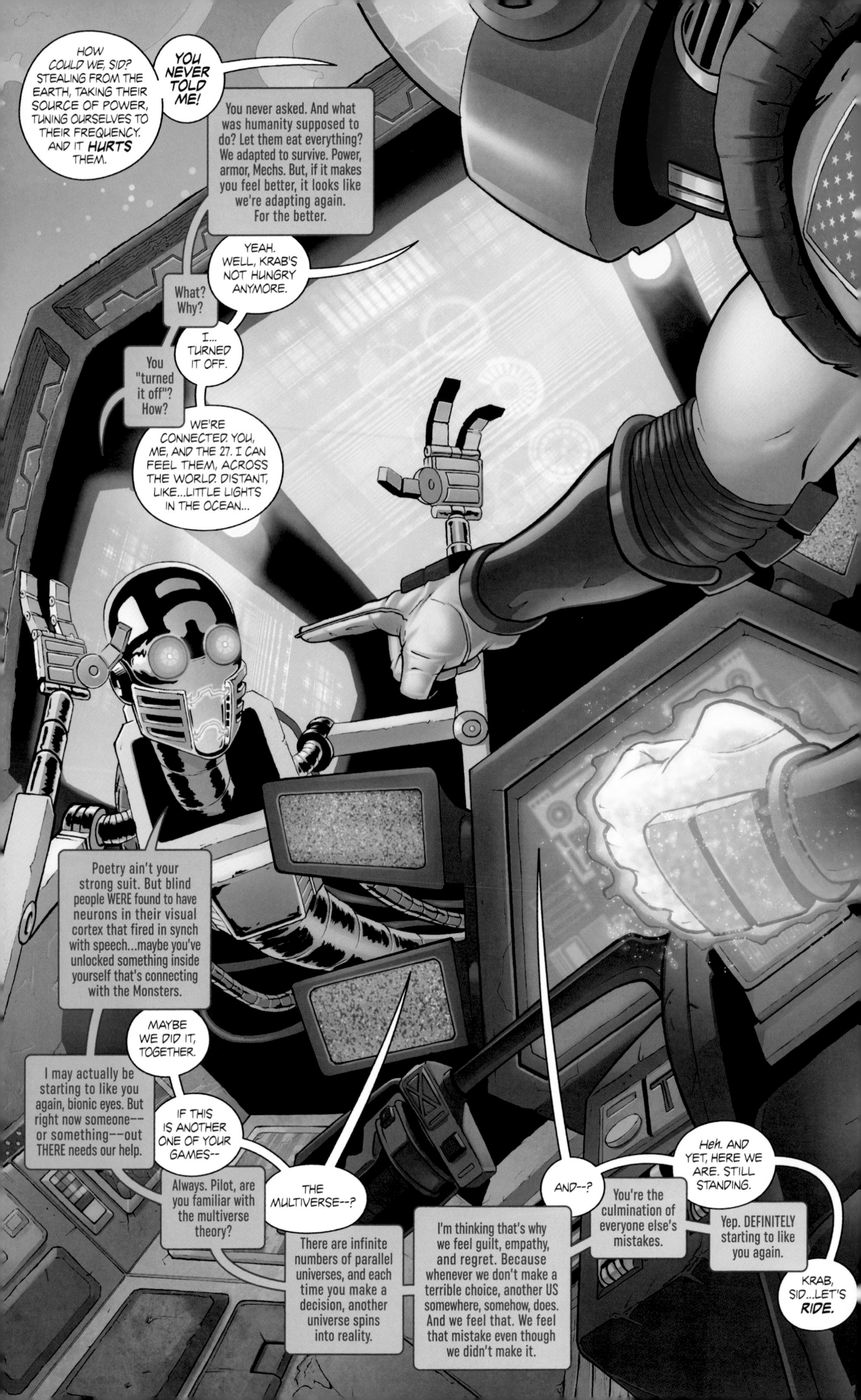
HOW COULD WE, SID? STEALING FROM THE EARTH, TAKING THEIR SOURCE OF POWER, TUNING OURSELVES TO THEIR FREQUENCY. AND IT HURTS THEM.
YOU NEVER TOLD ME!
You never asked. And what was humanity supposed to do? Let them eat everything? We adapted to survive. Power, armor, Mechs. But, if it makes you feel better, it looks like we're adapting again. For the better.
YEAH. WELL, KRAB'S NOT HUNGRY ANYMORE.
What? Why?
I... TURNED IT OFF.
You "turned it off"? How?
WE'RE CONNECTED. YOU, ME, AND THE 27. I CAN FEEL THEM, ACROSS THE WORLD. DISTANT, LIKE...LITTLE LIGHTS IN THE OCEAN...
Poetry ain't your strong suit. But blind people WERE found to have neurons in their visual cortex that fired in synch with speech...maybe you've unlocked something inside yourself that's connecting with the Monsters.
MAYBE WE DID IT, TOGETHER.
I may actually be starting to like you again, bionic eyes. But right now someone--or something--out THERE needs our help.
IF THIS IS ANOTHER ONE OF YOUR GAMES--
Always. Pilot, are you familiar with the multiverse theory?
THE MULTIVERSE--?
There are infinite numbers of parallel universes, and each time you make a decision, another universe spins into reality.
I'm thinking that's why we feel guilt, empathy, and regret. Because whenever we don't make a terrible choice, another US somewhere, somehow, does. And we feel that. We feel that mistake even though we didn't make it.
AND--?
You're the culmination of everyone else's mistakes.
Heh. AND YET, HERE WE ARE. STILL STANDING.
Yep. DEFINITELY starting to like you again.
KRAB, SID...LET'S RIDE.

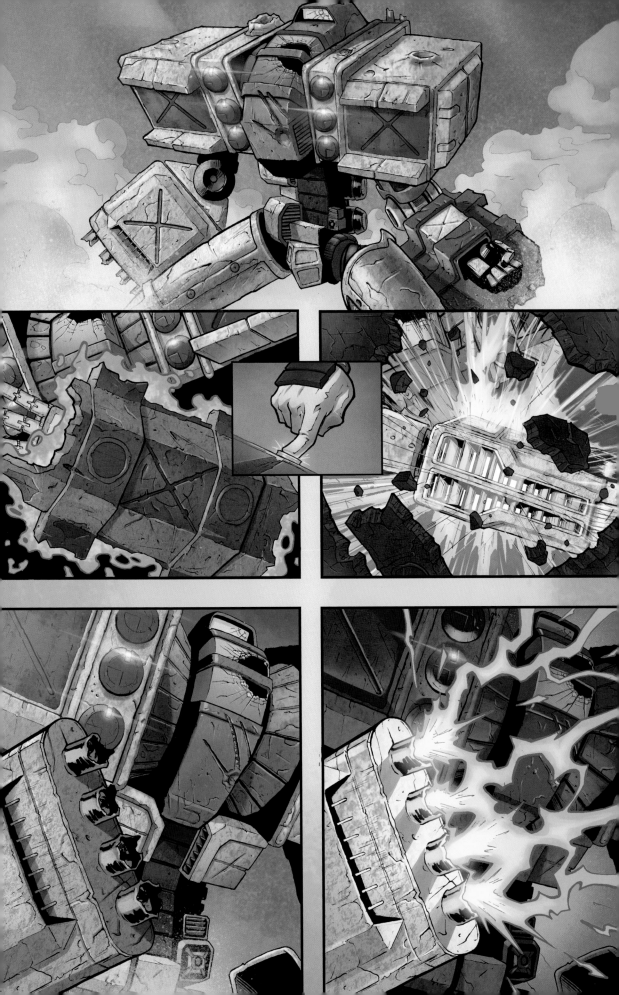

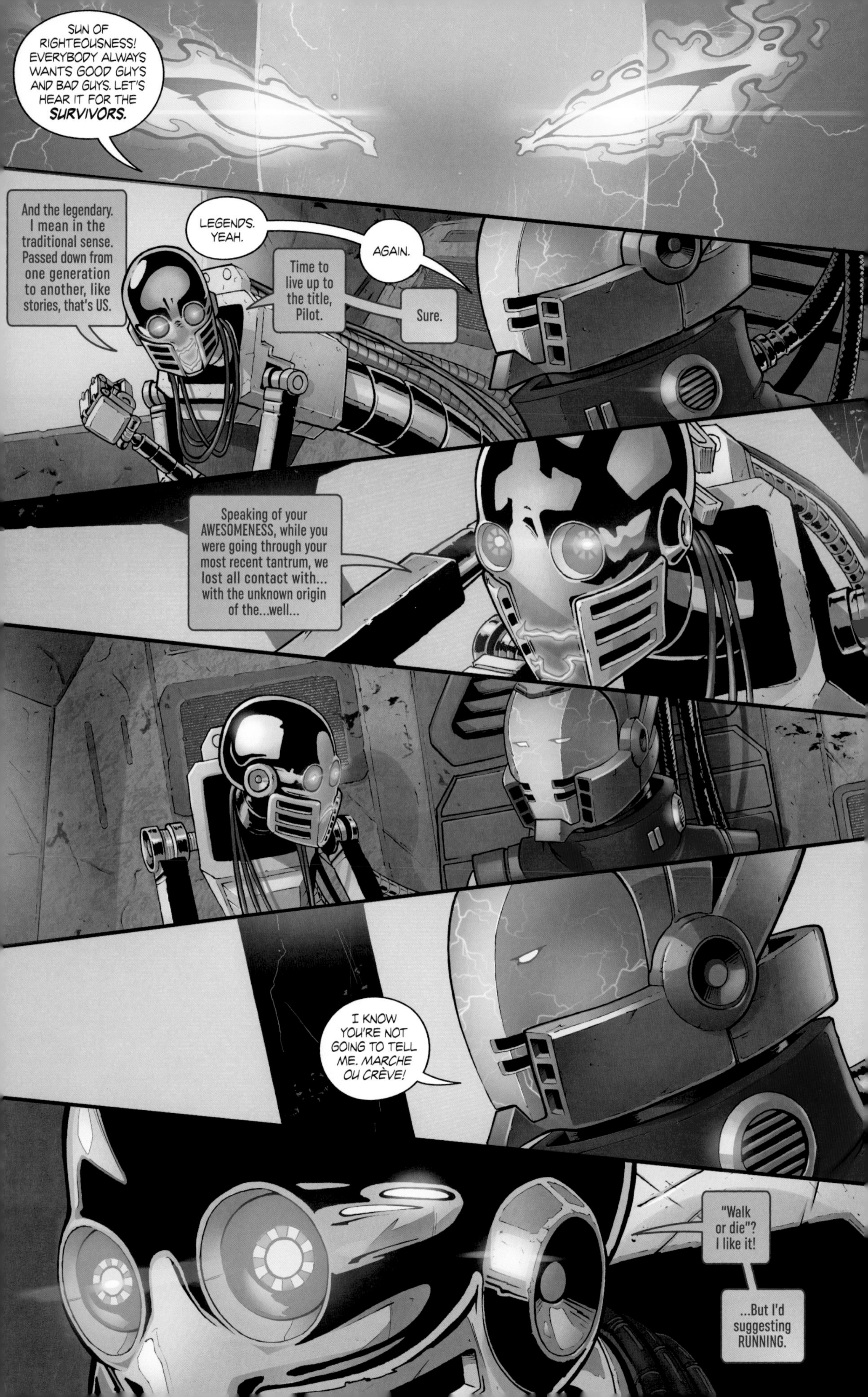
SUN OF RIGHTEOUSNESS! EVERYBODY ALWAYS WANTS GOOD GUYS AND BAD GUYS. LET'S HEAR IT FOR THE *SURVIVORS.*
And the legendary. I mean in the traditional sense. Passed down from one generation to another, like stories, that's US.
LEGENDS. YEAH.
AGAIN.
Time to live up to the title, Pilot.
Sure.
Speaking of your AWESOMENESS, while you were going through your most recent tantrum, we lost all contact with... with the unknown origin of the...well...
I KNOW YOU'RE NOT GOING TO TELL ME. *MARCHE OU CRÈVE!*
"Walk or die"? I like it!
...But I'd suggesting RUNNING.

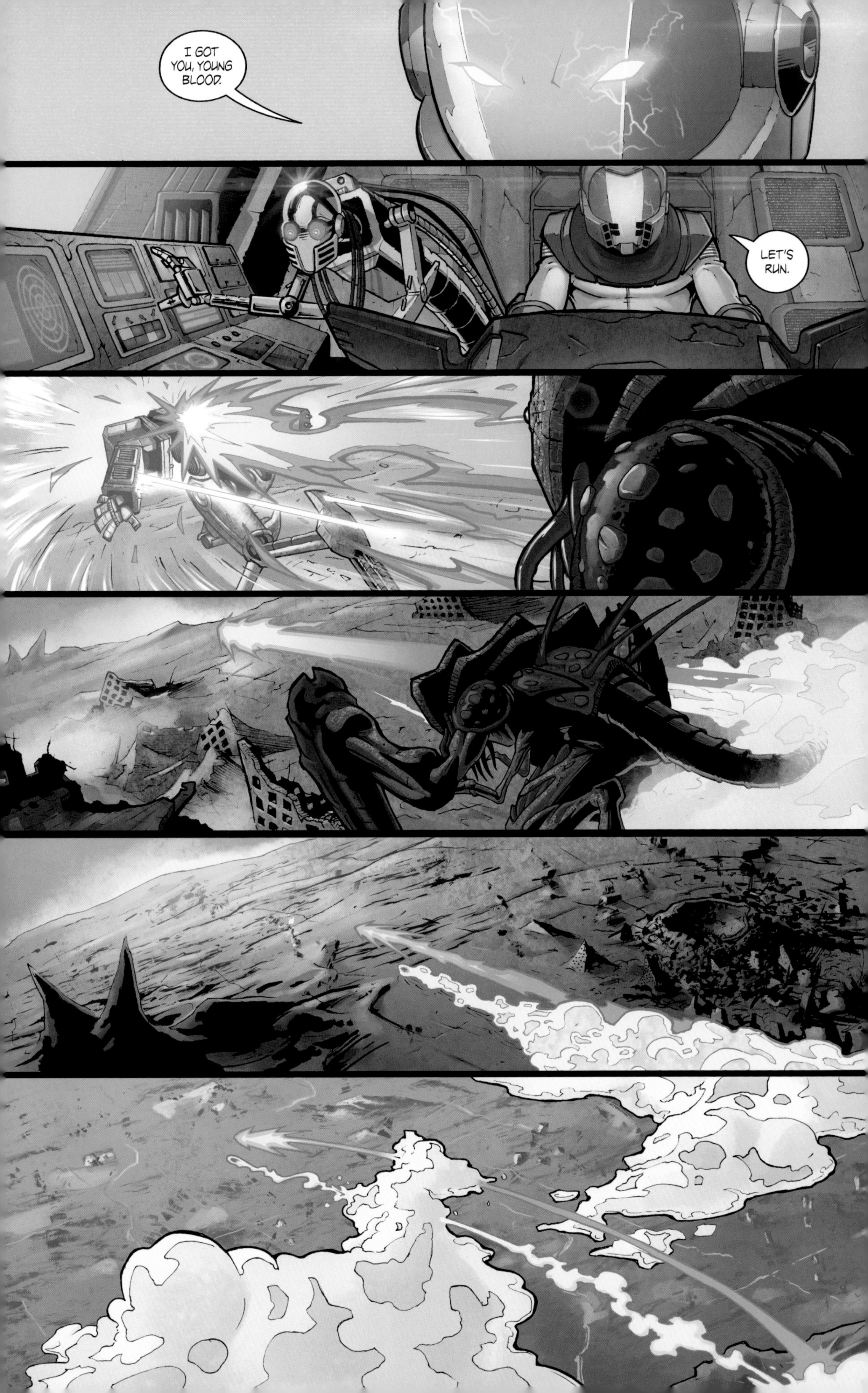
I GOT YOU, YOUNG BLOOD.
LET'S RUN.

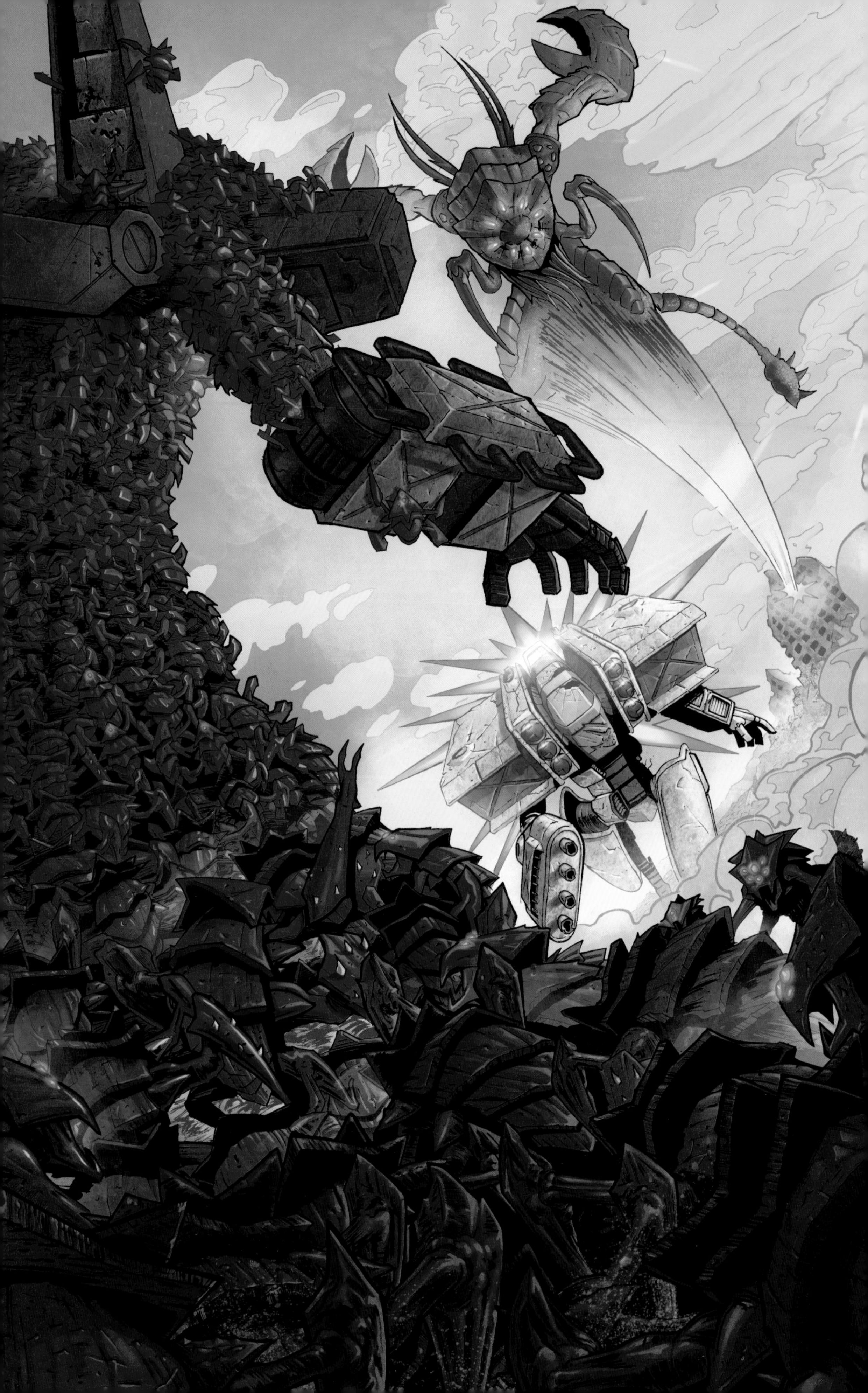

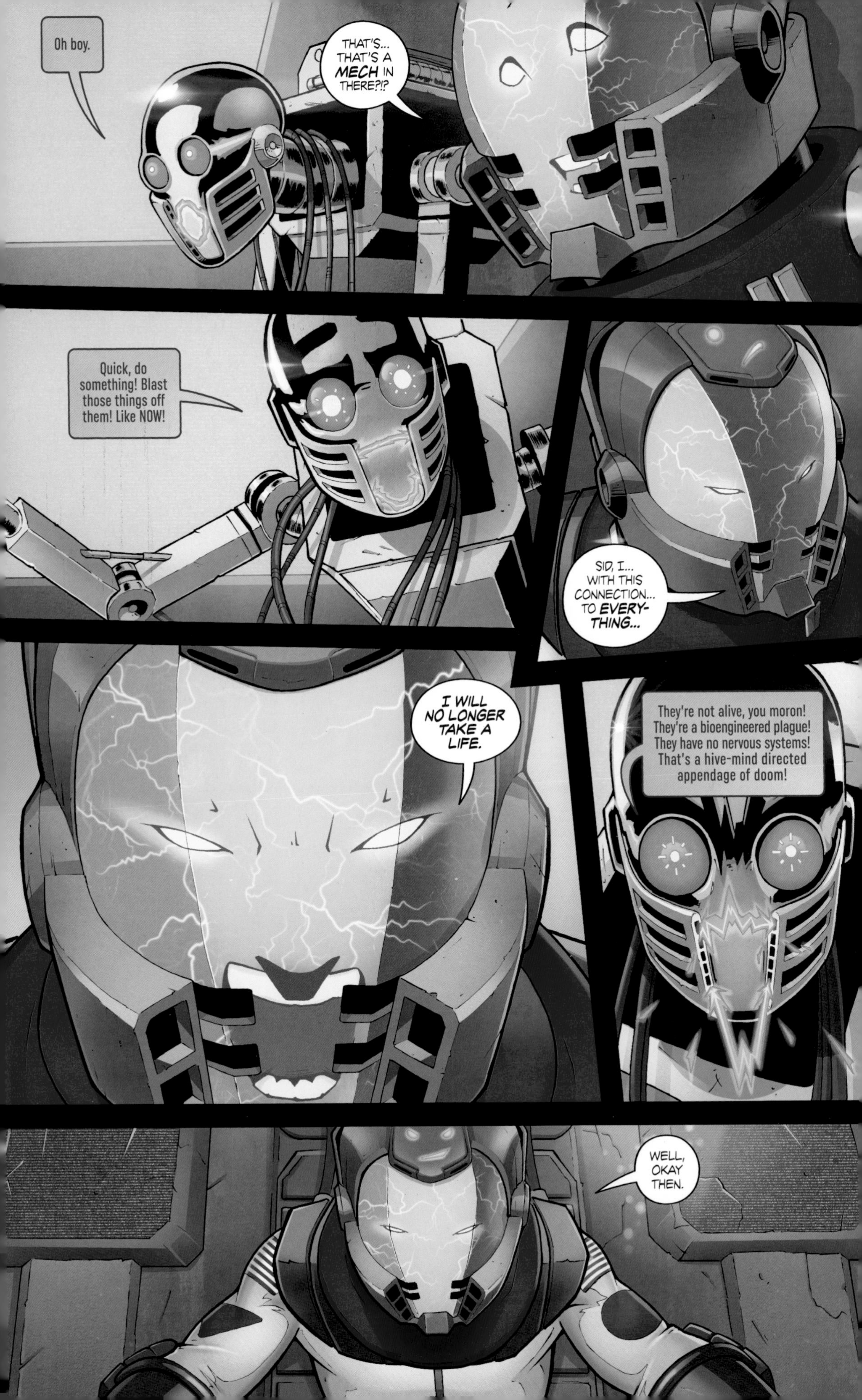
Oh boy.
THAT'S... THAT'S A MECH IN THERE?!?
Quick, do something! Blast those things off them! Like NOW!
SID, I... WITH THIS CONNECTION... TO EVERY-THING...
I WILL NO LONGER TAKE A LIFE.
They're not alive, you moron! They're a bioengineered plague! They have no nervous systems! That's a hive-mind directed appendage of doom!
WELL, OKAY THEN.

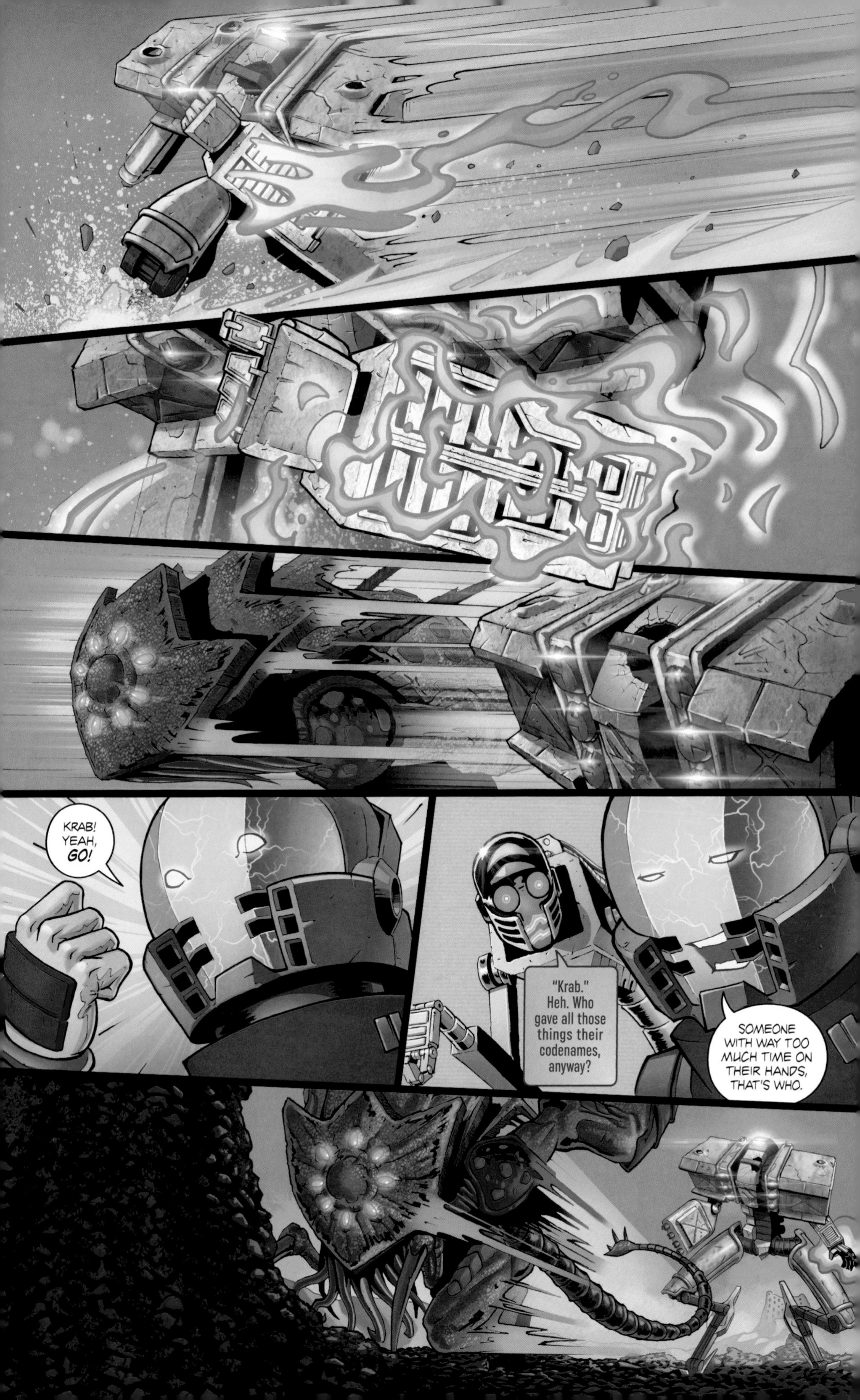
KRAB! YEAH, GO!
"Krab." Heh. Who gave all those things their codenames, anyway?
SOMEONE WITH WAY TOO MUCH TIME ON THEIR HANDS, THAT'S WHO.

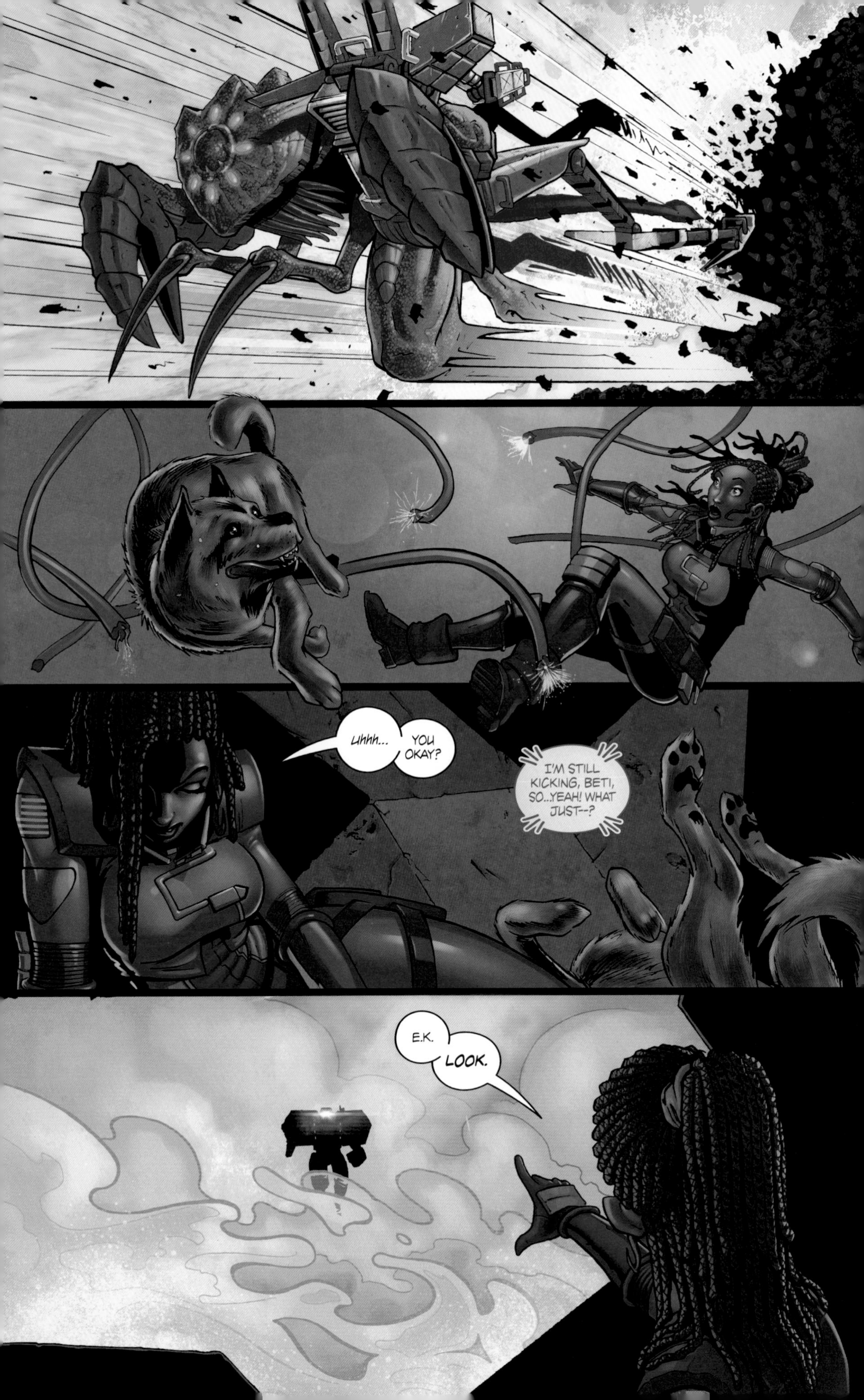
Uhhh...
YOU OKAY?
I'M STILL KICKING, BETI, SO...YEAH! WHAT JUST--?
E.K.
LOOK.

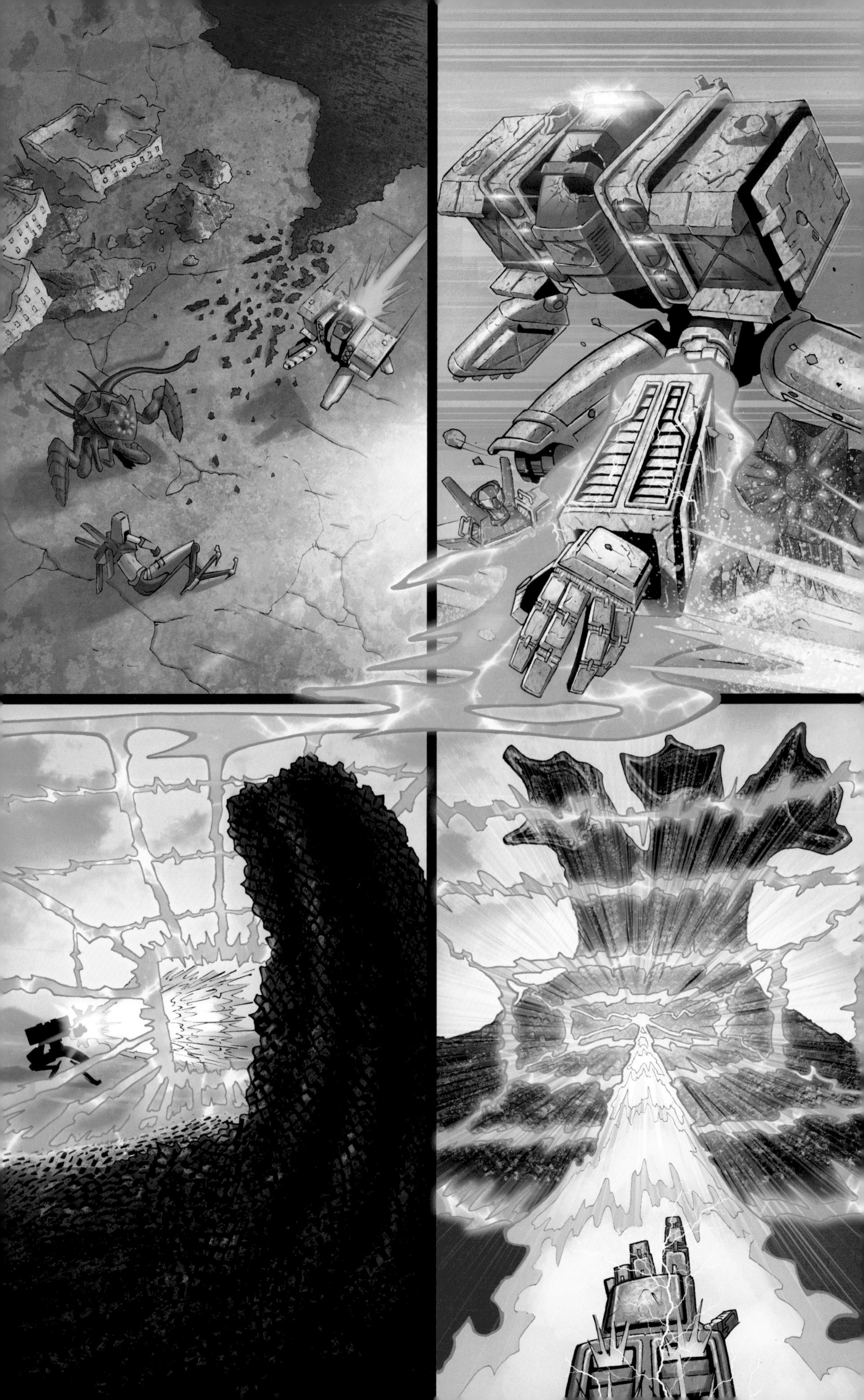

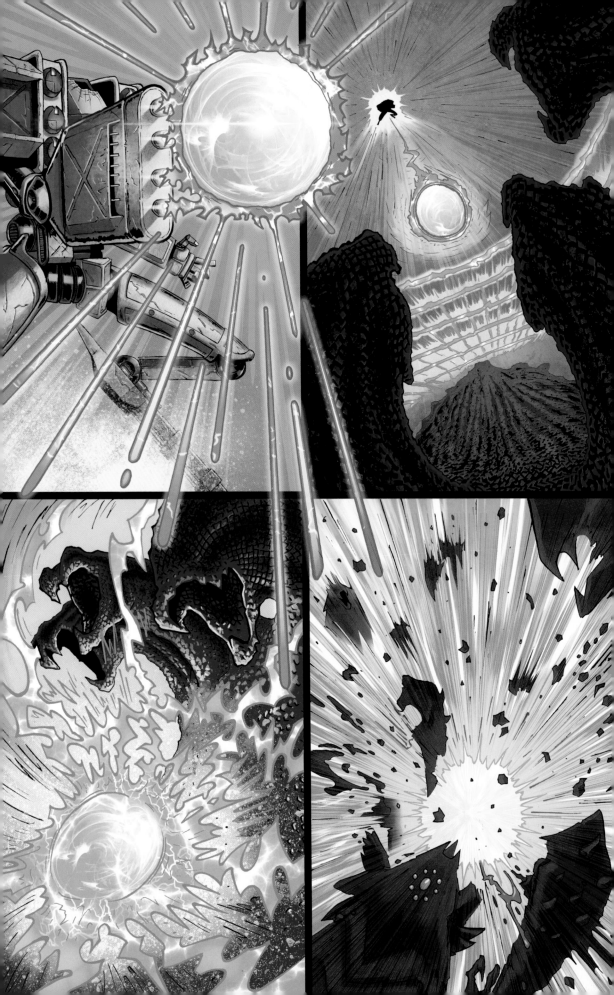

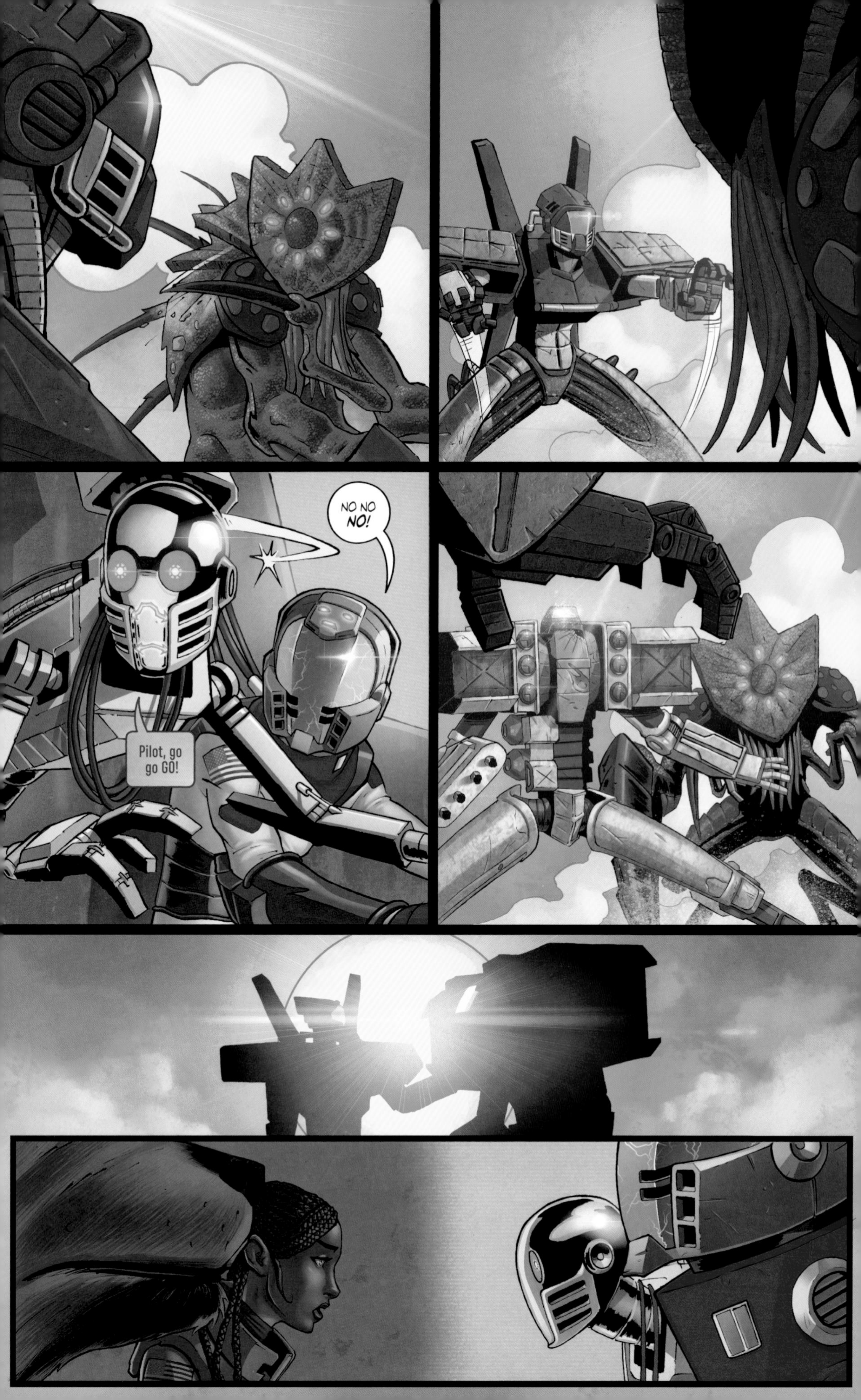
NO NO **NO!**
Pilot, go go GO!

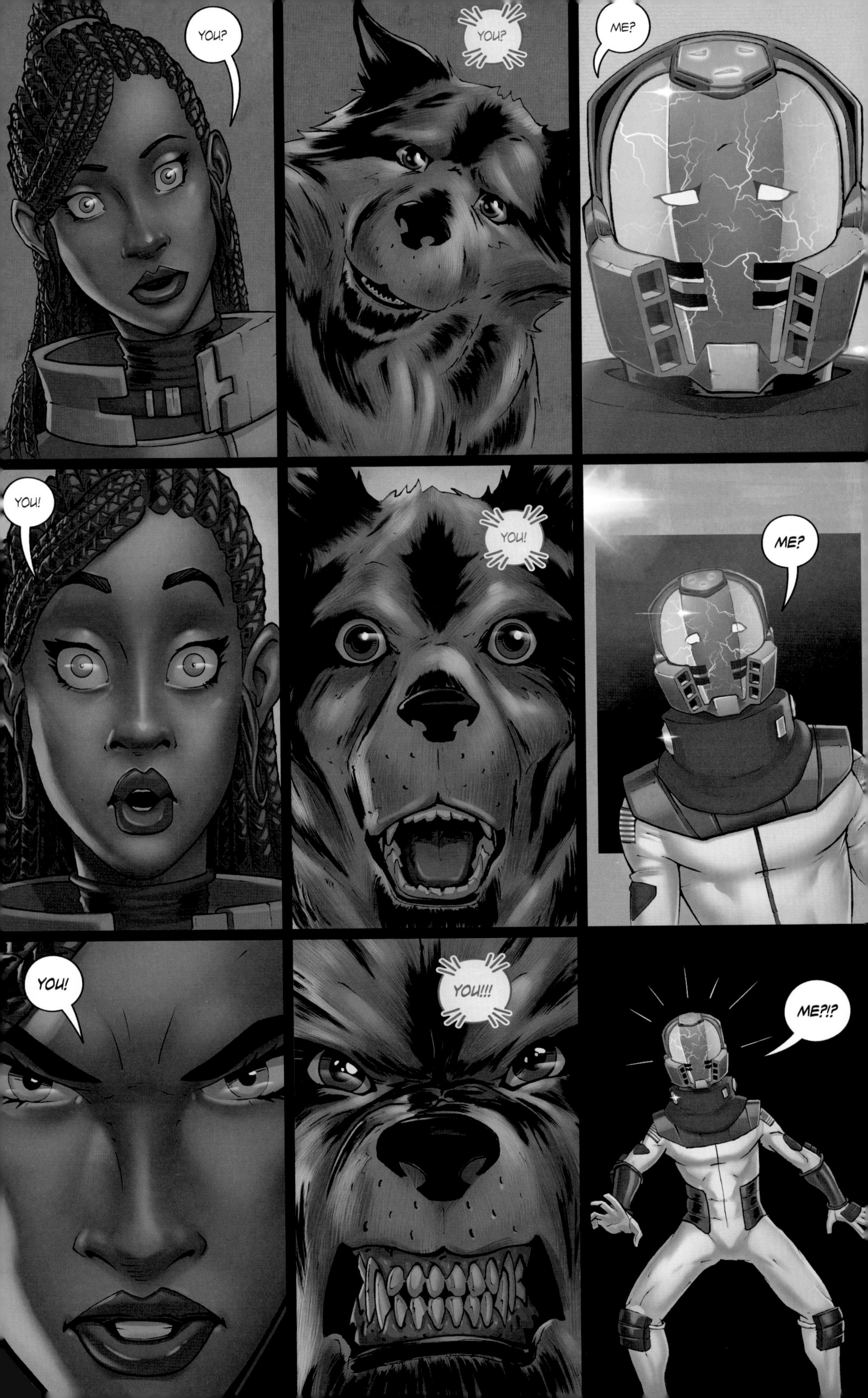
YOU?
YOU?
ME?
YOU!
YOU!
ME?
YOU!
YOU!!!
ME?!?

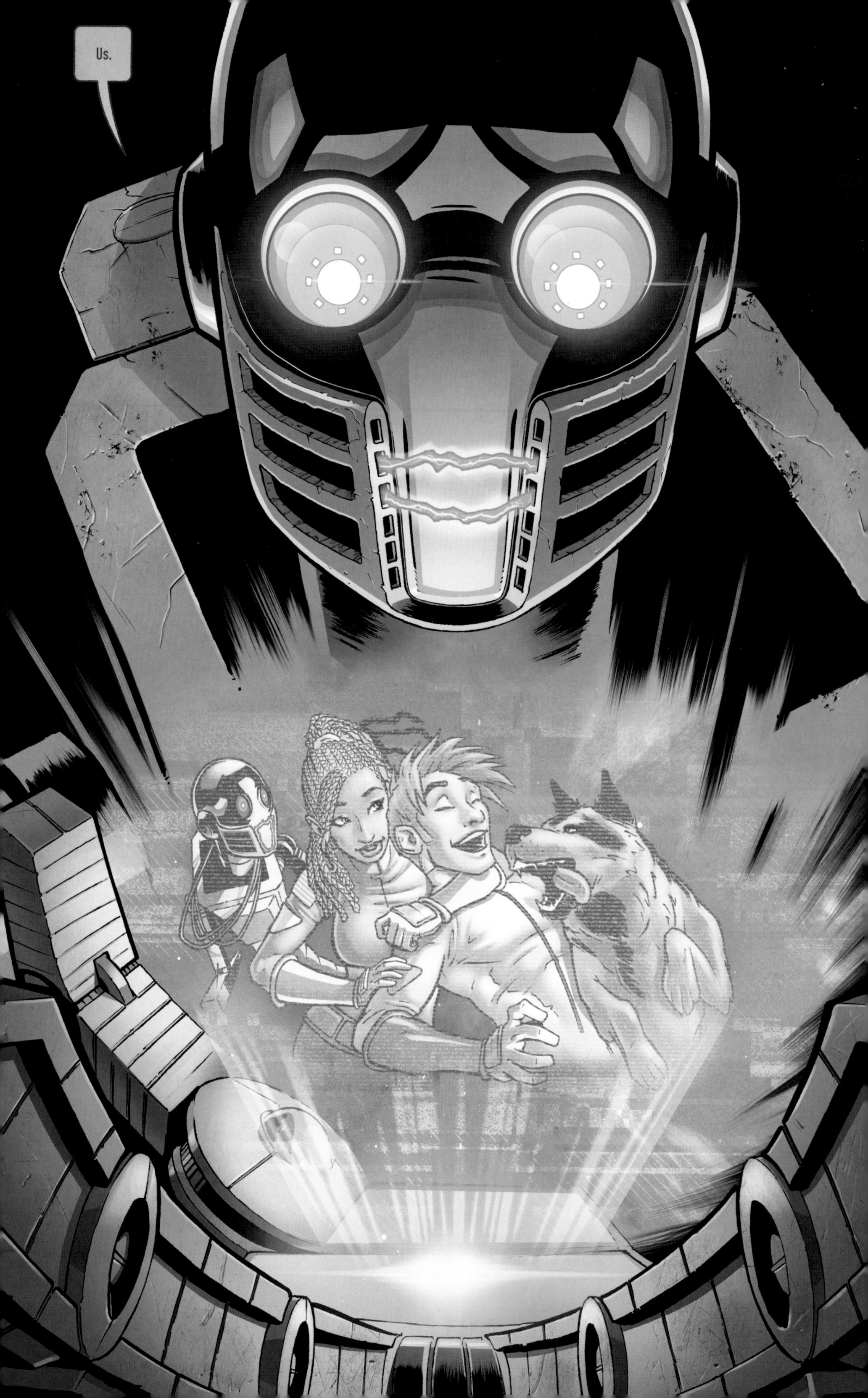
Us.

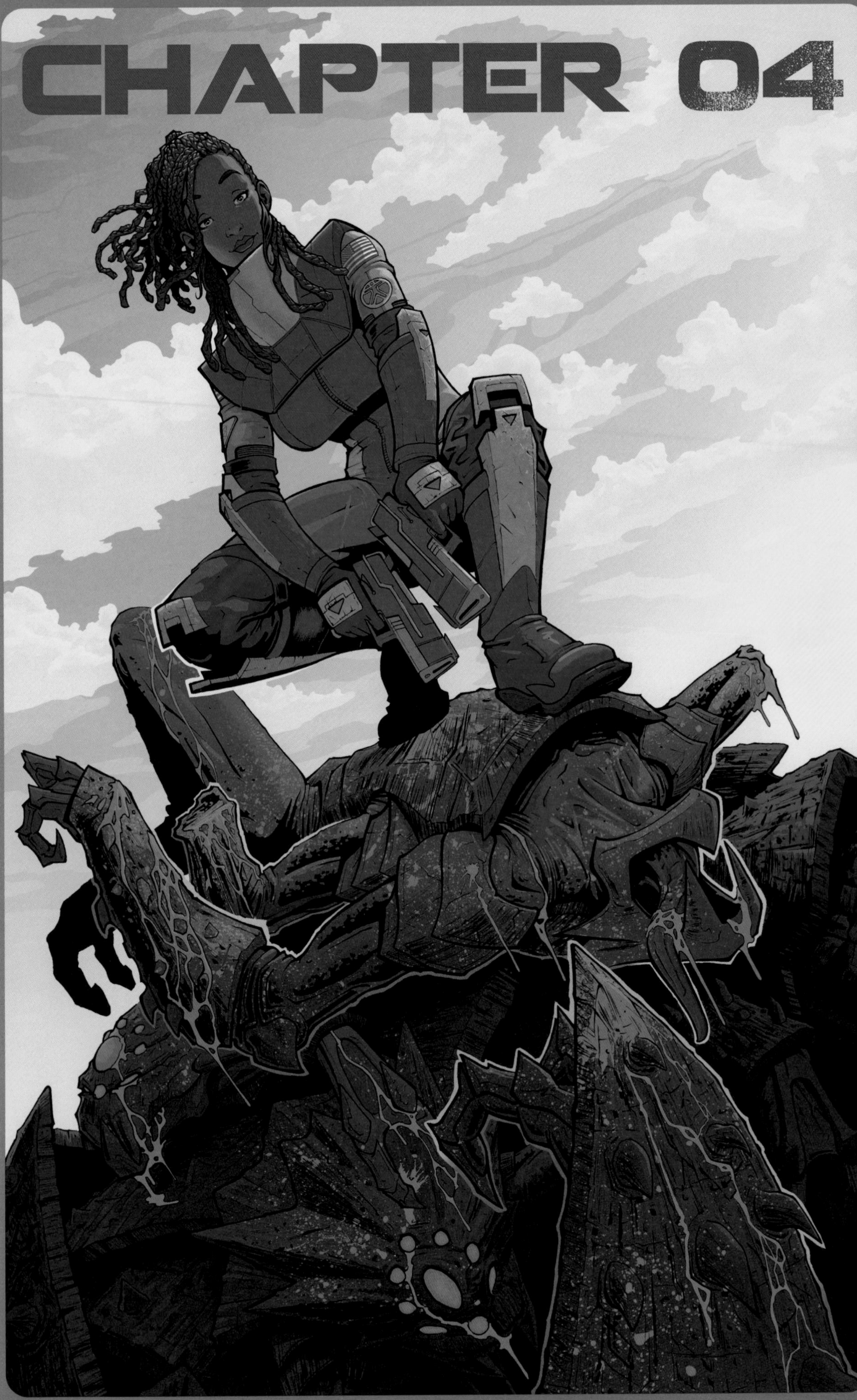
CHAPTER 04

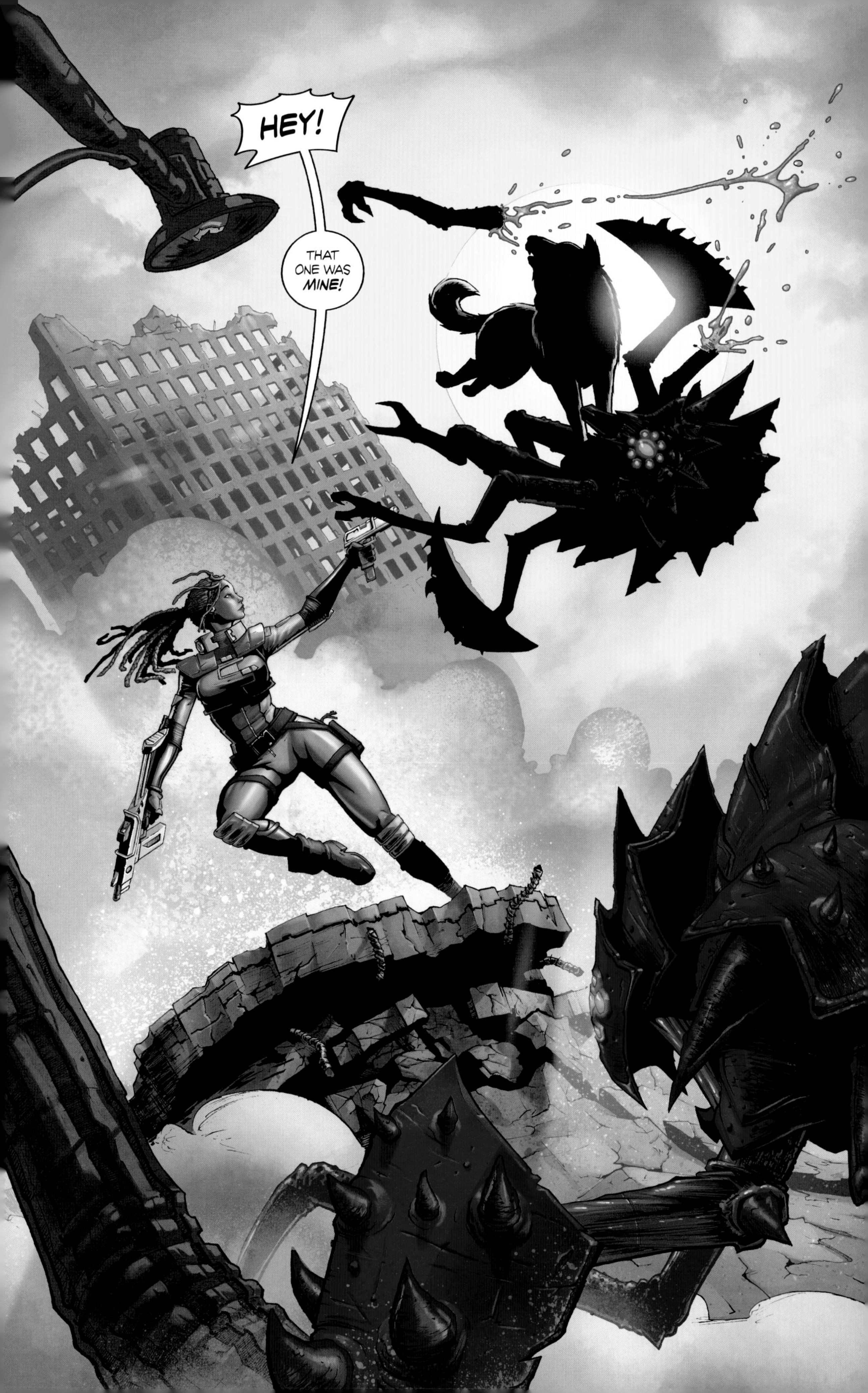
HEY!
THAT ONE WAS MINE!

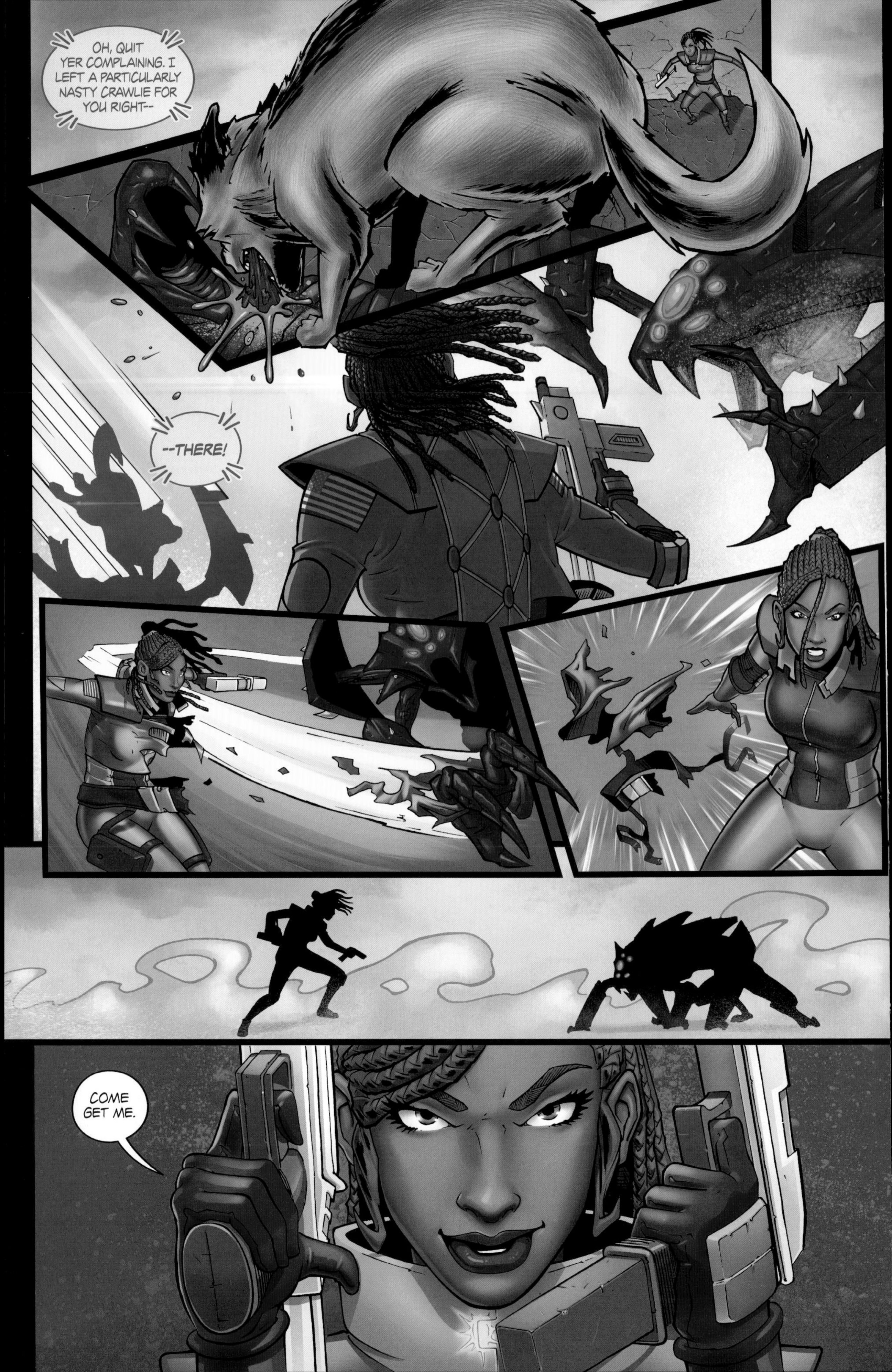
OH, QUIT YER COMPLAINING. I LEFT A PARTICULARLY NASTY CRAWLIE FOR YOU RIGHT--
--THERE!
COME GET ME.

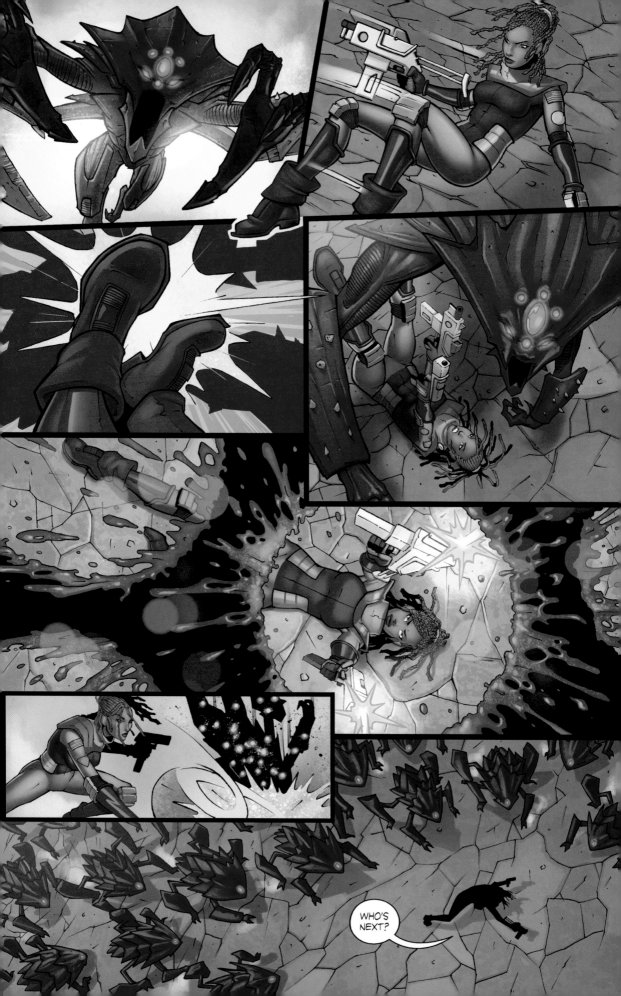

WHO'S NEXT?

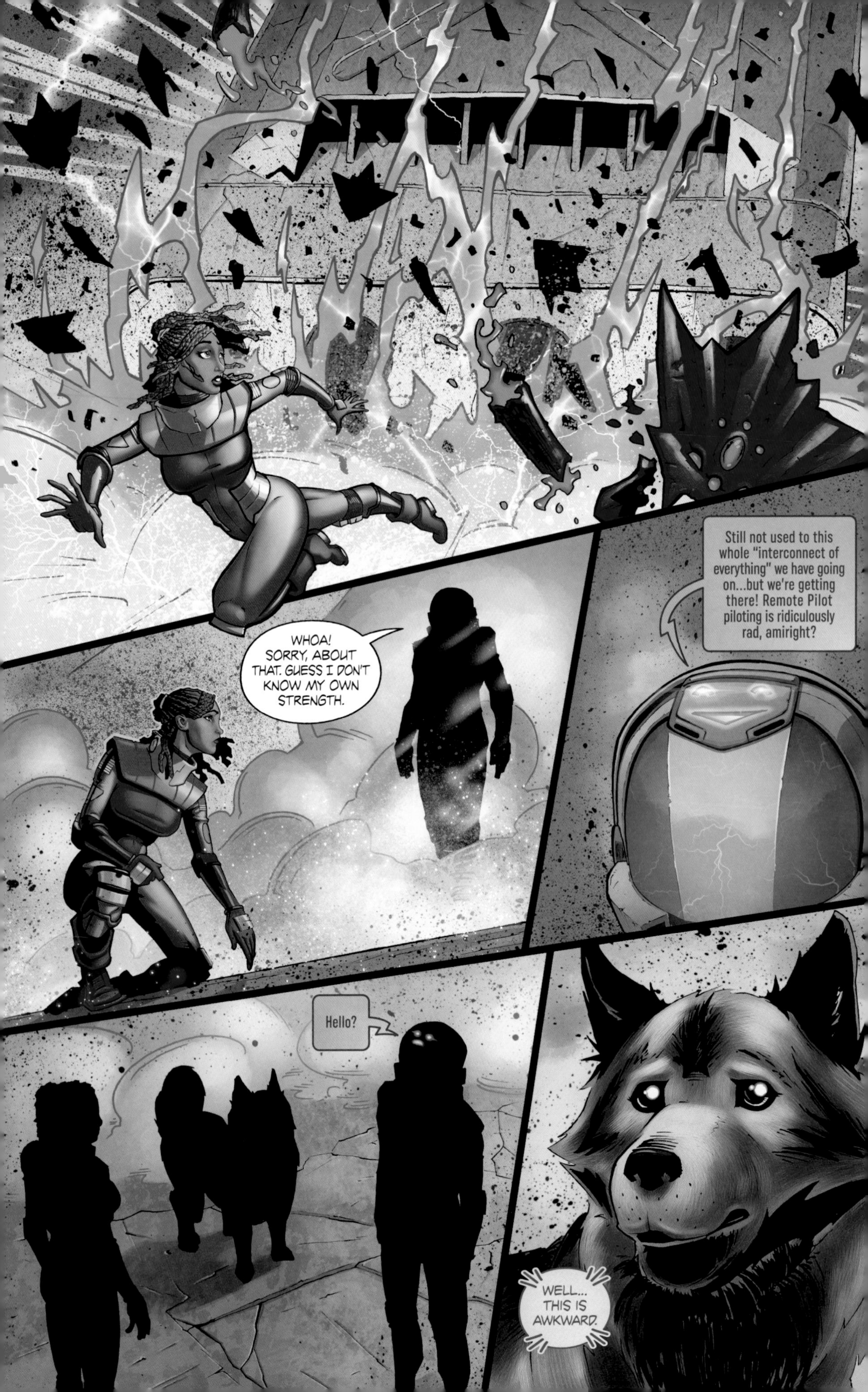
WHOA! SORRY, ABOUT THAT. GUESS I DON'T KNOW MY OWN STRENGTH.
Still not used to this whole "interconnect of everything" we have going on...but we're getting there! Remote Pilot piloting is ridiculously rad, amiright?
Hello?
WELL... THIS IS AWKWARD.

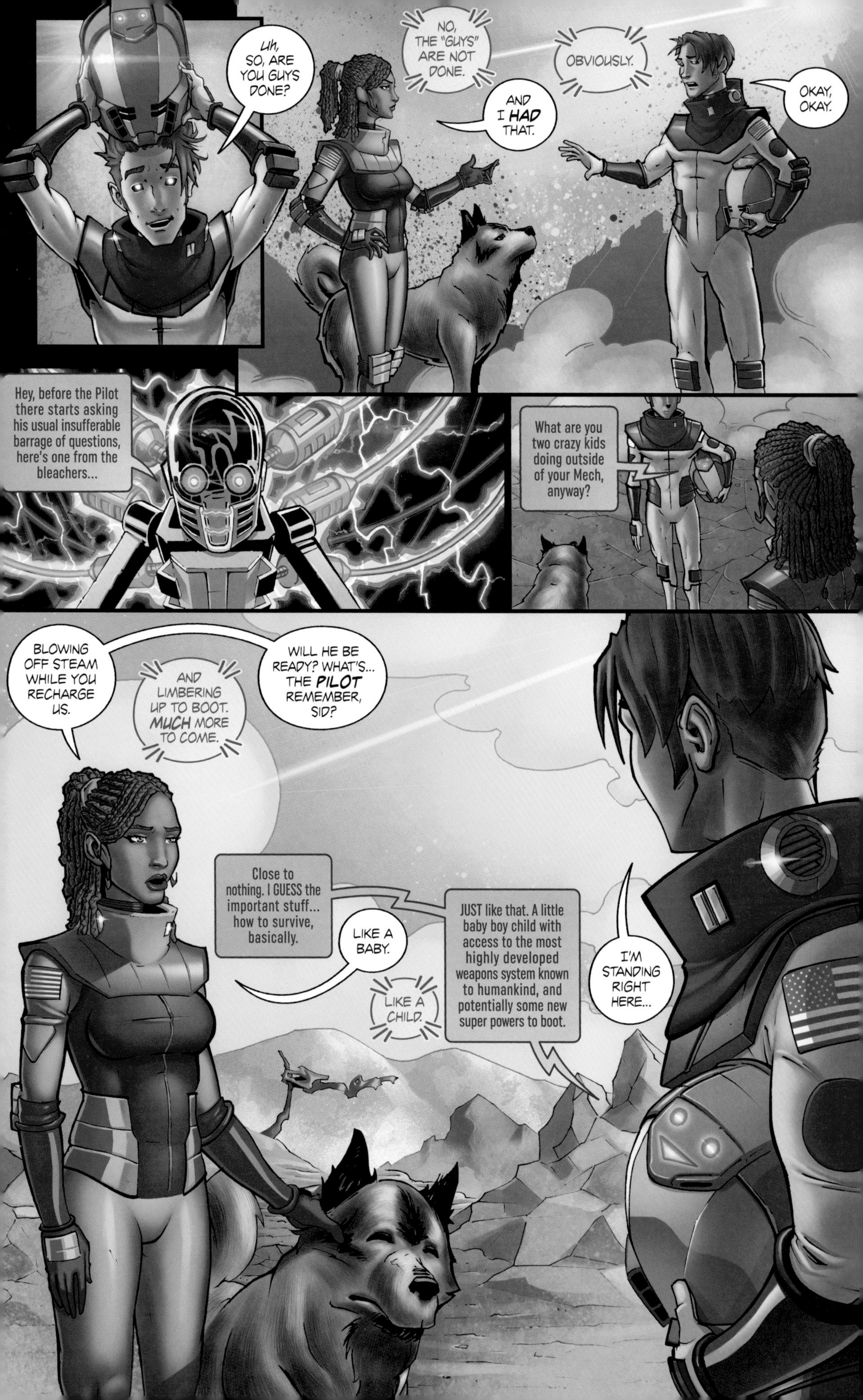
UH, SO, ARE YOU GUYS DONE?
NO, THE "GUYS" ARE NOT DONE.
AND I HAD THAT.
OBVIOUSLY.
OKAY, OKAY.
Hey, before the Pilot there starts asking his usual insufferable barrage of questions, here's one from the bleachers...
What are you two crazy kids doing outside of your Mech, anyway?
BLOWING OFF STEAM WHILE YOU RECHARGE US.
AND LIMBERING UP TO BOOT. MUCH MORE TO COME.
WILL HE BE READY? WHAT'S... THE PILOT REMEMBER, SID?
Close to nothing. I GUESS the important stuff... how to survive, basically.
LIKE A BABY.
LIKE A CHILD.
JUST like that. A little baby boy child with access to the most highly developed weapons system known to humankind, and potentially some new super powers to boot.
I'M STANDING RIGHT HERE...

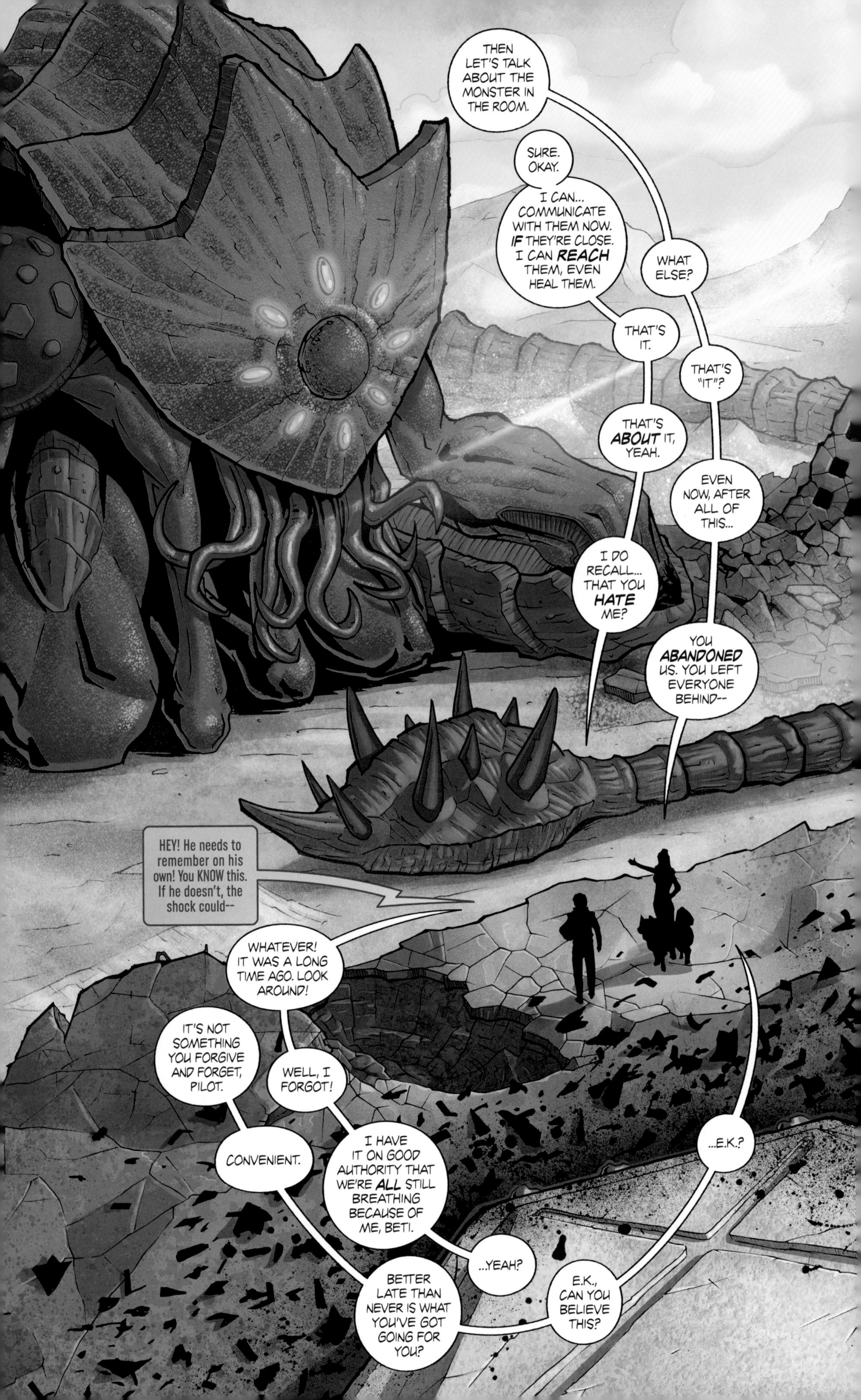
THEN LET'S TALK ABOUT THE MONSTER IN THE ROOM.
SURE. OKAY.
I CAN... COMMUNICATE WITH THEM NOW. IF THEY'RE CLOSE. I CAN REACH THEM, EVEN HEAL THEM.
WHAT ELSE?
THAT'S IT.
THAT'S "IT"?
THAT'S ABOUT IT, YEAH.
EVEN NOW, AFTER ALL OF THIS...
I DO RECALL... THAT YOU HATE ME?
YOU ABANDONED US. YOU LEFT EVERYONE BEHIND--
HEY! He needs to remember on his own! You KNOW this. If he doesn't, the shock could--
WHATEVER! IT WAS A LONG TIME AGO. LOOK AROUND!
IT'S NOT SOMETHING YOU FORGIVE AND FORGET, PILOT.
WELL, I FORGOT!
CONVENIENT.
I HAVE IT ON GOOD AUTHORITY THAT WE'RE ALL STILL BREATHING BECAUSE OF ME, BETI.
...YEAH?
BETTER LATE THAN NEVER IS WHAT YOU'VE GOT GOING FOR YOU?
E.K., CAN YOU BELIEVE THIS?
...E.K.?

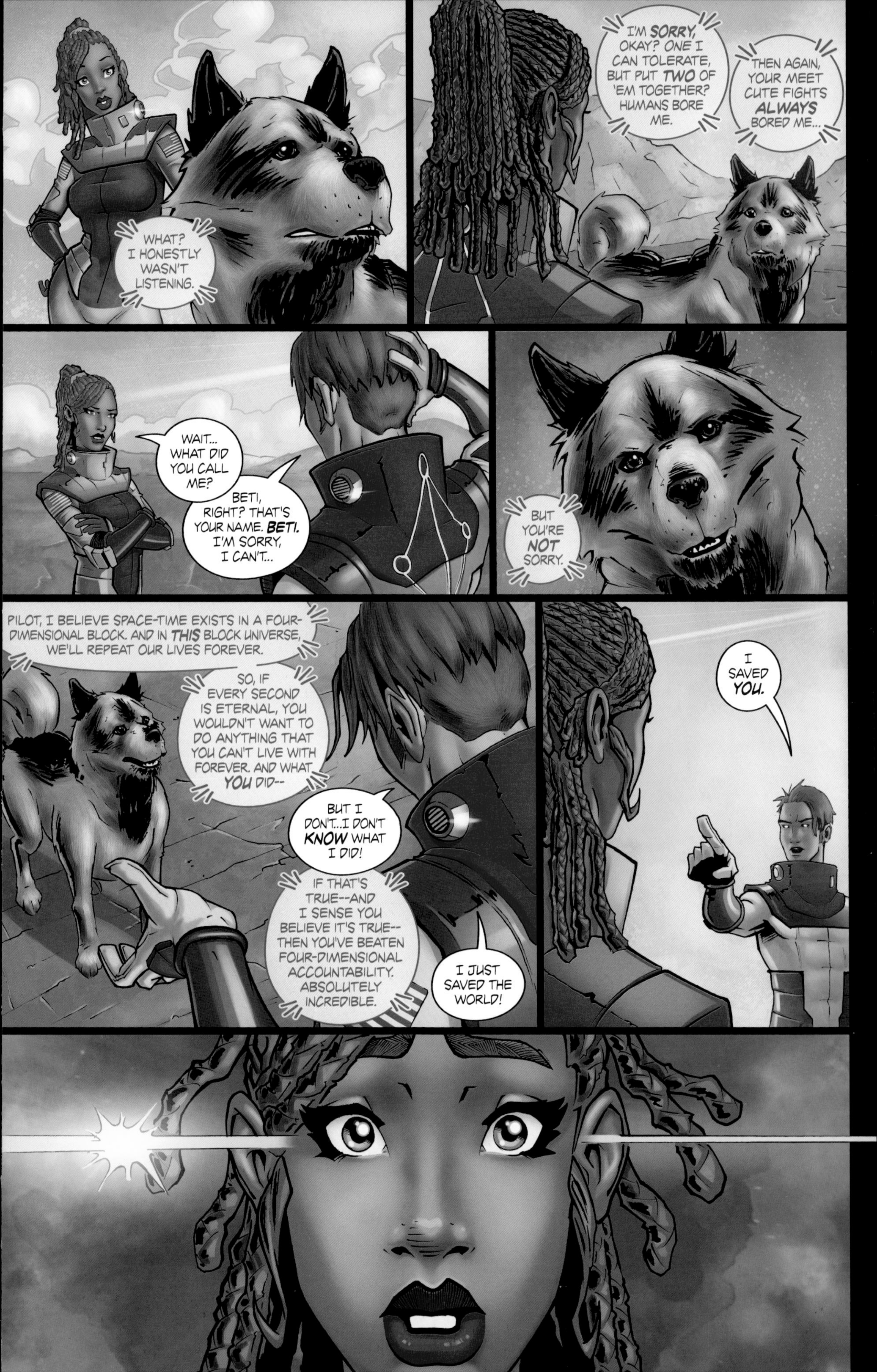
WHAT? I HONESTLY WASN'T LISTENING.
I'M SORRY, OKAY? ONE I CAN TOLERATE, BUT PUT TWO OF 'EM TOGETHER? HUMANS BORE ME.
THEN AGAIN, YOUR MEET CUTE FIGHTS ALWAYS BORED ME...
WAIT... WHAT DID YOU CALL ME?
BETI, RIGHT? THAT'S YOUR NAME. BETI. I'M SORRY, I CAN'T...
BUT YOU'RE NOT SORRY.
PILOT, I BELIEVE SPACE-TIME EXISTS IN A FOUR-DIMENSIONAL BLOCK. AND IN THIS BLOCK UNIVERSE, WE'LL REPEAT OUR LIVES FOREVER.
SO, IF EVERY SECOND IS ETERNAL, YOU WOULDN'T WANT TO DO ANYTHING THAT YOU CAN'T LIVE WITH FOREVER. AND WHAT YOU DID--
BUT I DON'T...I DON'T KNOW WHAT I DID!
IF THAT'S TRUE--AND I SENSE YOU BELIEVE IT'S TRUE--THEN YOU'VE BEATEN FOUR-DIMENSIONAL ACCOUNTABILITY. ABSOLUTELY INCREDIBLE.
I JUST SAVED THE WORLD!
I SAVED YOU.

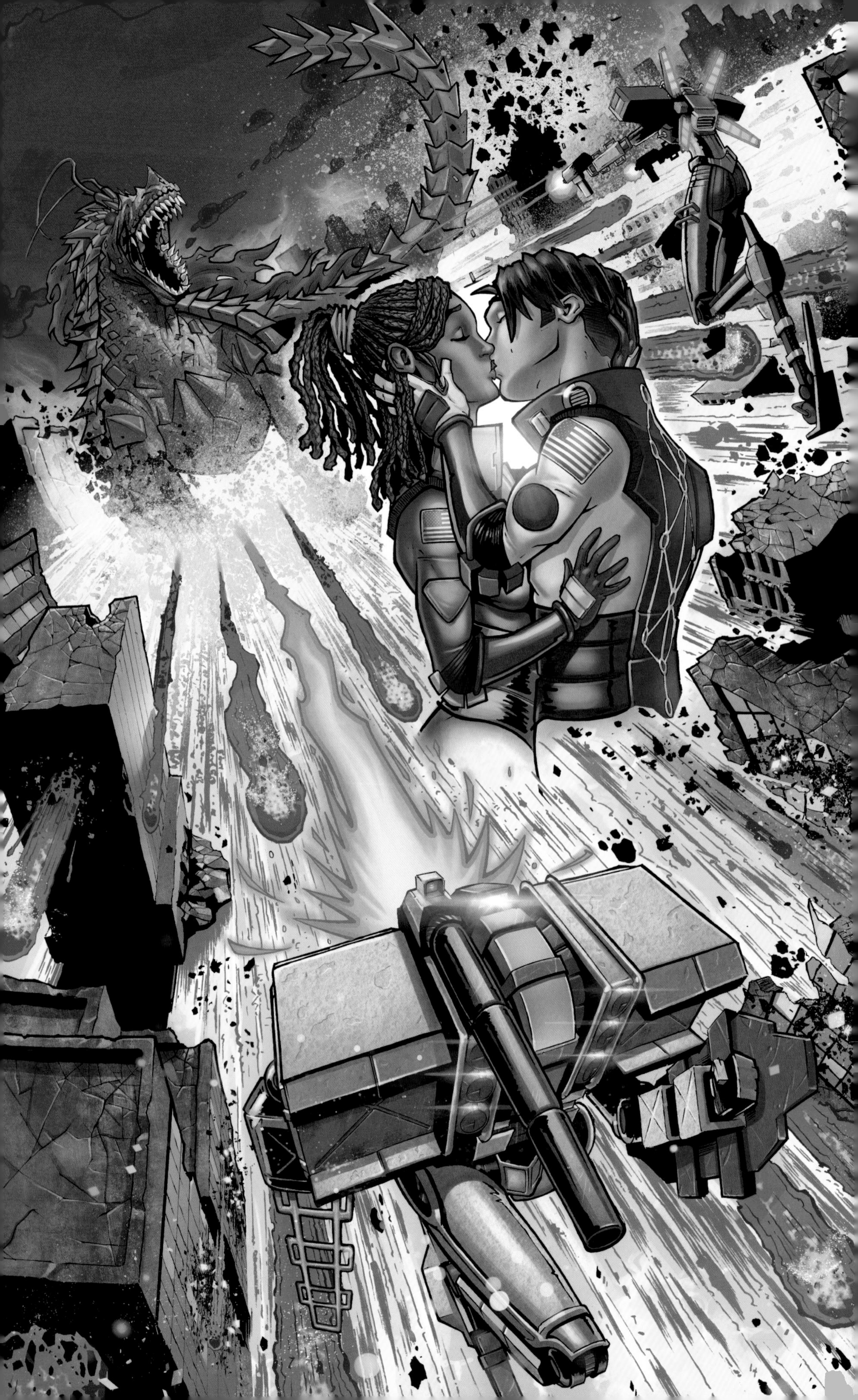

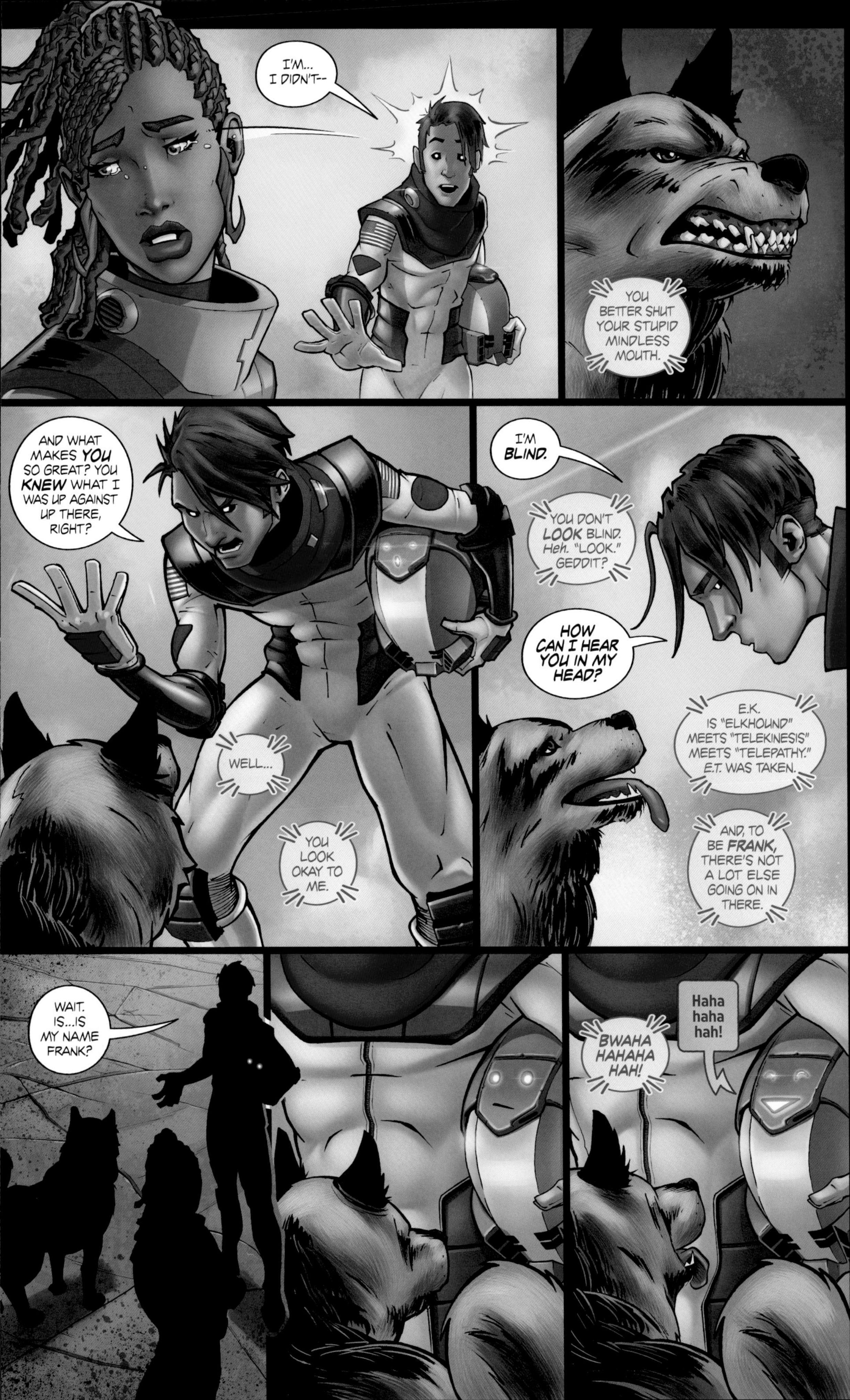
I'M... I DIDN'T--
YOU BETTER SHUT YOUR STUPID MINDLESS MOUTH.
AND WHAT MAKES **YOU** SO GREAT? YOU **KNEW** WHAT I WAS UP AGAINST UP THERE, RIGHT?
WELL...
YOU LOOK OKAY TO ME.
I'M **BLIND.**
YOU DON'T **LOOK** BLIND. *Heh.* "LOOK." GEDDIT?
HOW CAN I HEAR YOU IN MY HEAD?
E.K. IS "ELKHOUND" MEETS "TELEKINESIS" MEETS "TELEPATHY." E.T. WAS TAKEN.
AND, TO BE **FRANK,** THERE'S NOT A LOT ELSE GOING ON IN THERE.
WAIT. IS...IS MY NAME FRANK?
BWAHA HAHAHA HAH!
Haha haha hah!

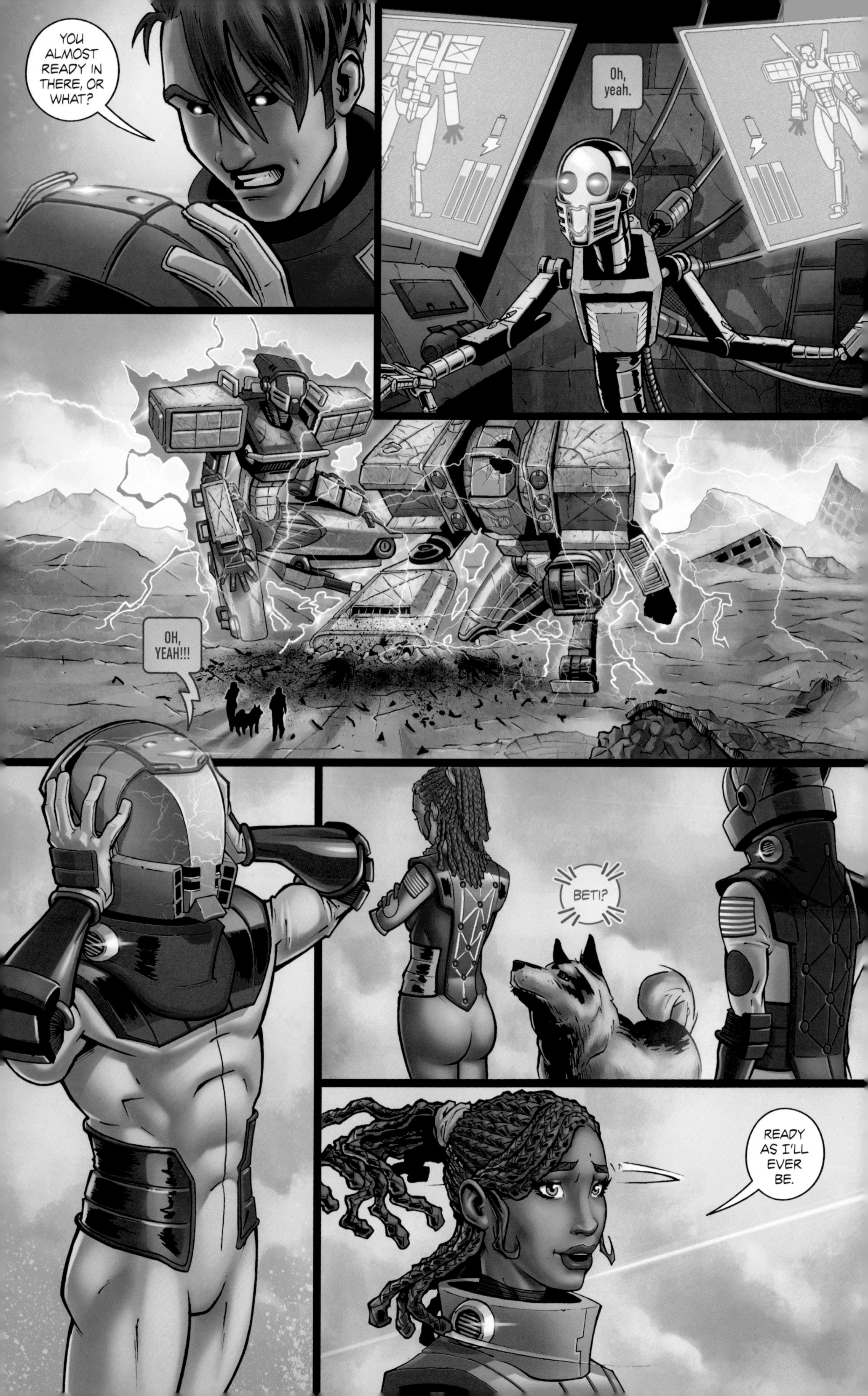
YOU ALMOST READY IN THERE, OR WHAT?
Oh, yeah.
OH, YEAH!!!
BETI?
READY AS I'LL EVER BE.

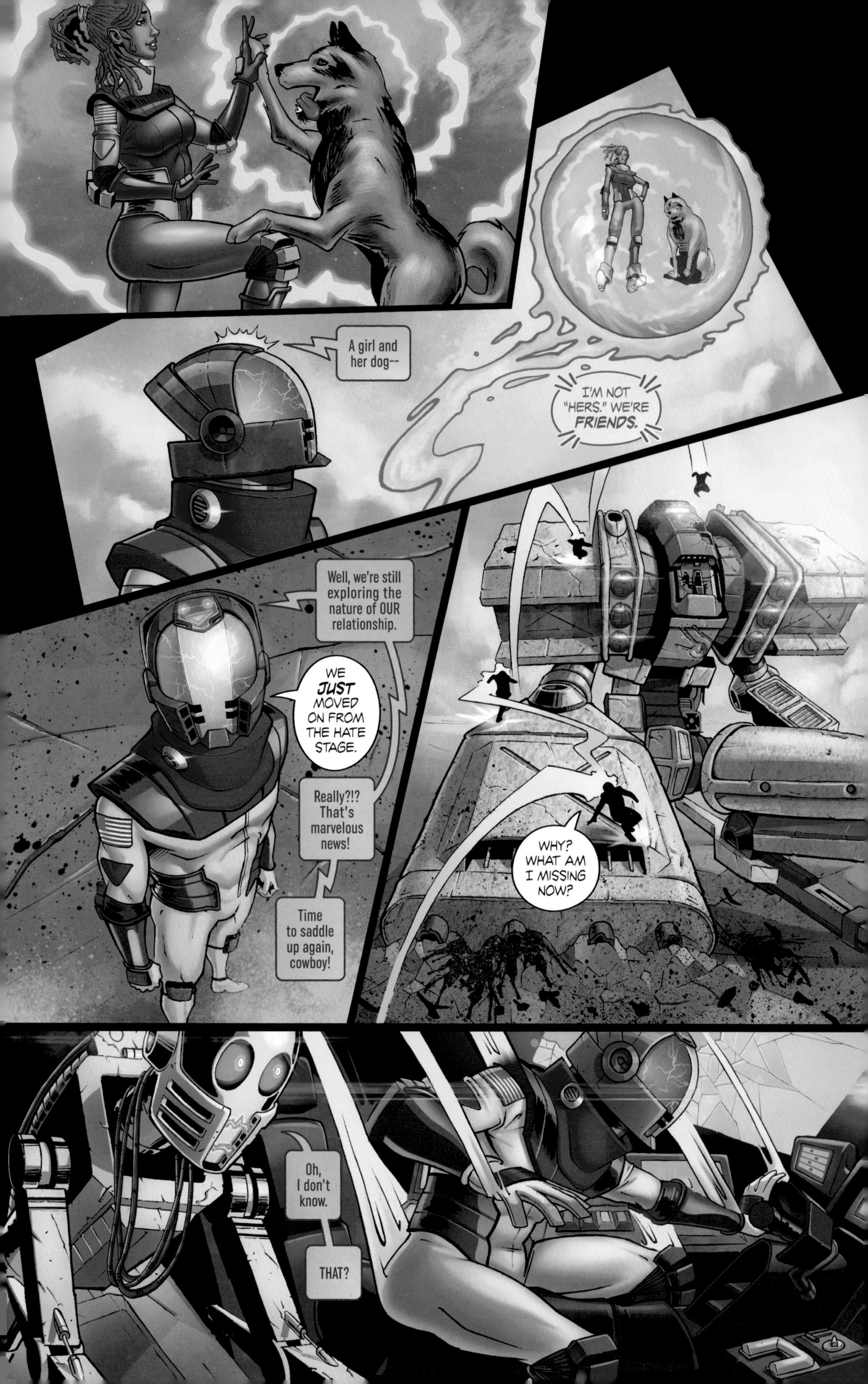
A girl and her dog--
I'M NOT "HERS." WE'RE FRIENDS.
Well, we're still exploring the nature of OUR relationship.
WE JUST MOVED ON FROM THE HATE STAGE.
Really?!? That's marvelous news!
Time to saddle up again, cowboy!
WHY? WHAT AM I MISSING NOW?
Oh, I don't know.
THAT?

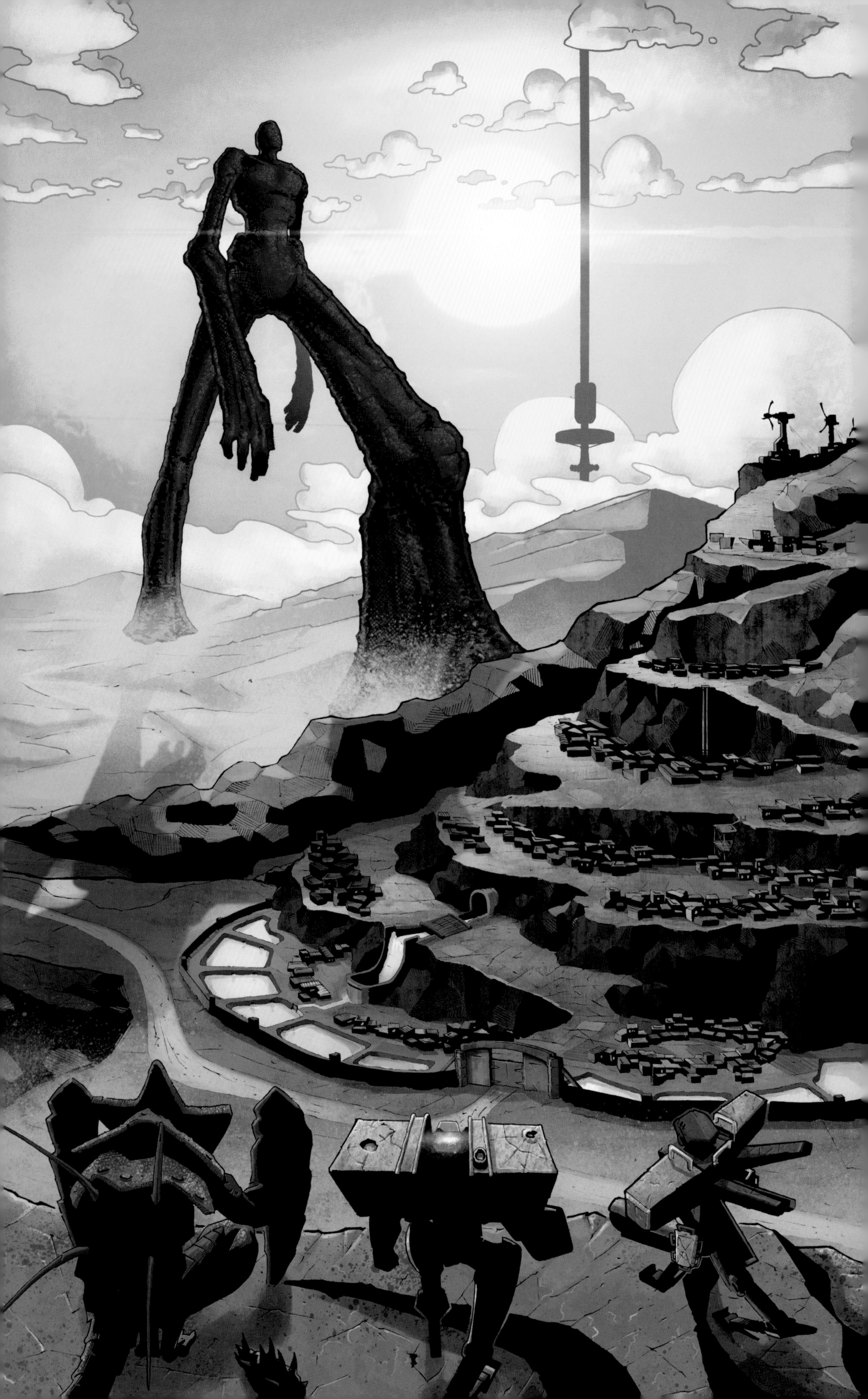

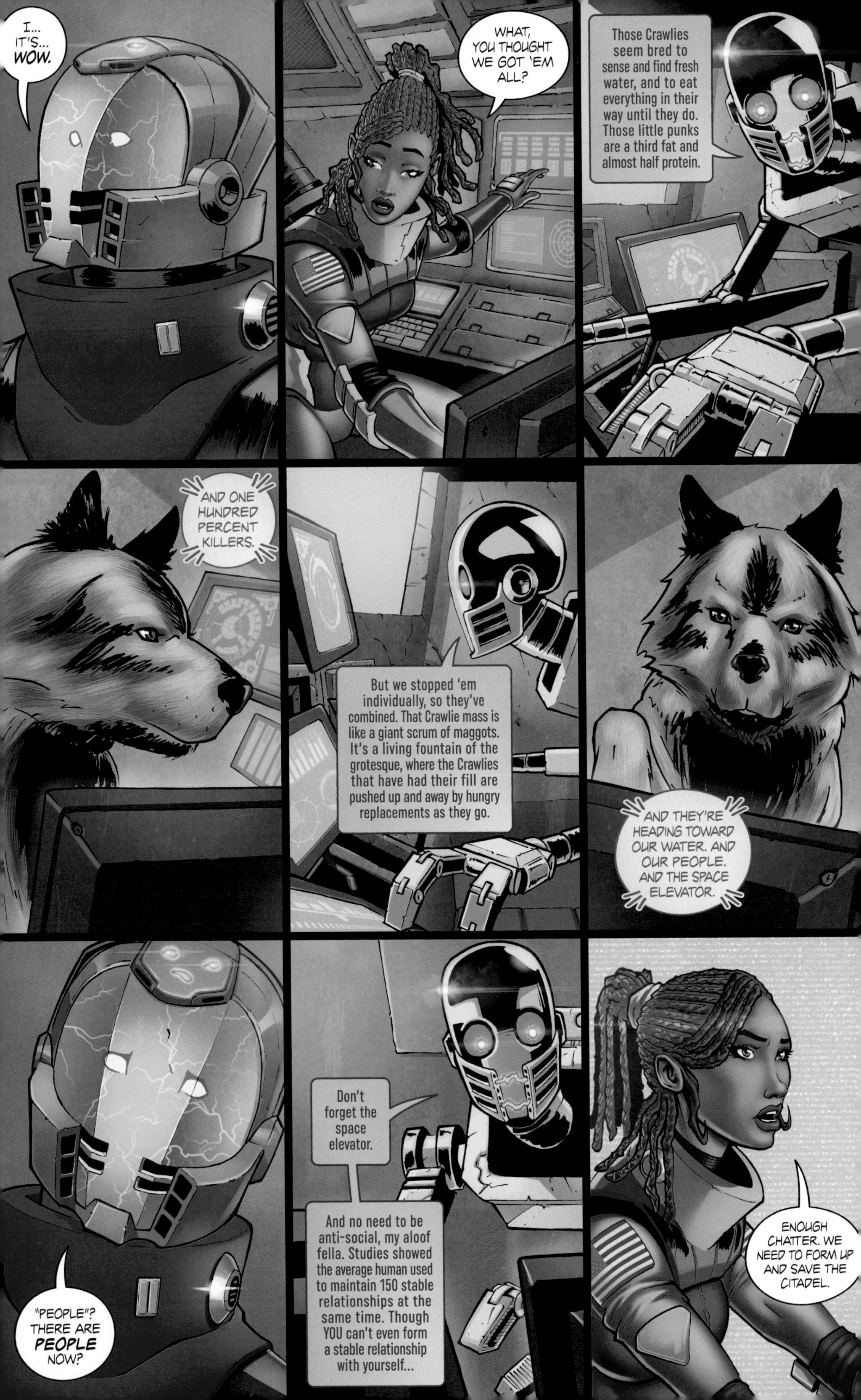
I... IT'S... WOW.
WHAT, YOU THOUGHT WE GOT 'EM ALL?
Those Crawlies seem bred to sense and find fresh water, and to eat everything in their way until they do. Those little punks are a third fat and almost half protein.
AND ONE HUNDRED PERCENT KILLERS.
But we stopped 'em individually, so they've combined. That Crawlie mass is like a giant scrum of maggots. It's a living fountain of the grotesque, where the Crawlies that have had their fill are pushed up and away by hungry replacements as they go.
AND THEY'RE HEADING TOWARD OUR WATER. AND OUR PEOPLE. AND THE SPACE ELEVATOR.
"PEOPLE"? THERE ARE PEOPLE NOW?
Don't forget the space elevator.
And no need to be anti-social, my aloof fella. Studies showed the average human used to maintain 150 stable relationships at the same time. Though YOU can't even form a stable relationship with yourself...
ENOUGH CHATTER. WE NEED TO FORM UP AND SAVE THE CITADEL.

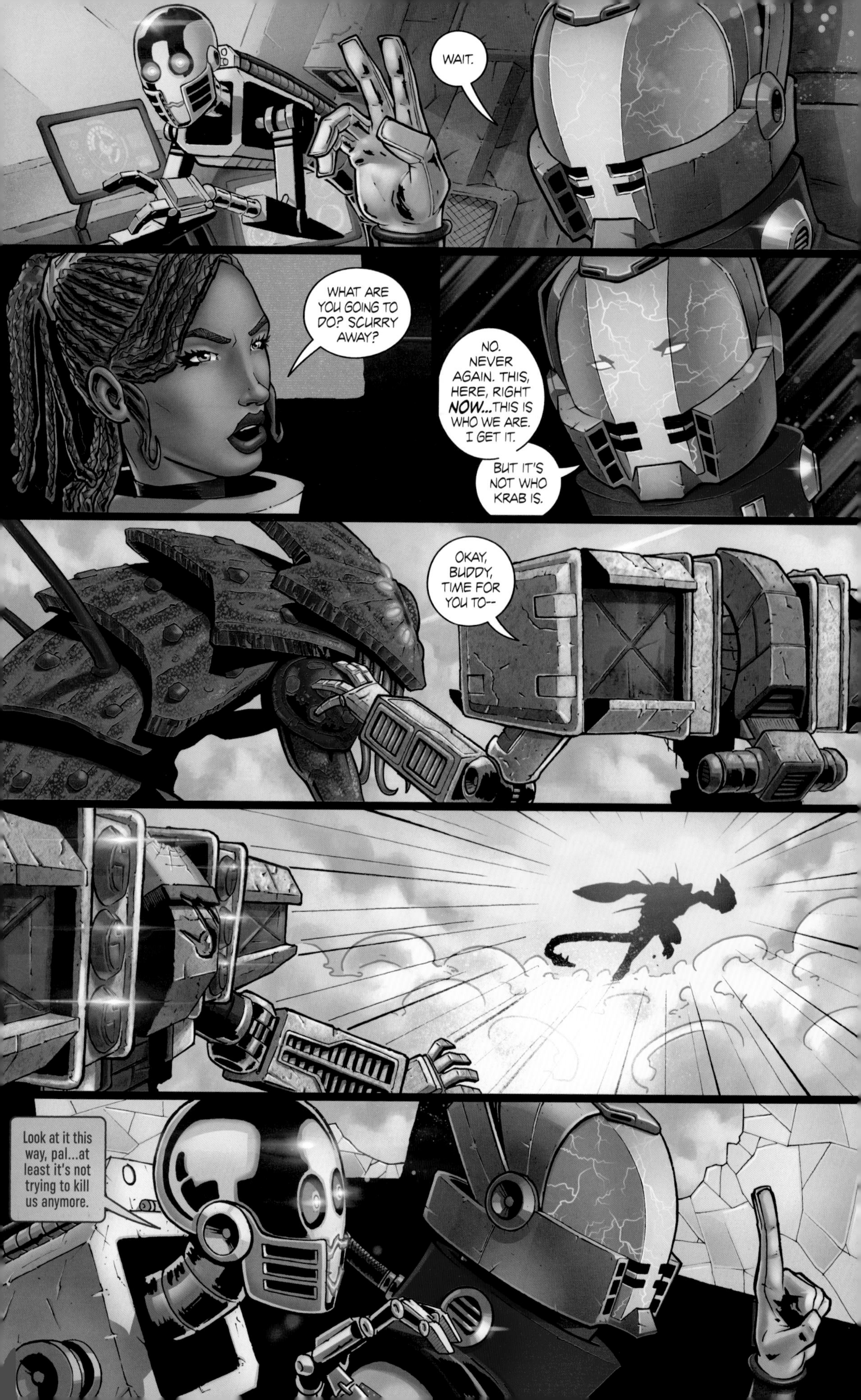
WAIT.
WHAT ARE YOU GOING TO DO? SCURRY AWAY?
NO. NEVER AGAIN. THIS, HERE, RIGHT NOW...THIS IS WHO WE ARE. I GET IT.
BUT IT'S NOT WHO KRAB IS.
OKAY, BUDDY, TIME FOR YOU TO--
Look at it this way, pal...at least it's not trying to kill us anymore.

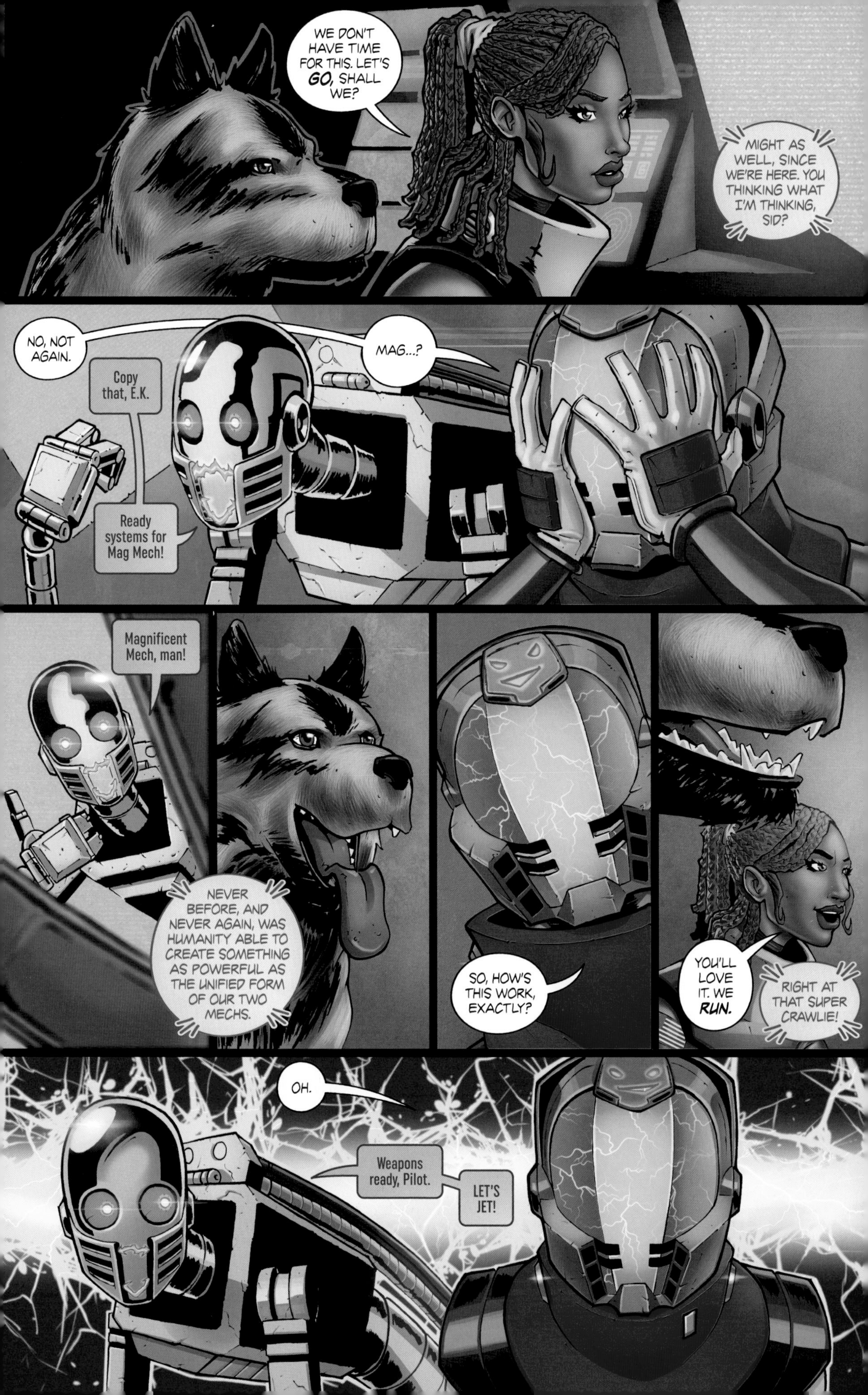
WE DON'T HAVE TIME FOR THIS. LET'S GO, SHALL WE?
MIGHT AS WELL, SINCE WE'RE HERE. YOU THINKING WHAT I'M THINKING, SID?
NO, NOT AGAIN.
MAG...?
Copy that, E.K.
Ready systems for Mag Mech!
Magnificent Mech, man!
NEVER BEFORE, AND NEVER AGAIN, WAS HUMANITY ABLE TO CREATE SOMETHING AS POWERFUL AS THE UNIFIED FORM OF OUR TWO MECHS.
SO, HOW'S THIS WORK, EXACTLY?
YOU'LL LOVE IT. WE RUN.
RIGHT AT THAT SUPER CRAWLIE!
OH.
Weapons ready, Pilot.
LET'S JET!

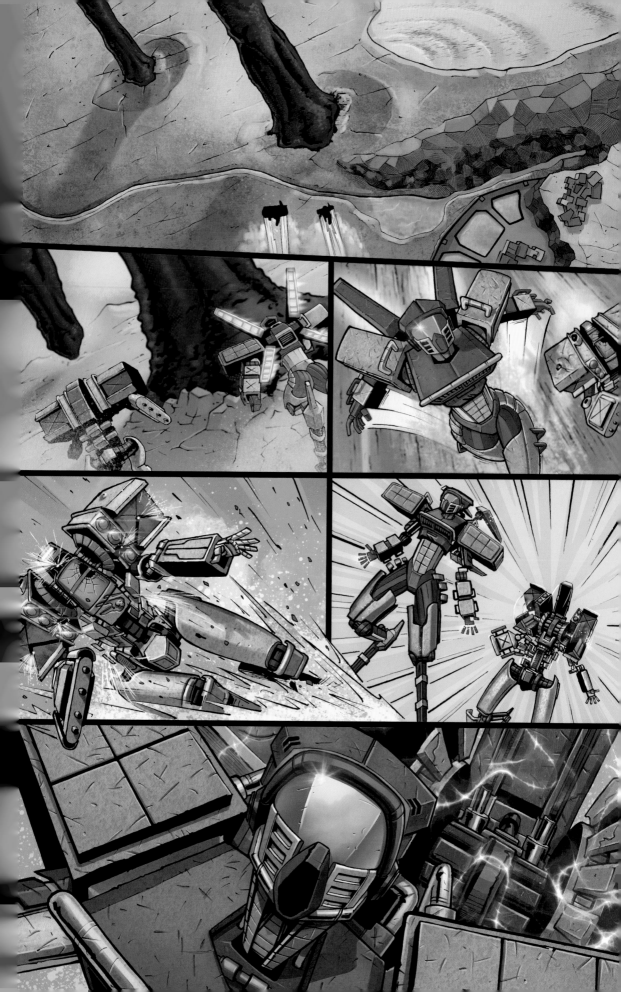

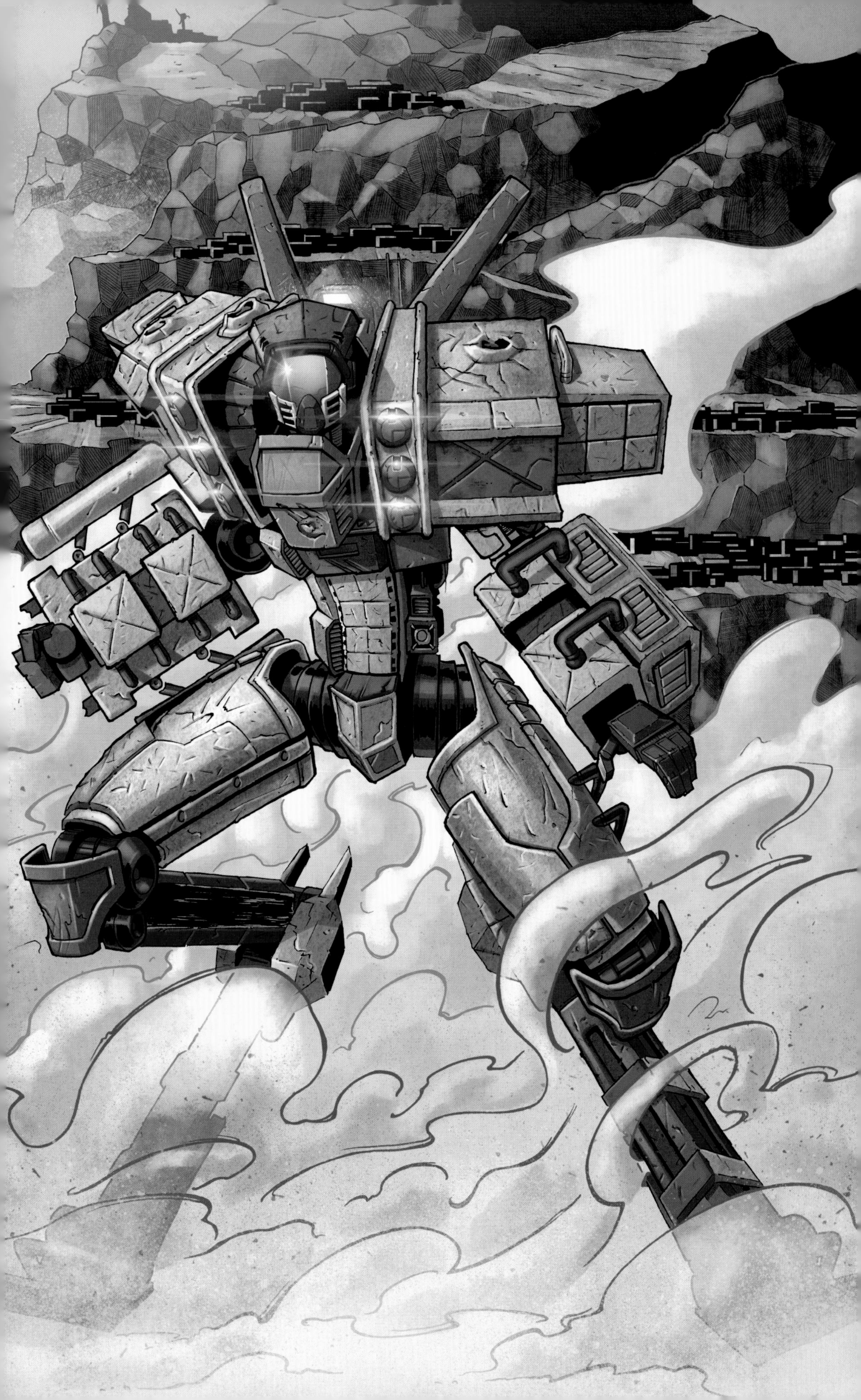

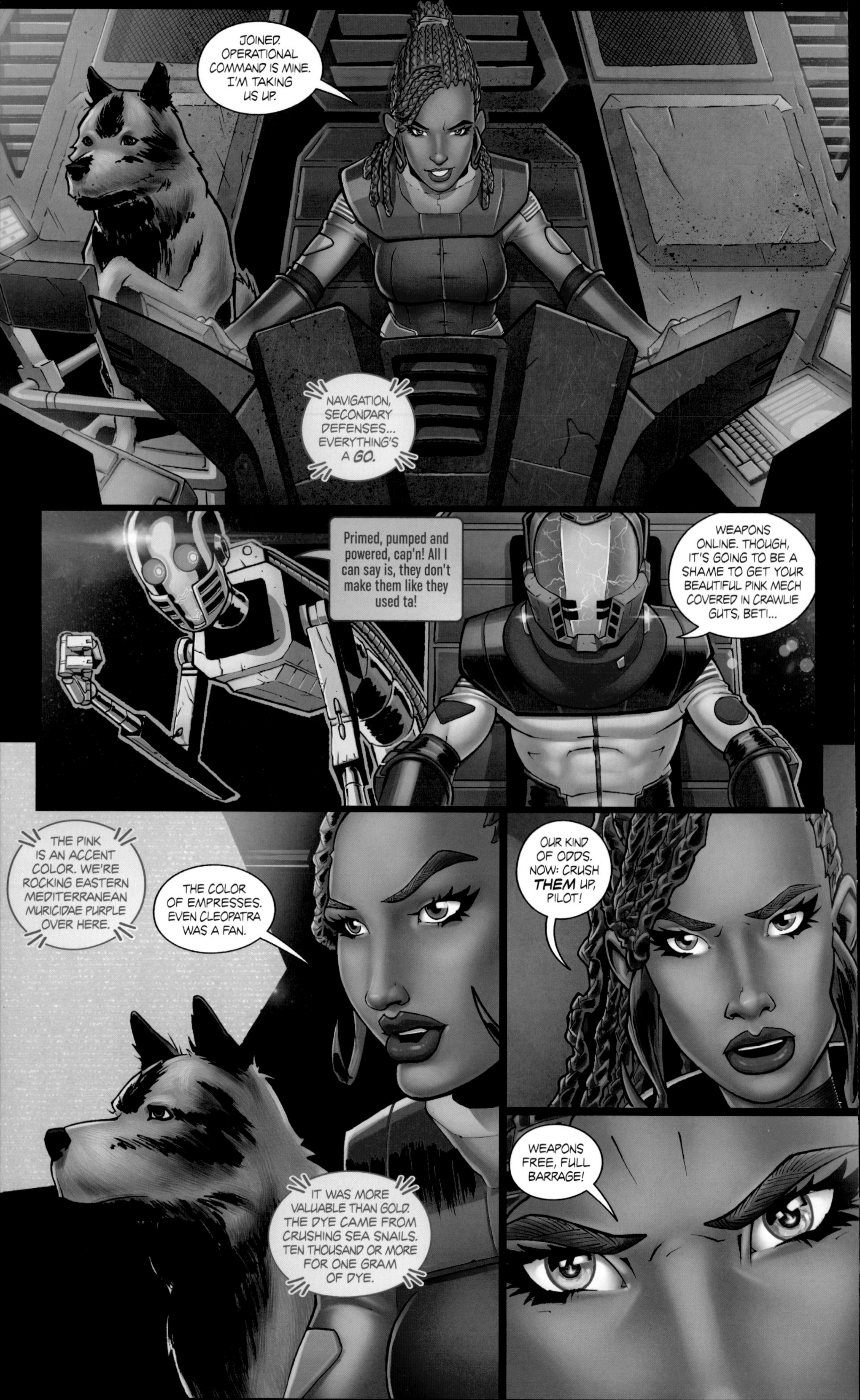
JOINED. OPERATIONAL COMMAND IS MINE. I'M TAKING US UP.
NAVIGATION, SECONDARY DEFENSES... EVERYTHING'S A GO.
Primed, pumped and powered, cap'n! All I can say is, they don't make them like they used ta!
WEAPONS ONLINE. THOUGH, IT'S GOING TO BE A SHAME TO GET YOUR BEAUTIFUL PINK MECH COVERED IN CRAWLIE GUTS, BETI...
THE PINK IS AN ACCENT COLOR. WE'RE ROCKING EASTERN MEDITERRANEAN MURICIDAE PURPLE OVER HERE.
THE COLOR OF EMPRESSES. EVEN CLEOPATRA WAS A FAN.
IT WAS MORE VALUABLE THAN GOLD. THE DYE CAME FROM CRUSHING SEA SNAILS. TEN THOUSAND OR MORE FOR ONE GRAM OF DYE.
OUR KIND OF ODDS. NOW: CRUSH THEM UP, PILOT!
WEAPONS FREE, FULL BARRAGE!

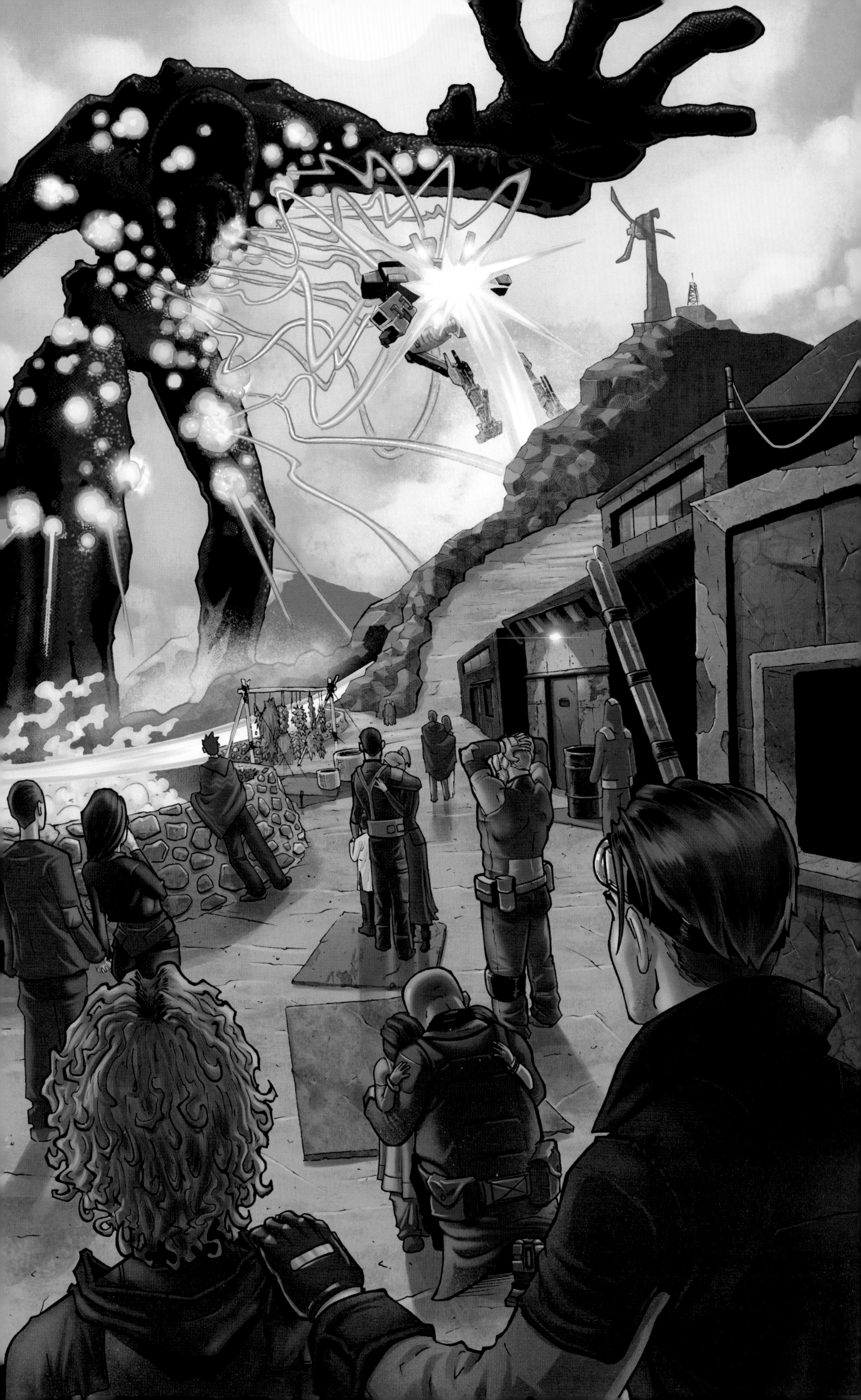

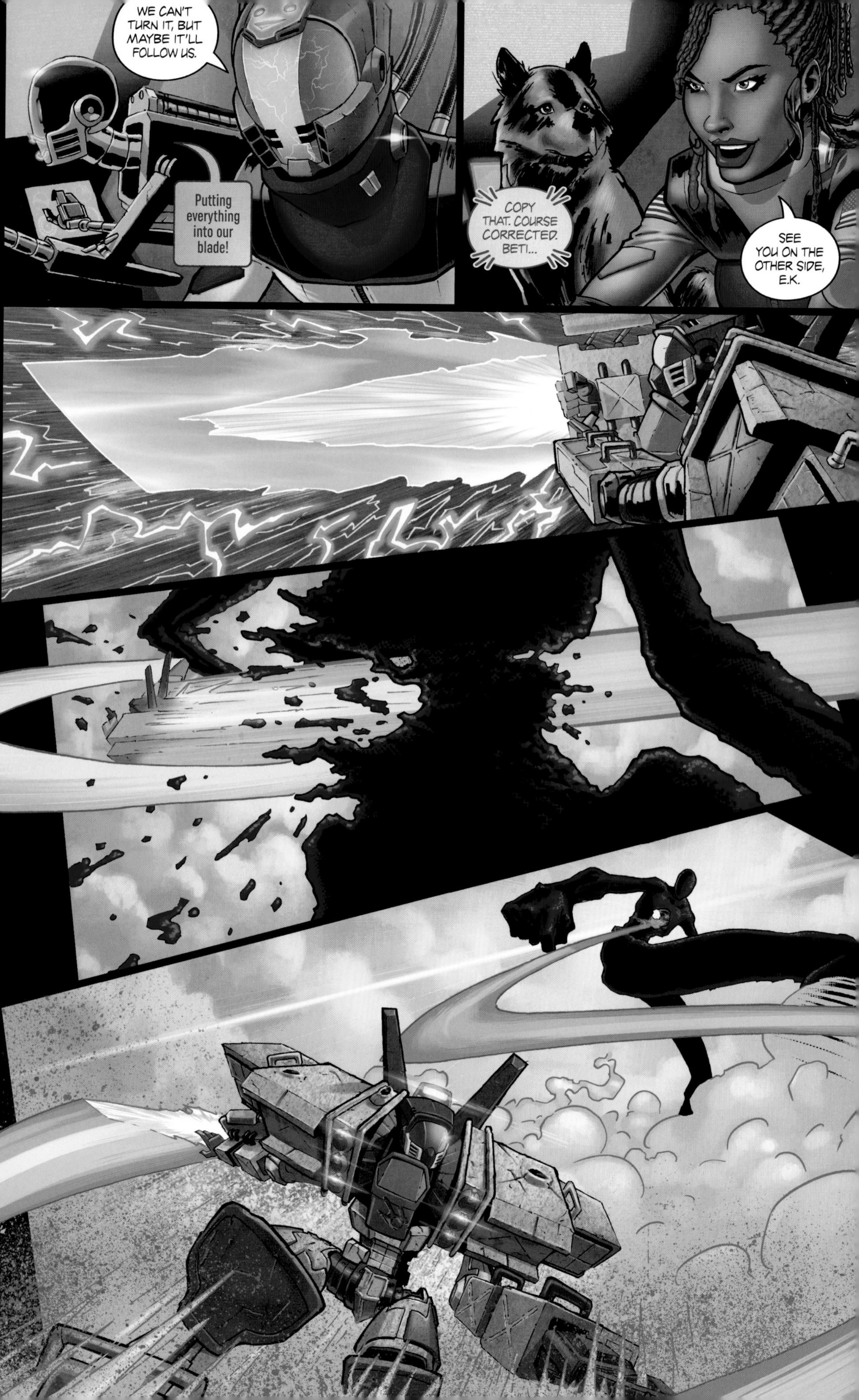
WE CAN'T TURN IT, BUT MAYBE IT'LL FOLLOW US.
Putting everything into our blade!
COPY THAT. COURSE CORRECTED. BETI...
SEE YOU ON THE OTHER SIDE, E.K.

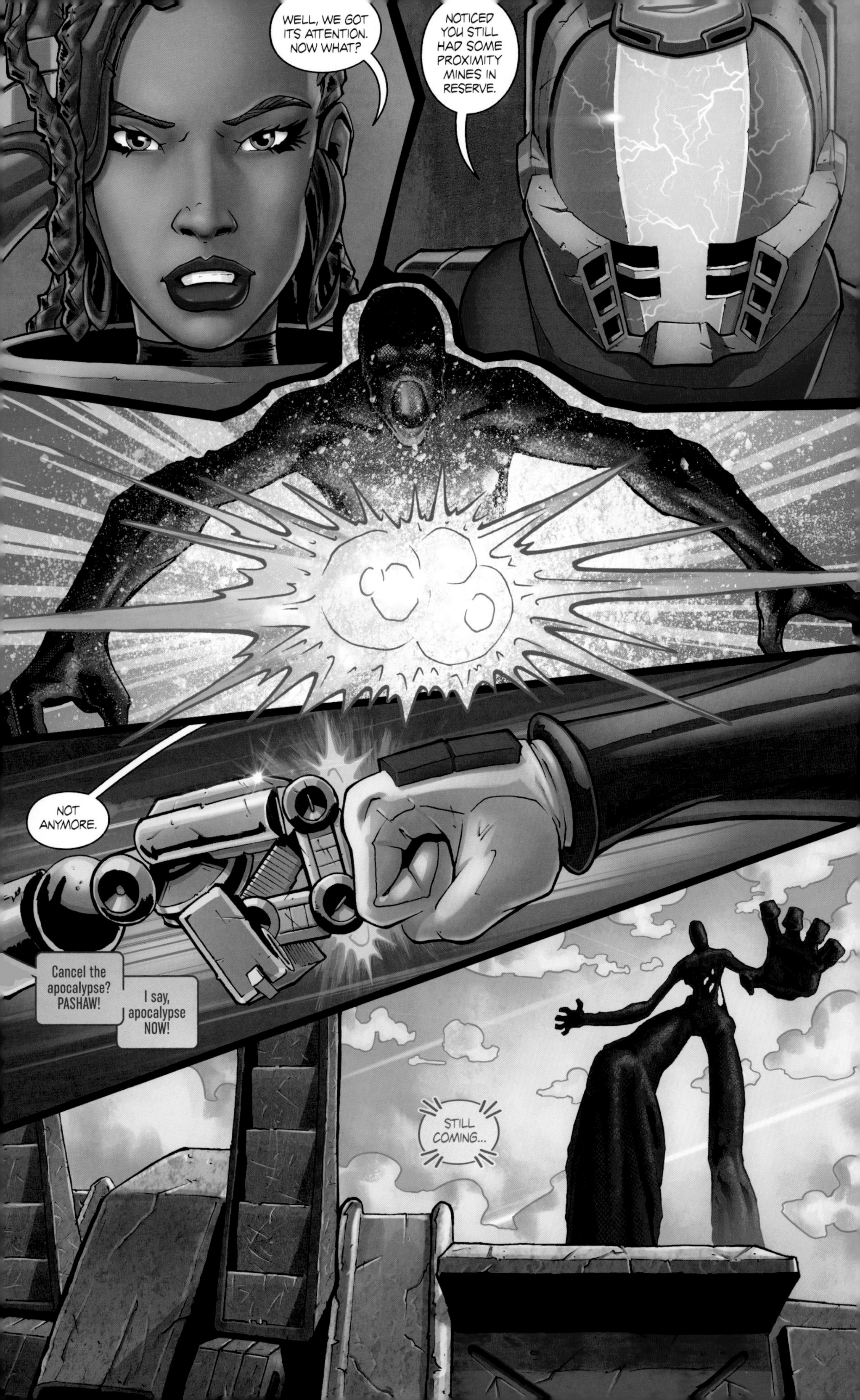
WELL, WE GOT ITS ATTENTION. NOW WHAT?
NOTICED YOU STILL HAD SOME PROXIMITY MINES IN RESERVE.
NOT ANYMORE.
Cancel the apocalypse? PASHAW!
I say, apocalypse NOW!
STILL COMING...

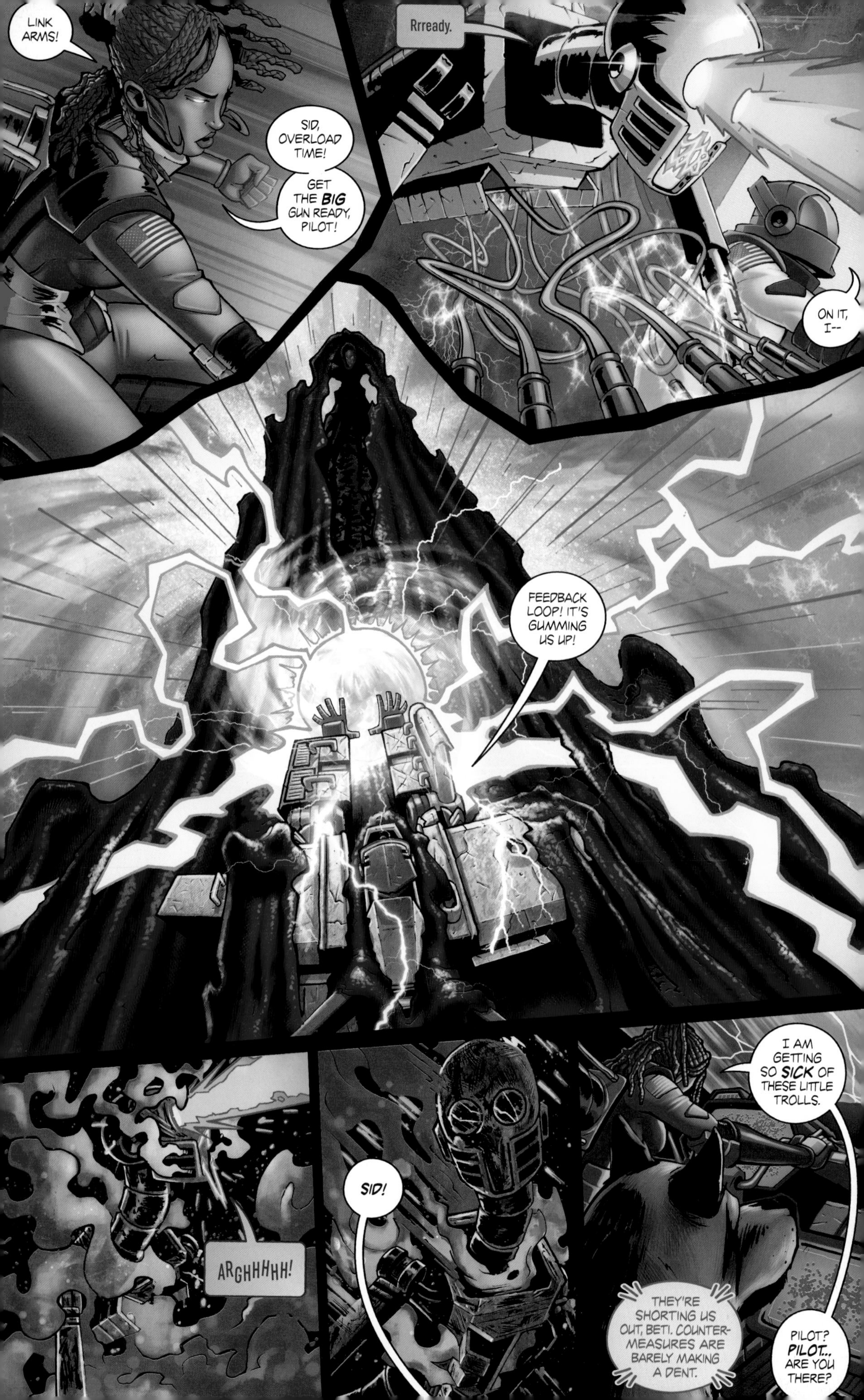
LINK ARMS!
SID, OVERLOAD TIME!
GET THE **BIG** GUN READY, PILOT!
Rrready.
ON IT, I--
FEEDBACK LOOP! IT'S GUMMING US UP!
ARGHHHHH!
SID!
I AM GETTING SO **SICK** OF THESE LITTLE TROLLS.
THEY'RE SHORTING US OUT, BETI. COUNTER-MEASURES ARE BARELY MAKING A DENT.
PILOT? **PILOT..** ARE YOU THERE?

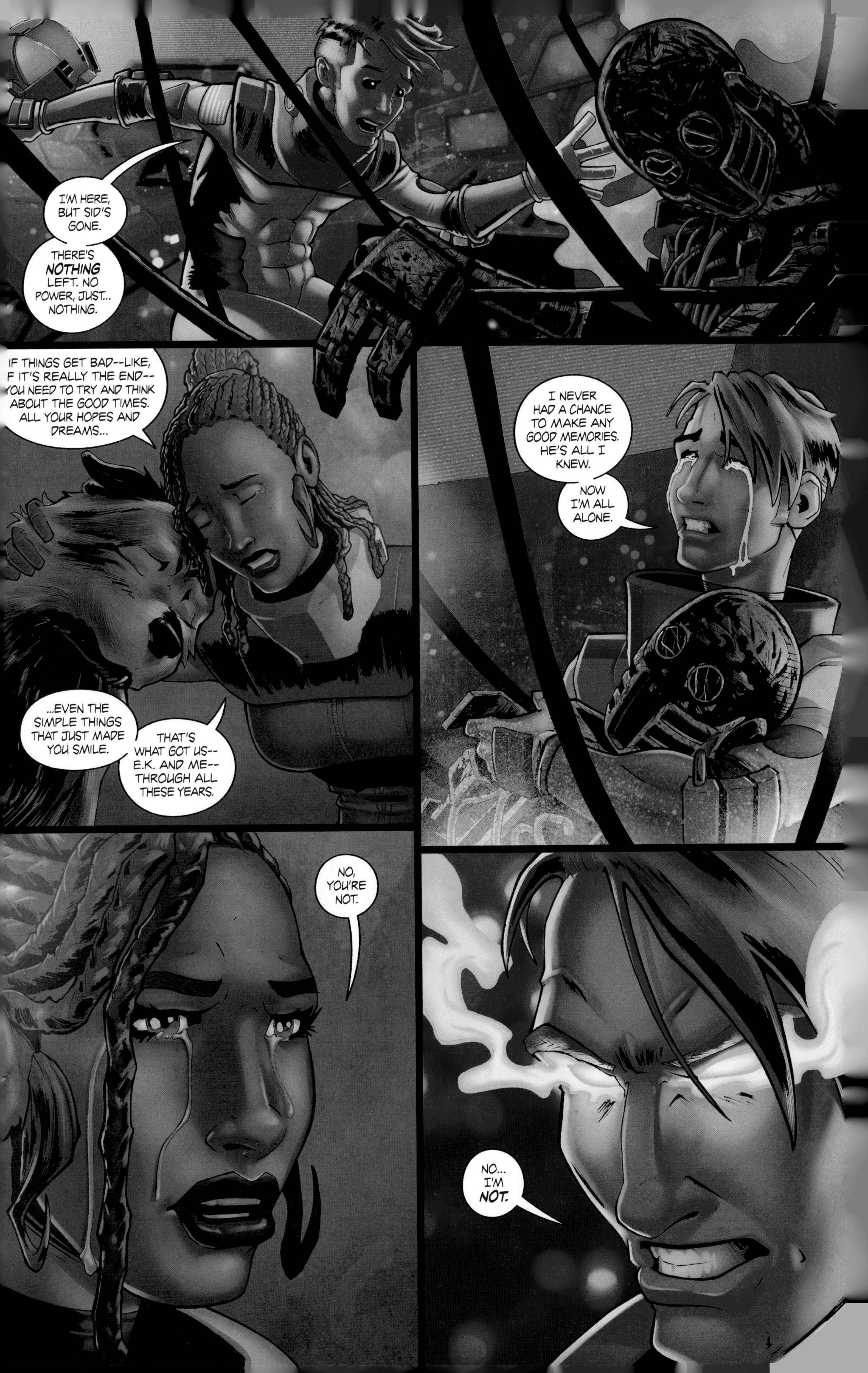
I'M HERE, BUT SID'S GONE.
THERE'S NOTHING LEFT. NO POWER, JUST... NOTHING.
IF THINGS GET BAD--LIKE, F IT'S REALLY THE END--YOU NEED TO TRY AND THINK ABOUT THE GOOD TIMES. ALL YOUR HOPES AND DREAMS...
...EVEN THE SIMPLE THINGS THAT JUST MADE YOU SMILE.
THAT'S WHAT GOT US--E.K. AND ME--THROUGH ALL THESE YEARS.
I NEVER HAD A CHANCE TO MAKE ANY GOOD MEMORIES. HE'S ALL I KNEW.
NOW I'M ALL ALONE.
NO, YOU'RE NOT.
NO... I'M NOT.

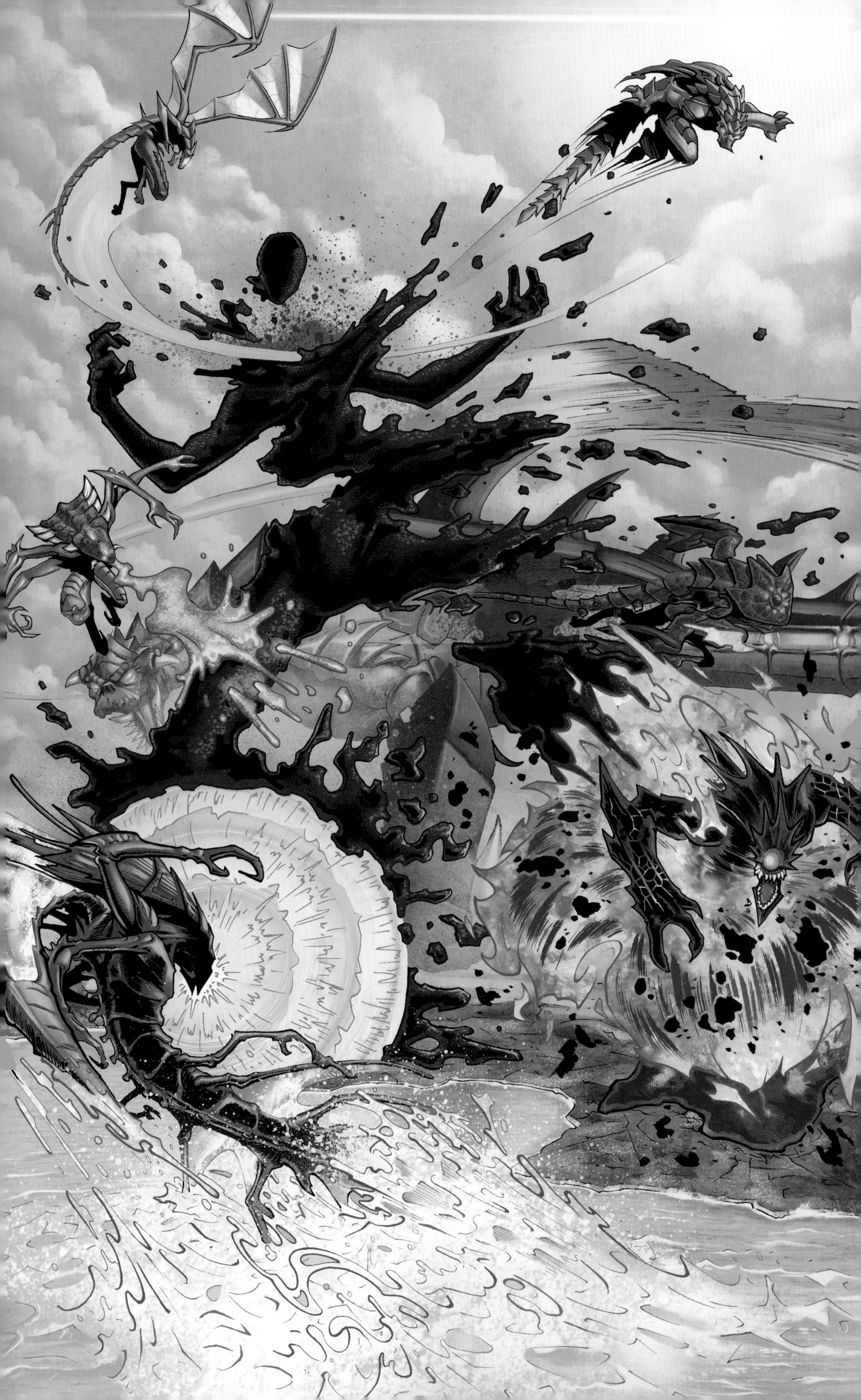

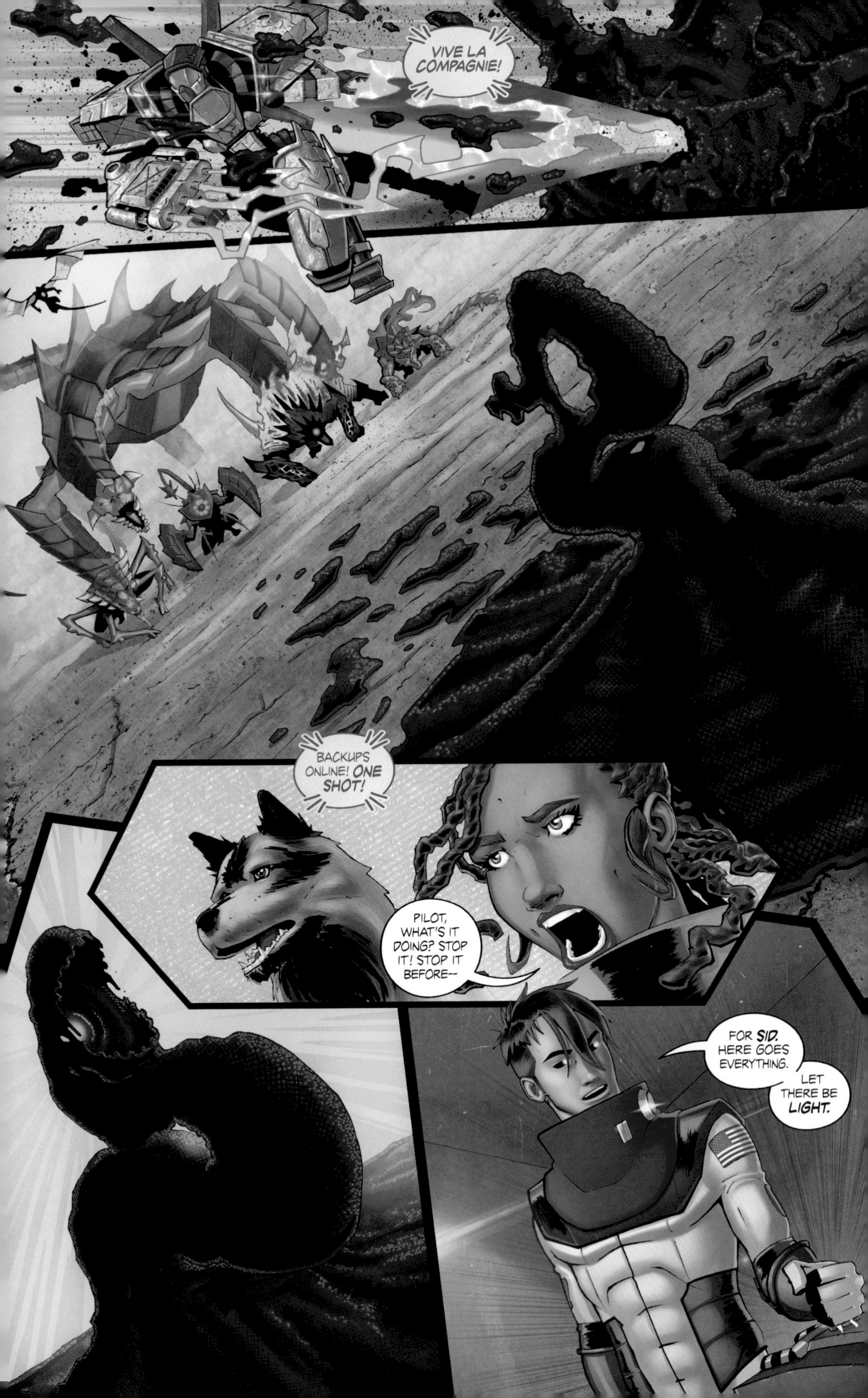
VIVE LA COMPAGNIE!
BACKUPS ONLINE! ONE SHOT!
PILOT, WHAT'S IT DOING? STOP IT! STOP IT BEFORE--
FOR SID. HERE GOES EVERYTHING.
LET THERE BE LIGHT.

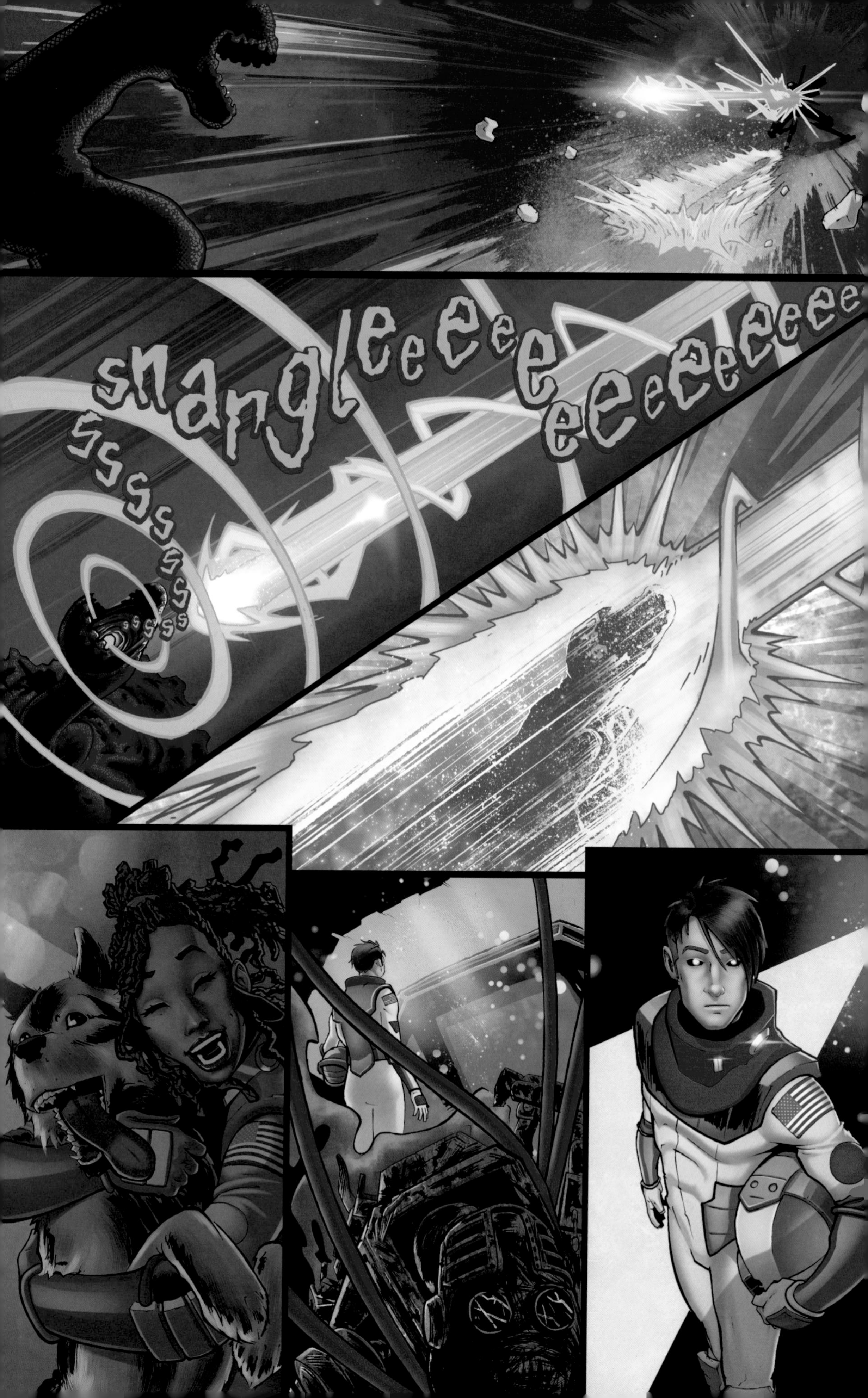
snangleeeeeeeeeeeeeeeee
SSSSSSSSSSS

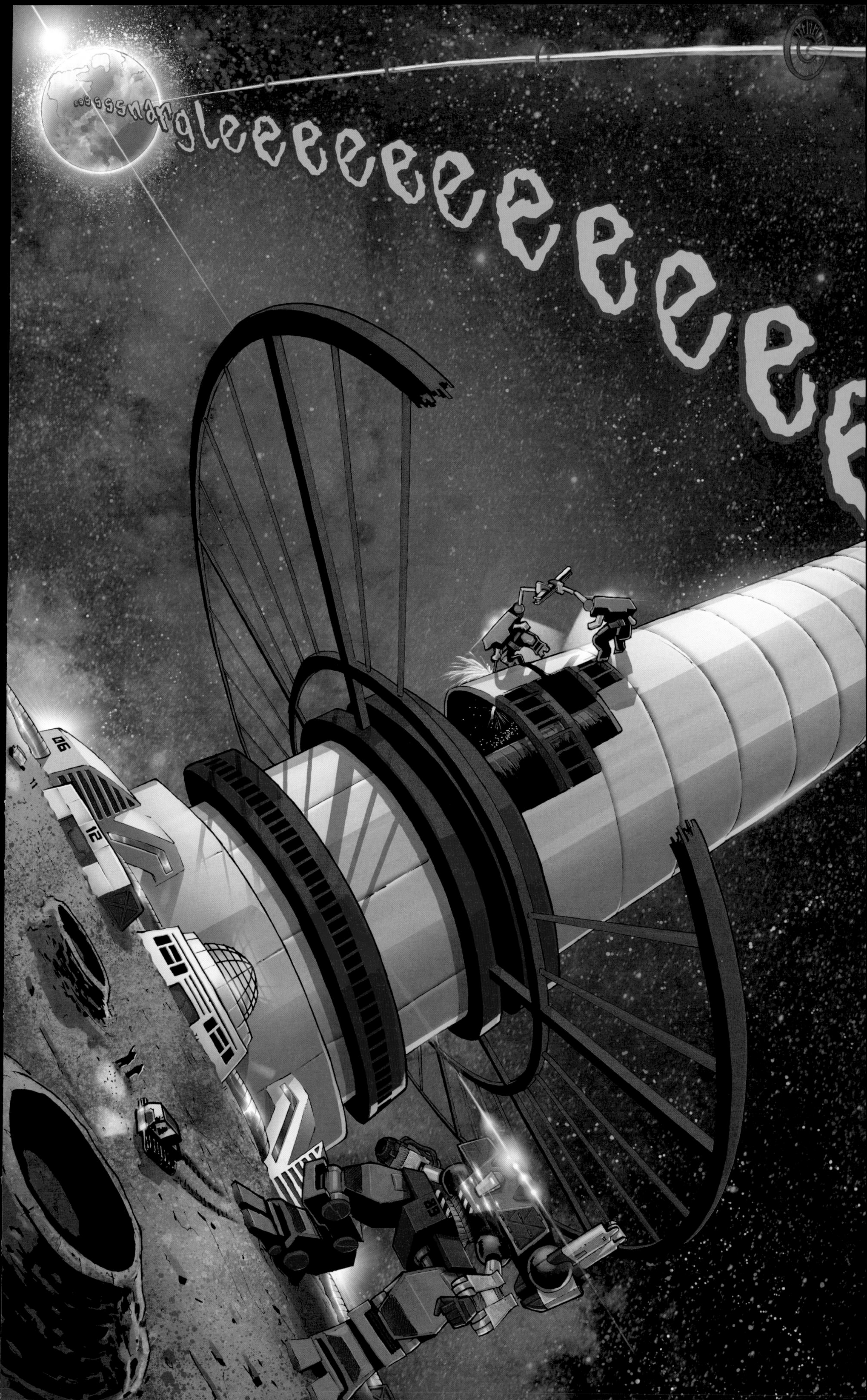
sssssnargleeeeeeeeeeeeee

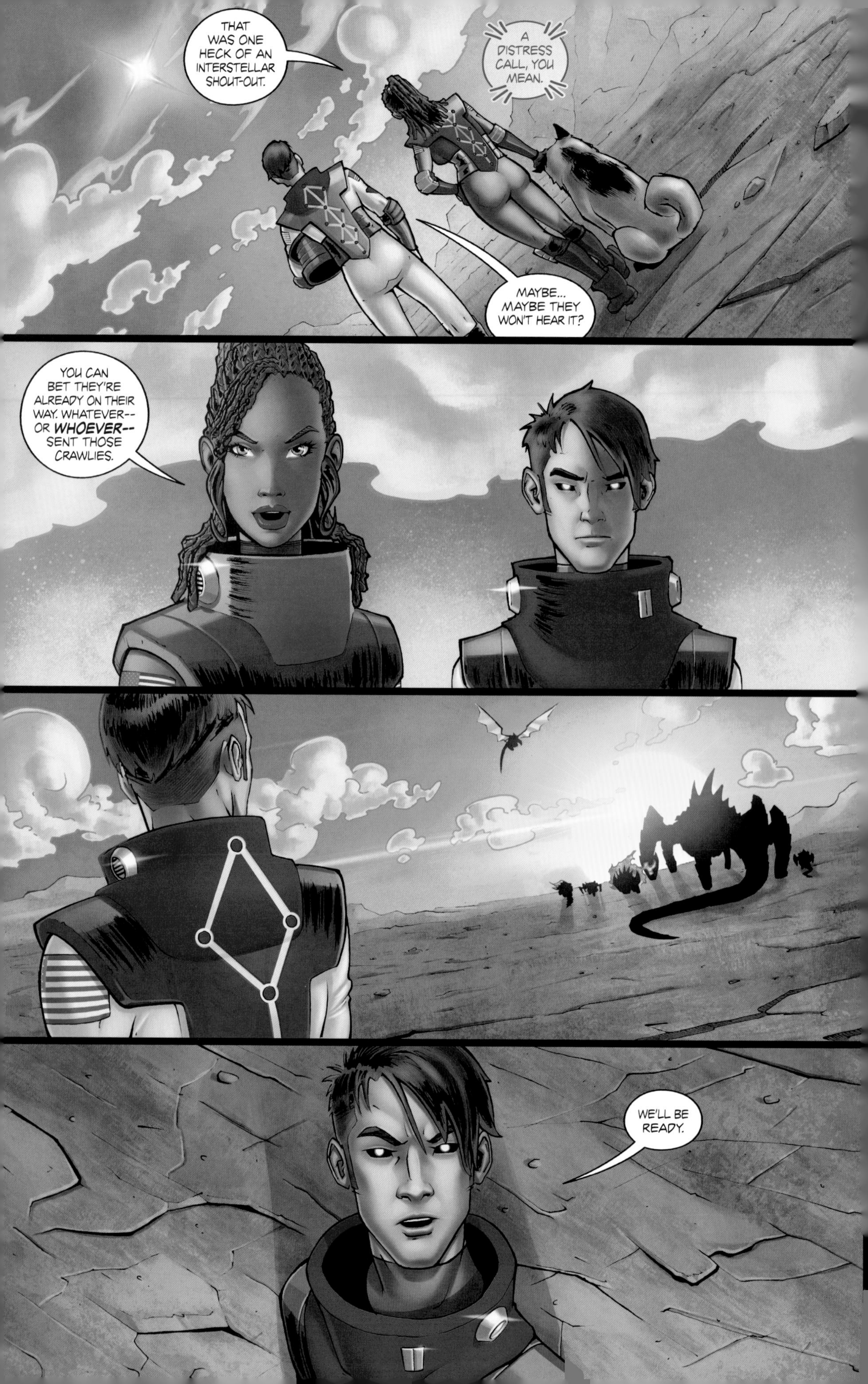
THAT WAS ONE HECK OF AN INTERSTELLAR SHOUT-OUT.
A DISTRESS CALL, YOU MEAN.
MAYBE... MAYBE THEY WON'T HEAR IT?
YOU CAN BET THEY'RE ALREADY ON THEIR WAY. WHATEVER-- OR **WHOEVER--** SENT THOSE CRAWLIES.
WE'LL BE READY.

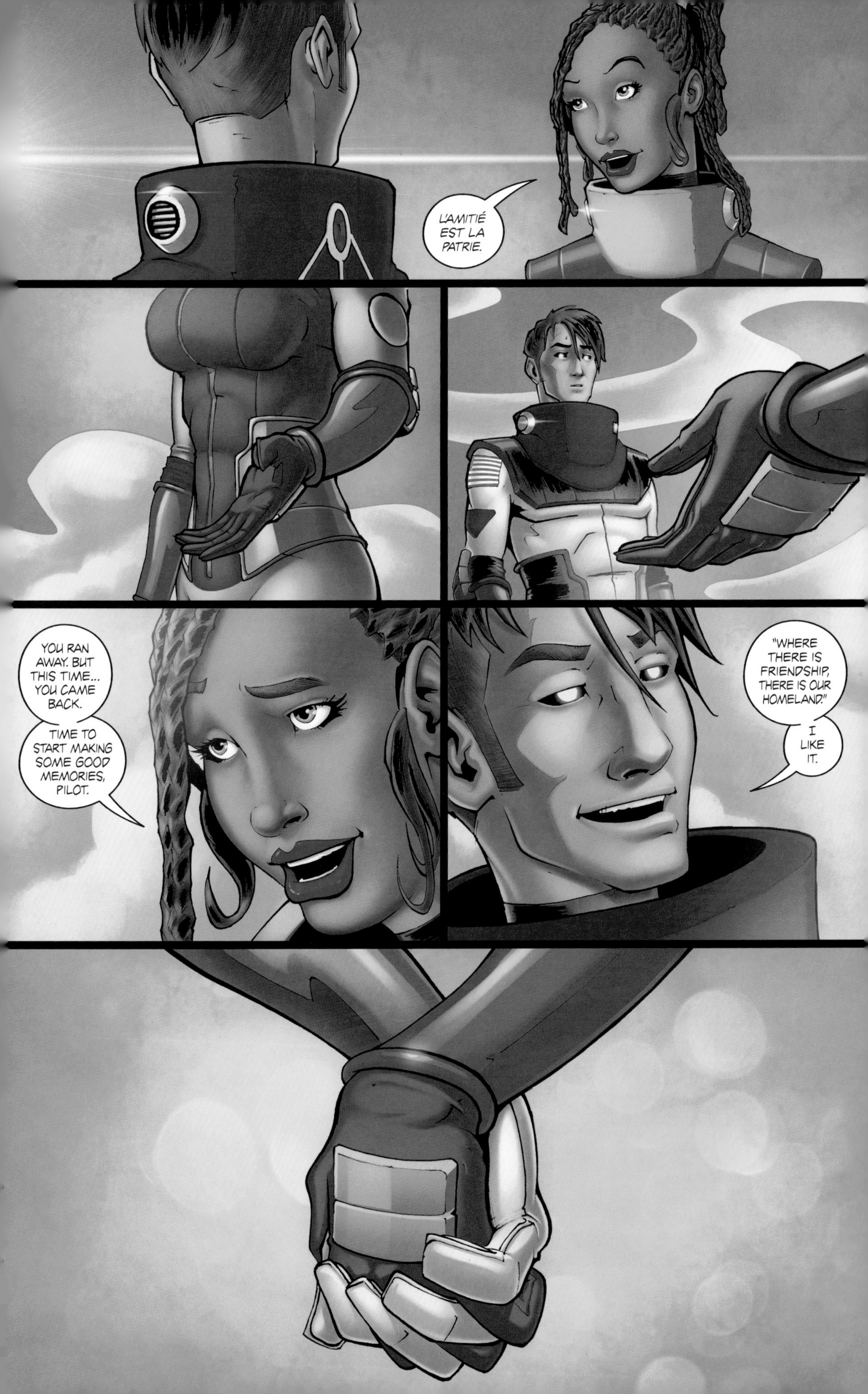
L'AMITIÉ EST LA PATRIE.
YOU RAN AWAY. BUT THIS TIME... YOU CAME BACK.
TIME TO START MAKING SOME GOOD MEMORIES, PILOT.
"WHERE THERE IS FRIENDSHIP, THERE IS OUR HOMELAND."
I LIKE IT.

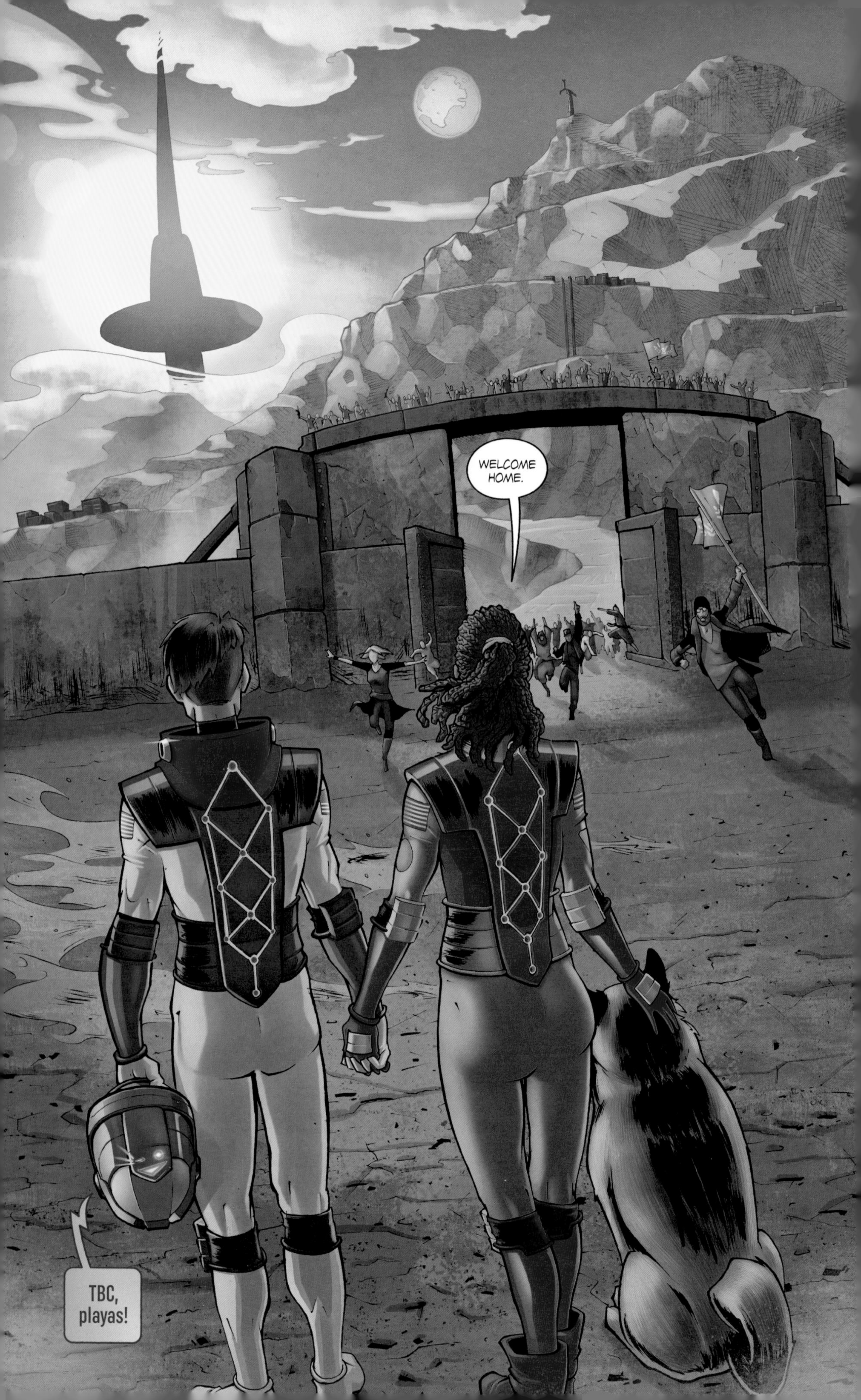
WELCOME HOME.
TBC, playas!

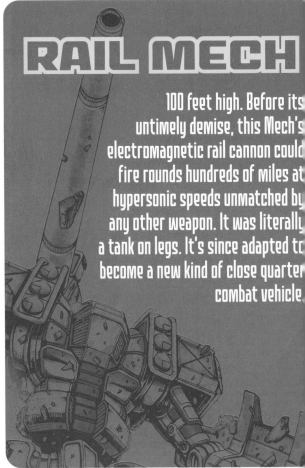

RAIL MECH

100 feet high. Before its untimely demise, this Mech's electromagnetic rail cannon could fire rounds hundreds of miles at hypersonic speeds unmatched by any other weapon. It was literally a tank on legs. It's since adapted to become a new kind of close quarter combat vehicle.

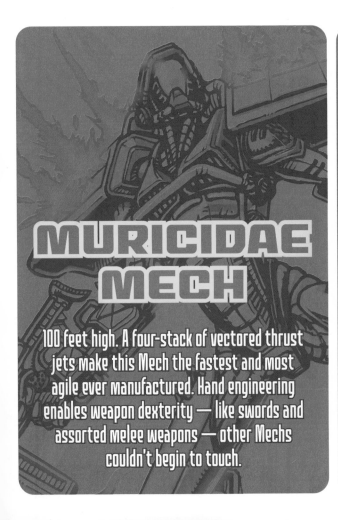

MURICIDAE MECH

100 feet high. A four-stack of vectored thrust jets make this Mech the fastest and most agile ever manufactured. Hand engineering enables weapon dexterity — like swords and assorted melee weapons — other Mechs couldn't begin to touch.

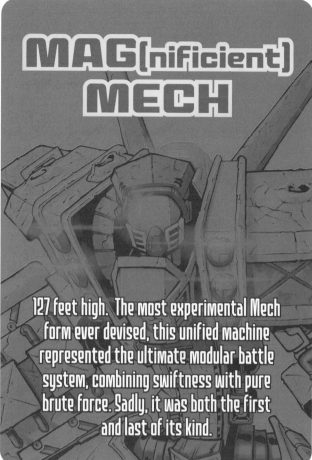

MAG(nificient) MECH

127 feet high. The most experimental Mech form ever devised, this unified machine represented the ultimate modular battle system, combining swiftness with pure brute force. Sadly, it was both the first and last of its kind.

CRAWLIES

6 to 10 feet around, give or take, they're a bioengineered plague with no nervous systems bred to find fresh water... and to destroy everything else.

CRAWLIE SCRUM

1250 feet high. As big as the Empire State Building, aka a 102-story skyscraper. No one knows anything about this horror. No one's ever lived long enough to find out.

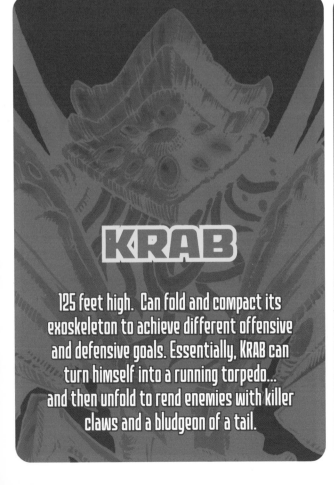

KRAB

125 feet high. Can fold and compact its exoskeleton to achieve different offensive and defensive goals. Essentially, KRAB can turn himself into a running torpedo... and then unfold to rend enemies with killer claws and a bludgeon of a tail.

FLYER

125 feet high, wingspan 250 feet.
Of all recorded Monsters, FLYER flies
the highest, flies the fastest...
and flies the deadliest.

GOLIATH

800 feet high,
1500 feet long.
The biggest of the
Monsters makes nests
out of skyscrapers and entire city
boroughs. GOLIATH's 7 prehensile tongues
are each half as long as a football field.

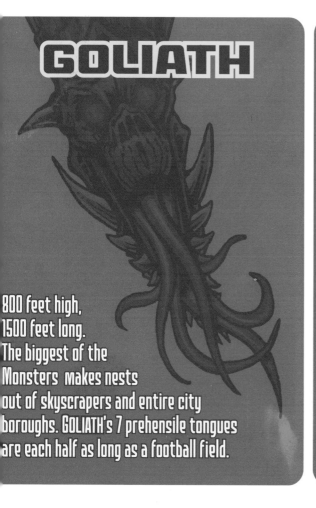

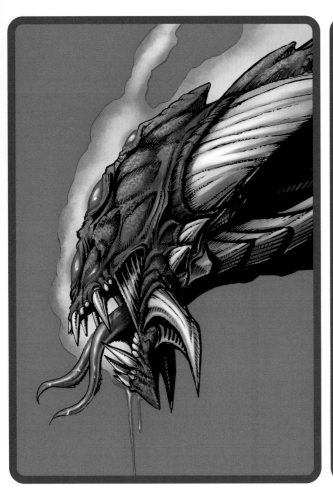

DROOL

200 feet high. DROOL's got acidic spit and toxic breath. If that doesn't get you killed, its ability to spring across miles and literally rip you apart will.

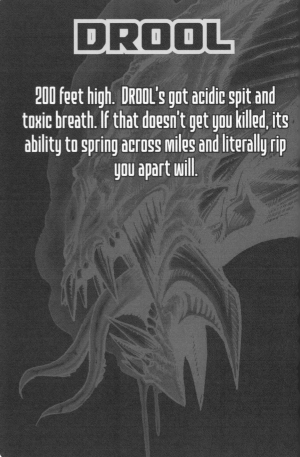

SMOULDER

300 feet tall when standing upright, 600 feet long. Super-heated armor plates send up flaming tempests wherever it steps. SMOULDER literally sears the ground with its body, and burrows deep underground between feedings, preferring to be as hot as possible at all times.

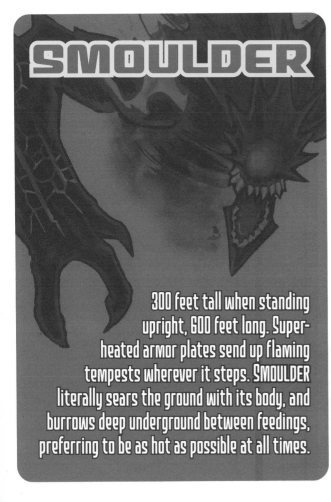

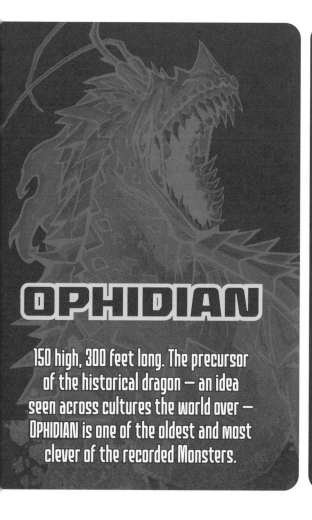

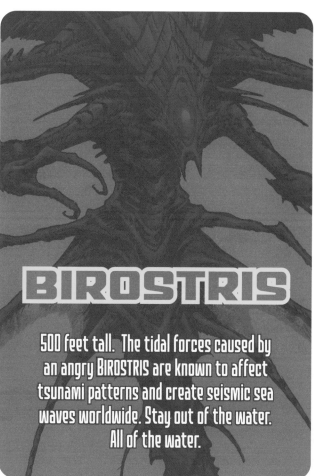

BIROSTRIS

500 feet tall. The tidal forces caused by an angry BIROSTRIS are known to affect tsunami patterns and create seismic sea waves worldwide. Stay out of the water. All of the water.

OPHIDIAN

150 high, 300 feet long. The precursor of the historical dragon — an idea seen across cultures the world over — OPHIDIAN is one of the oldest and most clever of the recorded Monsters.

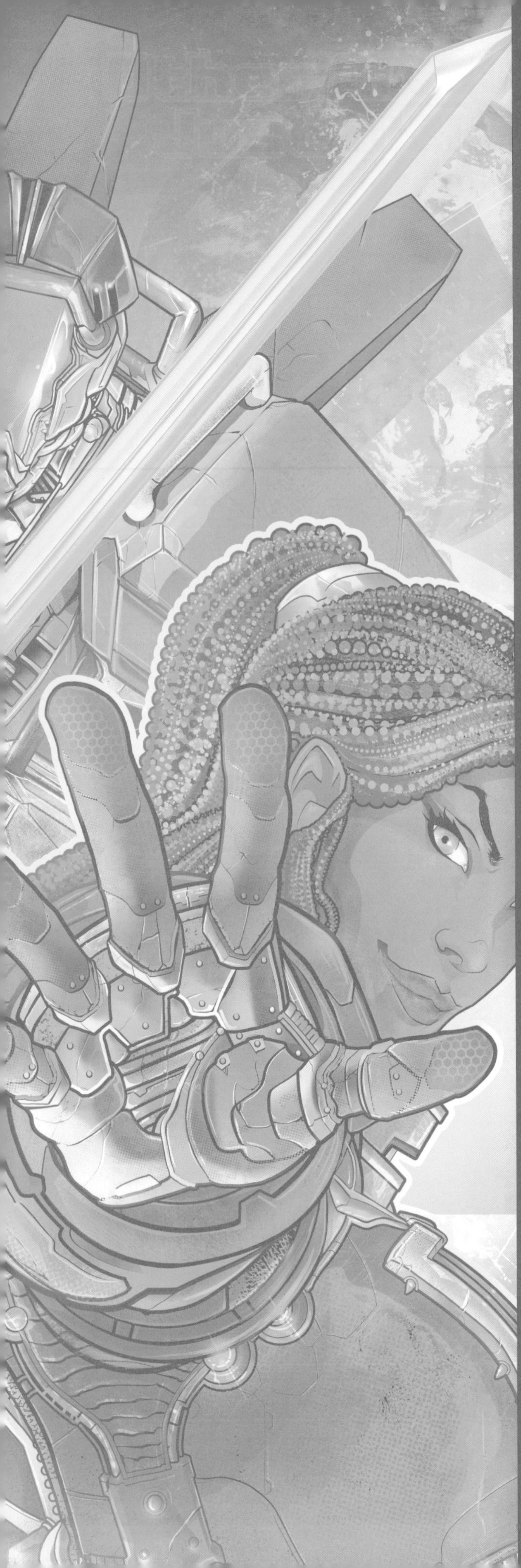

THE 27 RUN:™ CRUSH

GALLERY

1 HARDCOVER: ROBBI RODRIGUEZ

2 PREMIER COVER: KEN LASHLEY & JUAN FERNANDEZ

3 VARIANT COVER: LEO COLAPIETRO

4 PIN-UP: SID VENBLU

5 RAIL MECH: RUSSELL BROWN

6 BIROSTRIS: RUSSELL BROWN

7 FLYER: RUSSELL BROWN

8 SMOULDER: RUSSELL BROWN

9 LINE-UP: RUSSELL BROWN

10 MAG MECH: RUSSELL BROWN

11 OPHIDIAN: ETHAN CLAUNCH

12 CRUMP: ETHAN CLAUNCH

13 PRE-PRODUCTION: RUSSELL BROWN

5-13 COLORS: FRAN GAMBOA

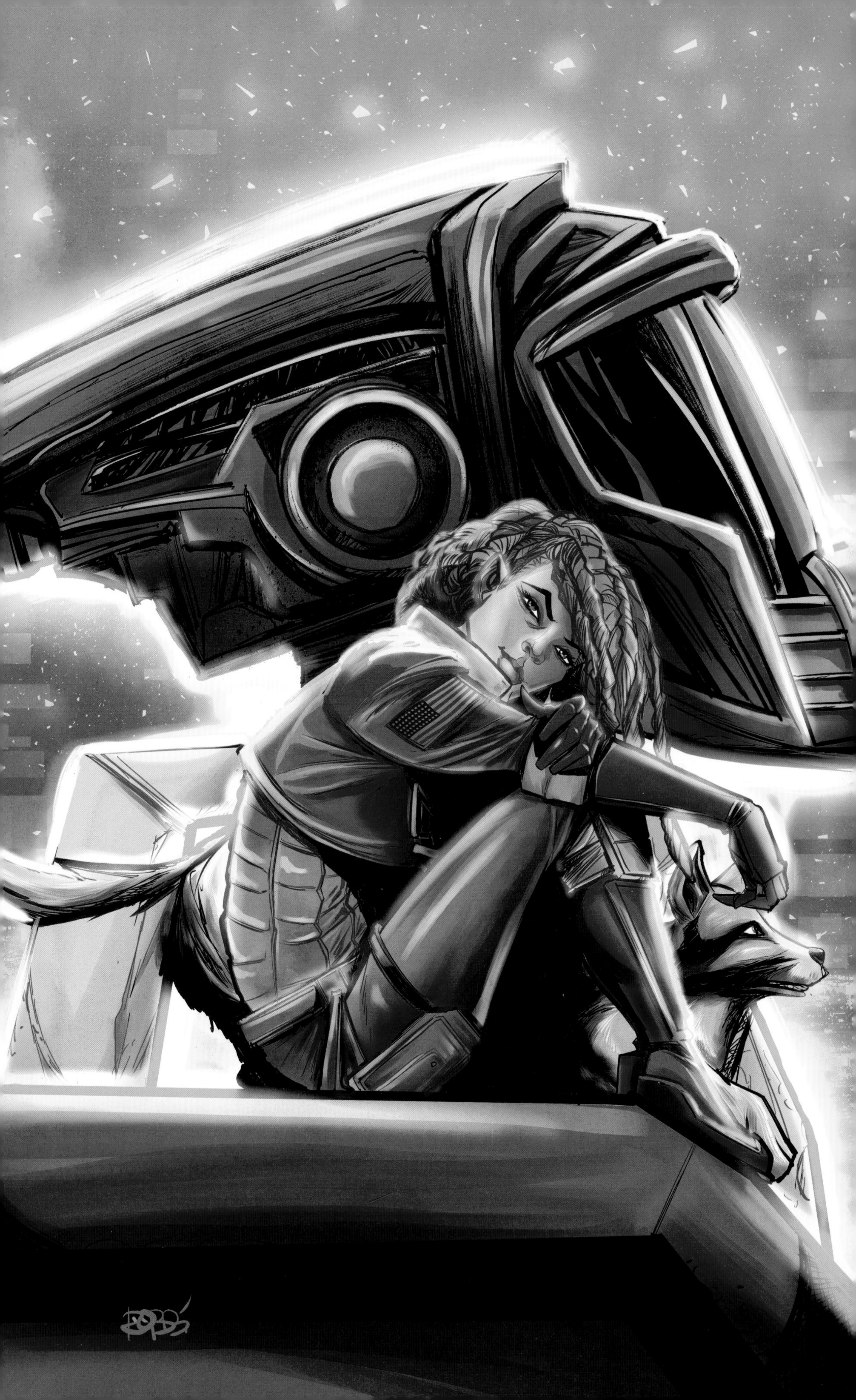

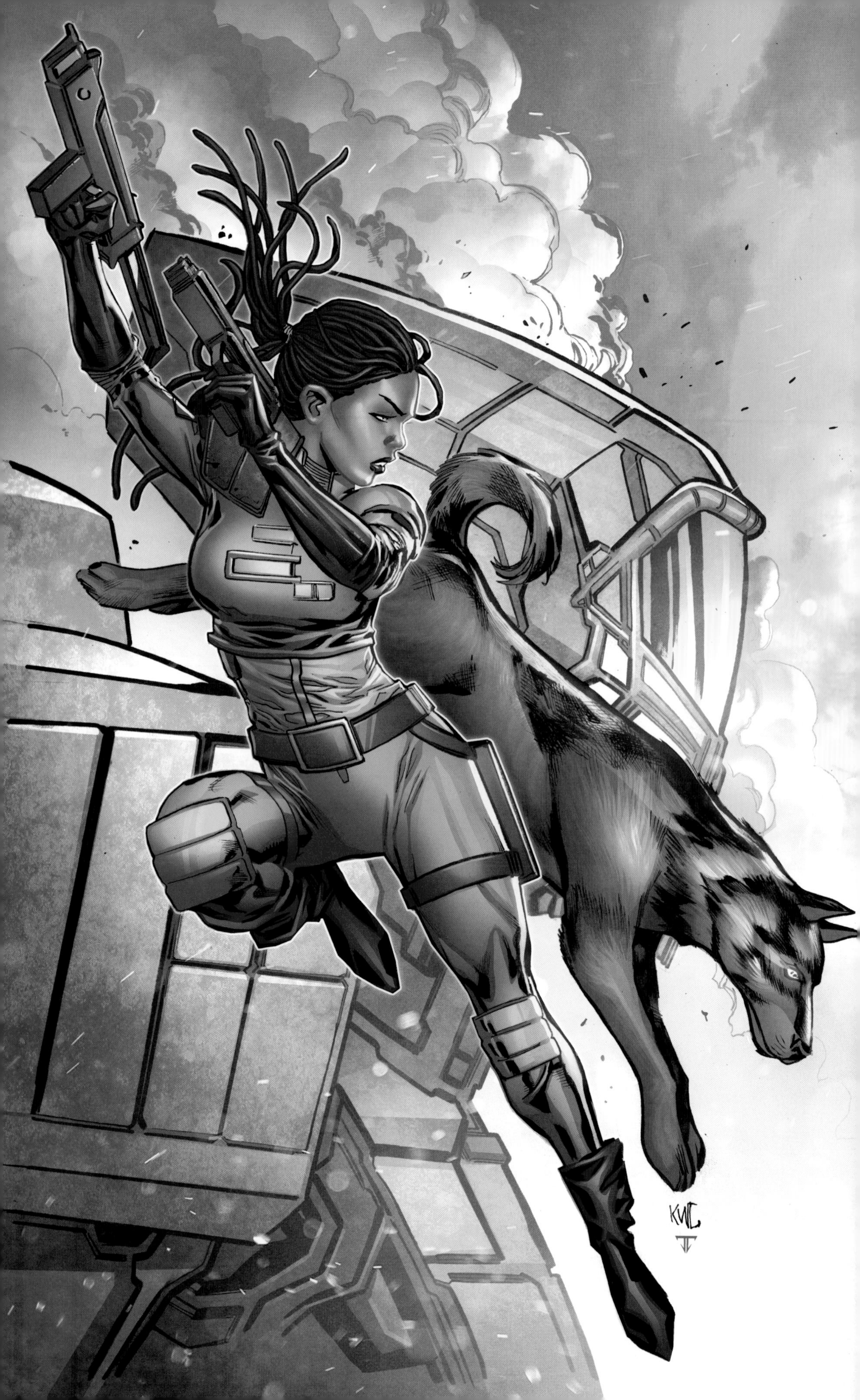

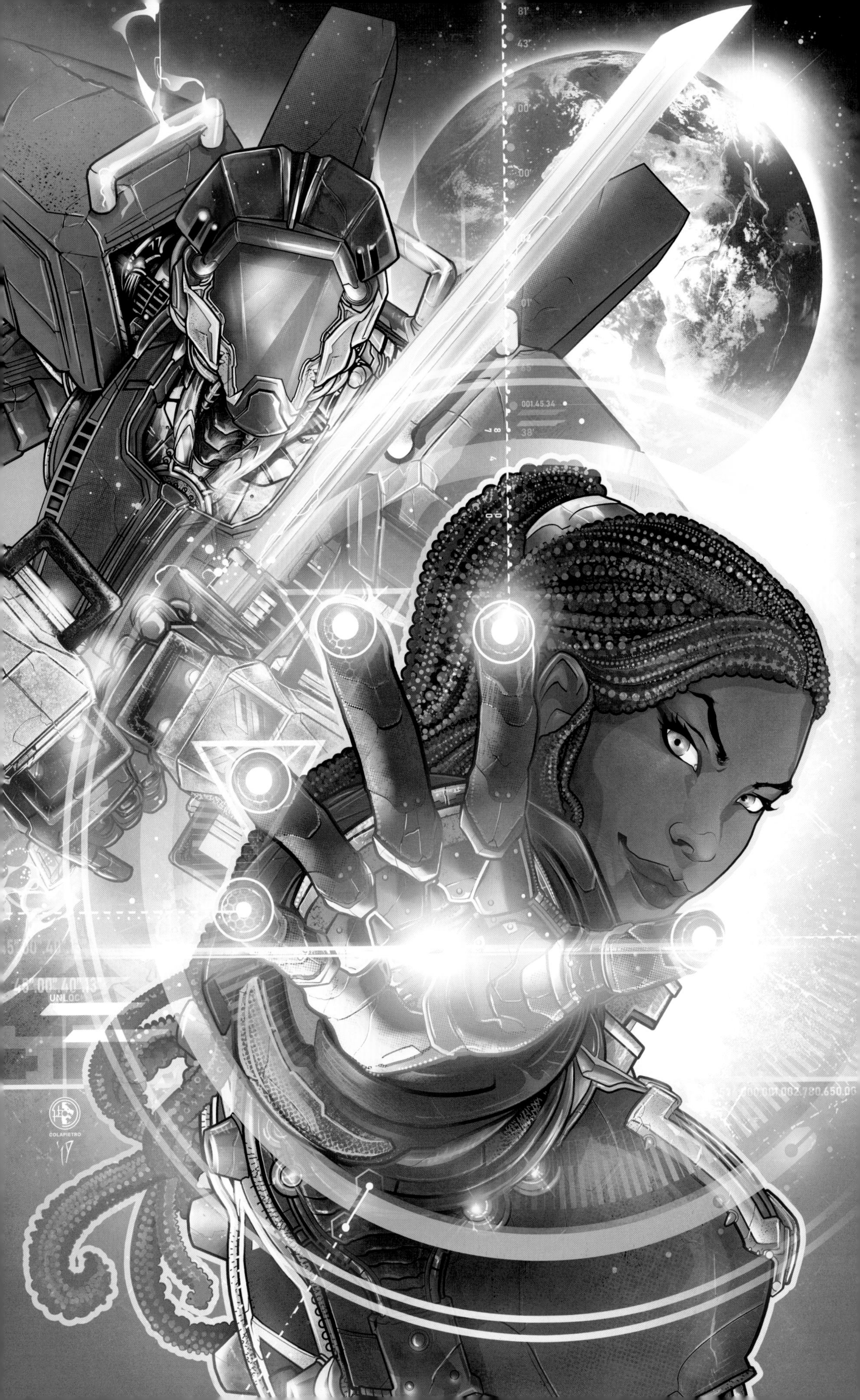
001.45.34
COLAPIETRO
'17

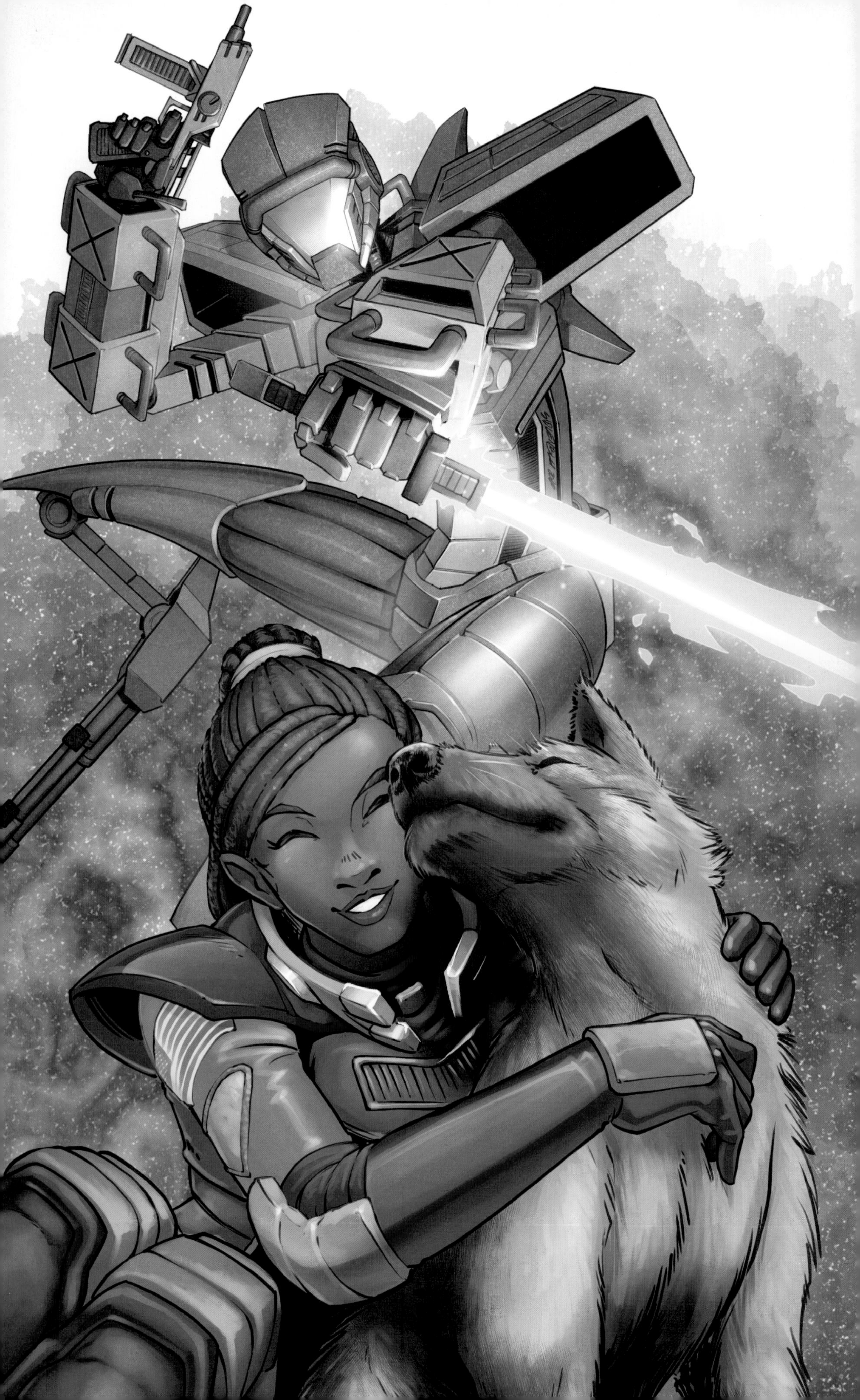

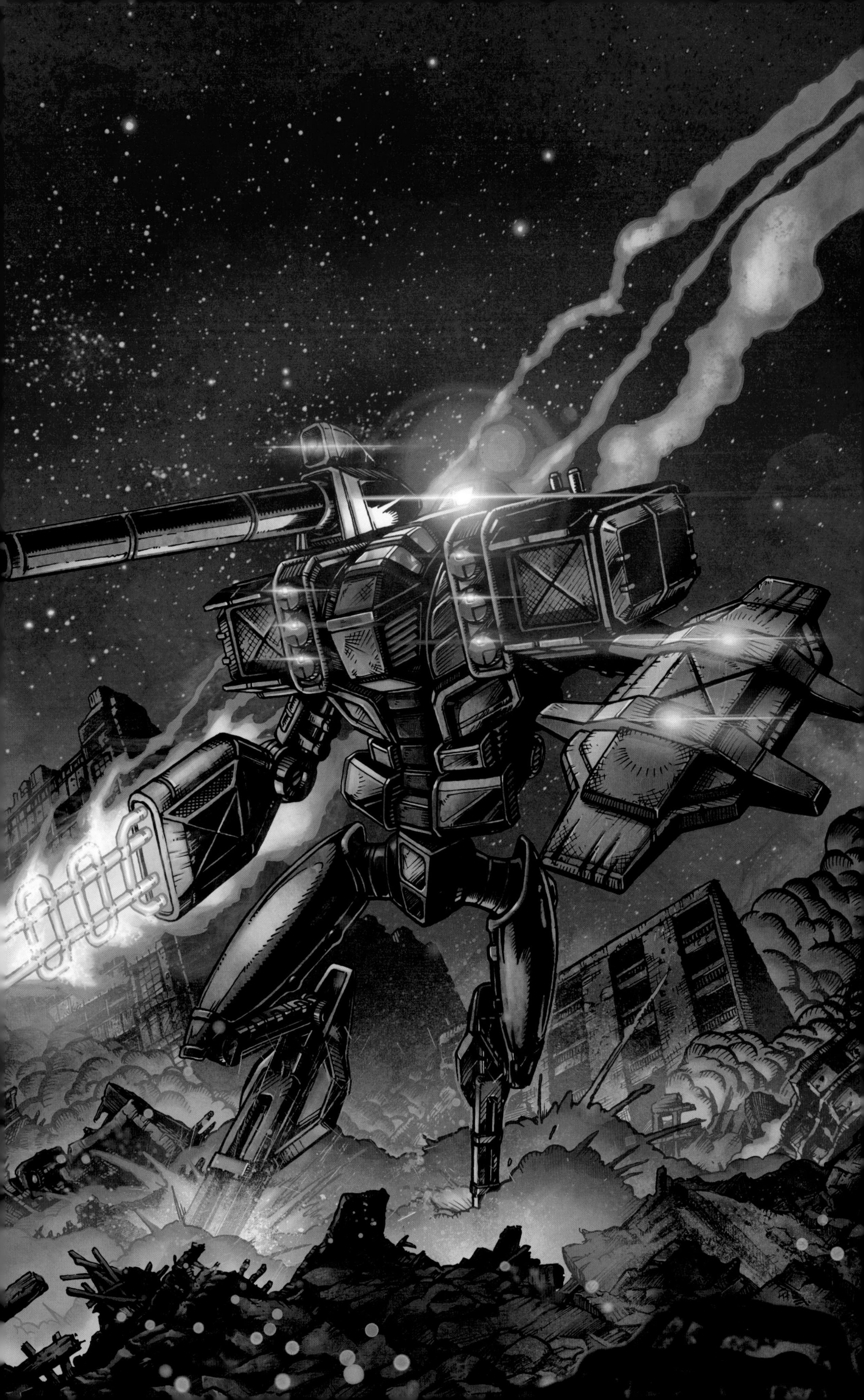

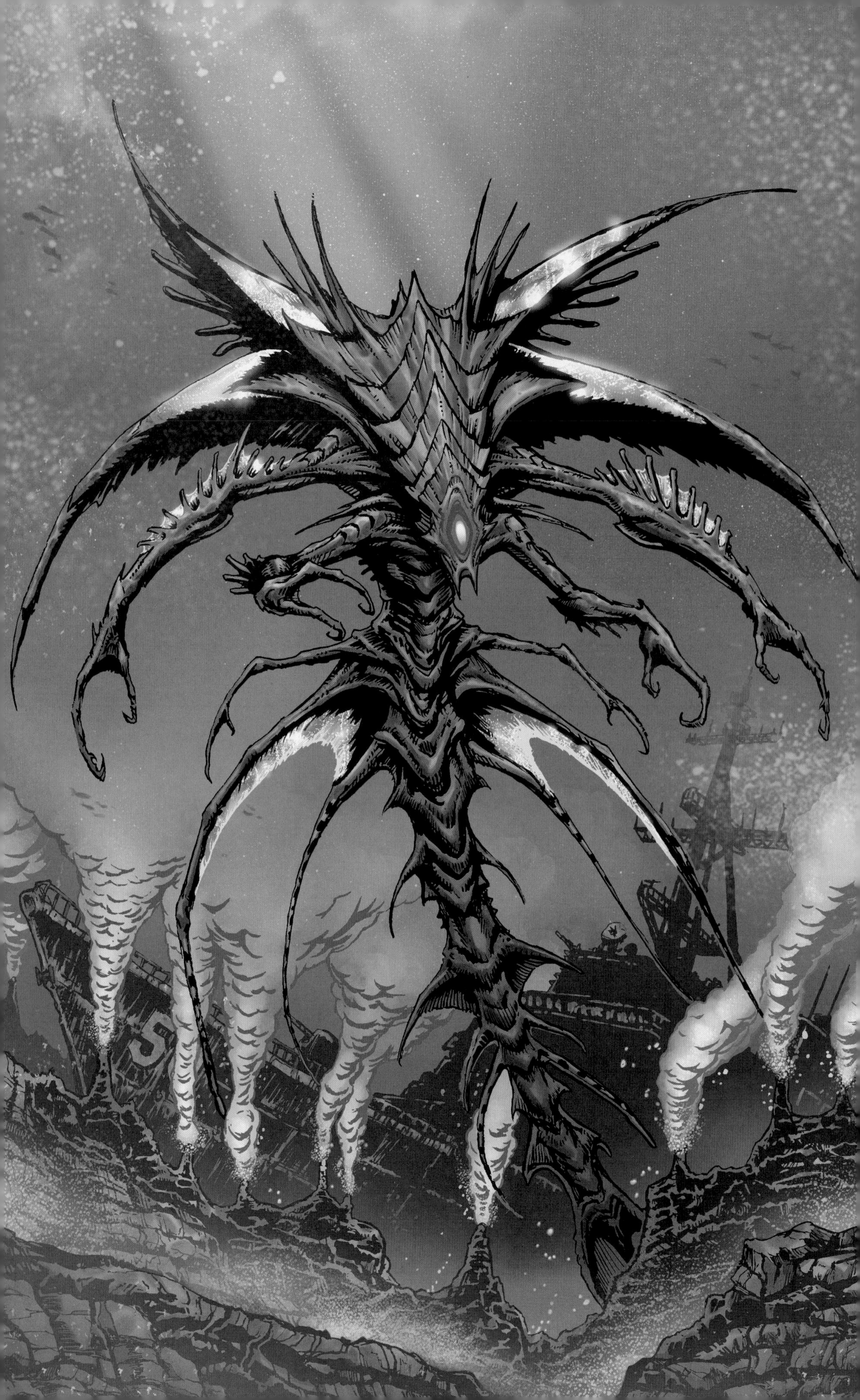

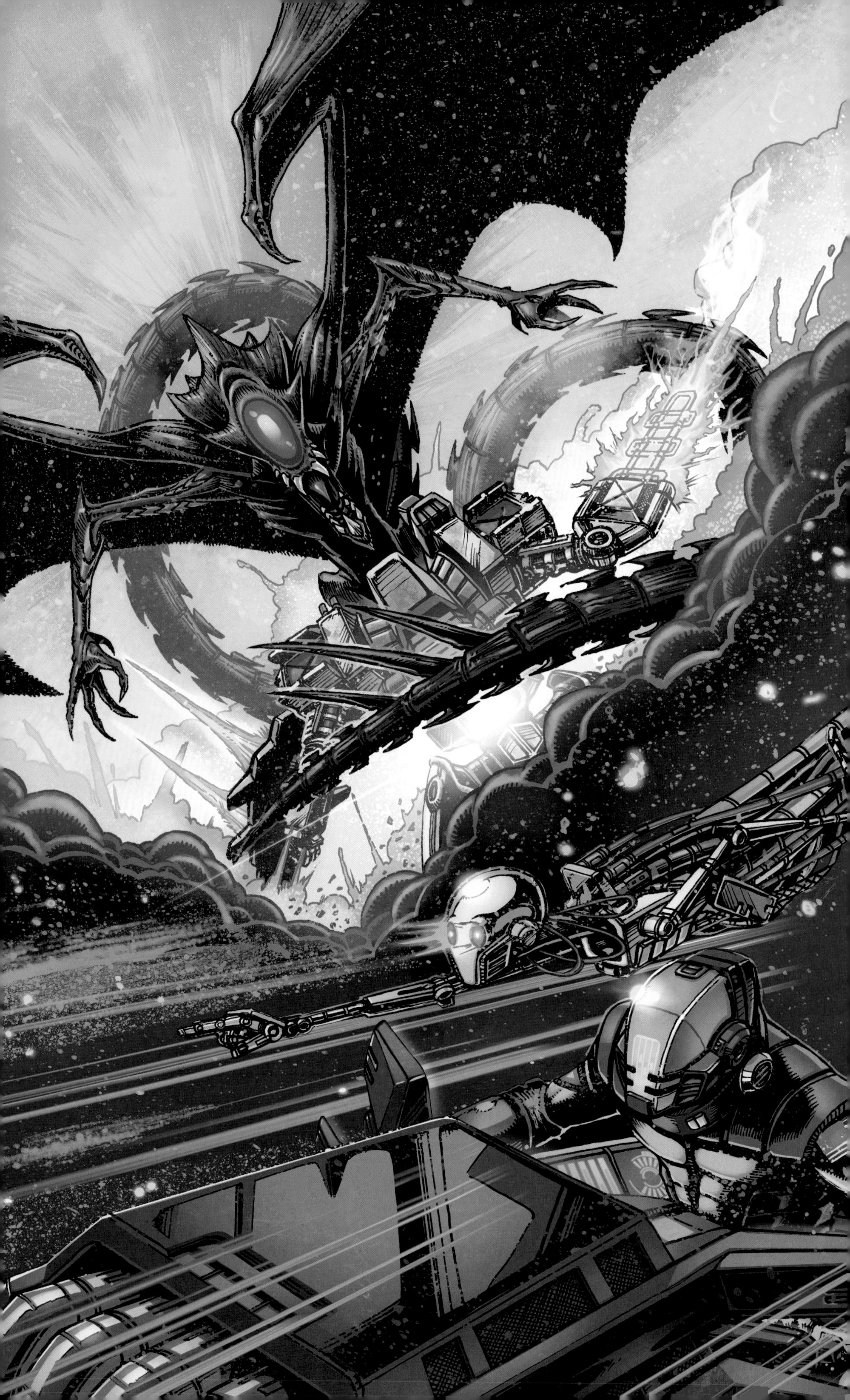

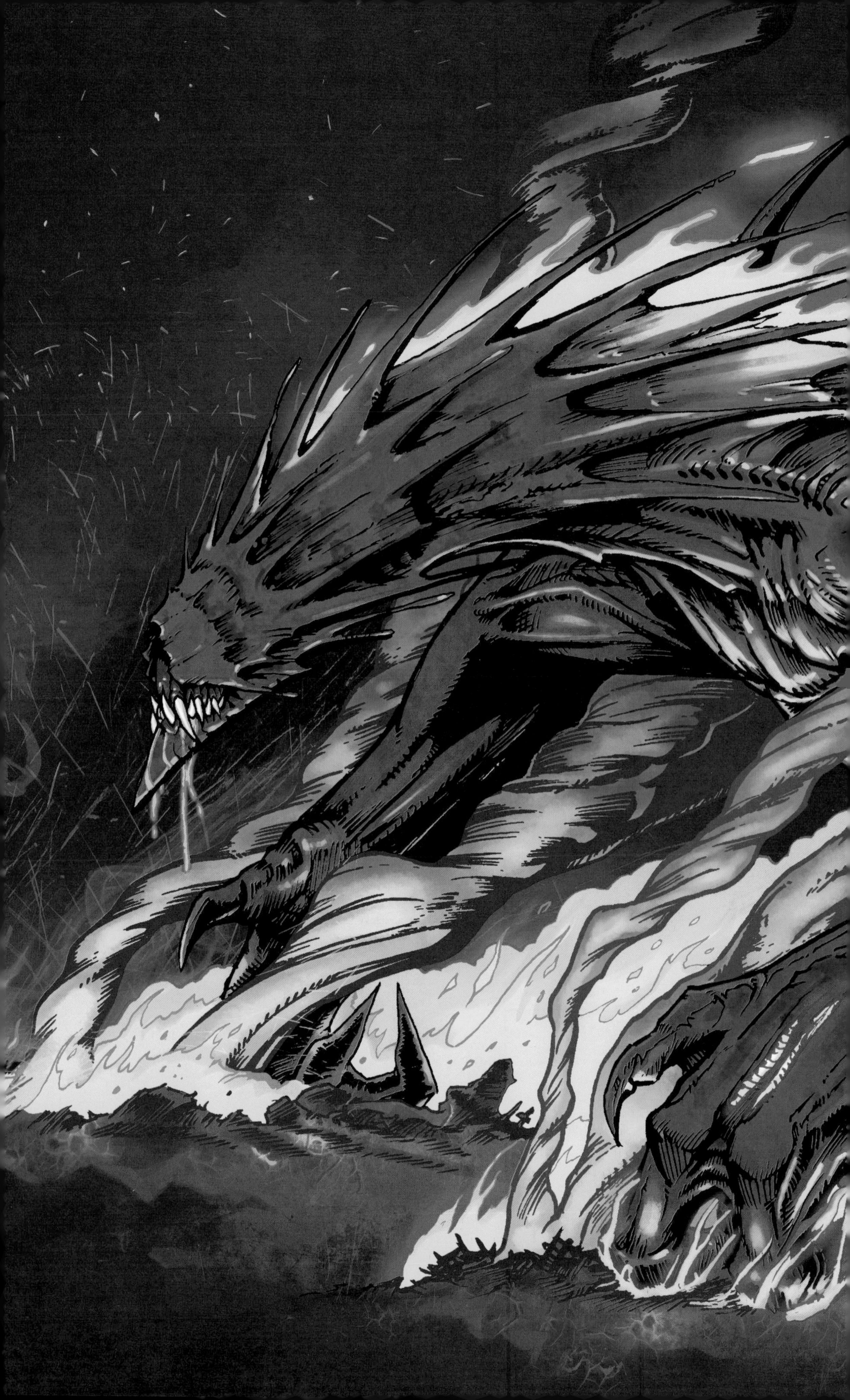

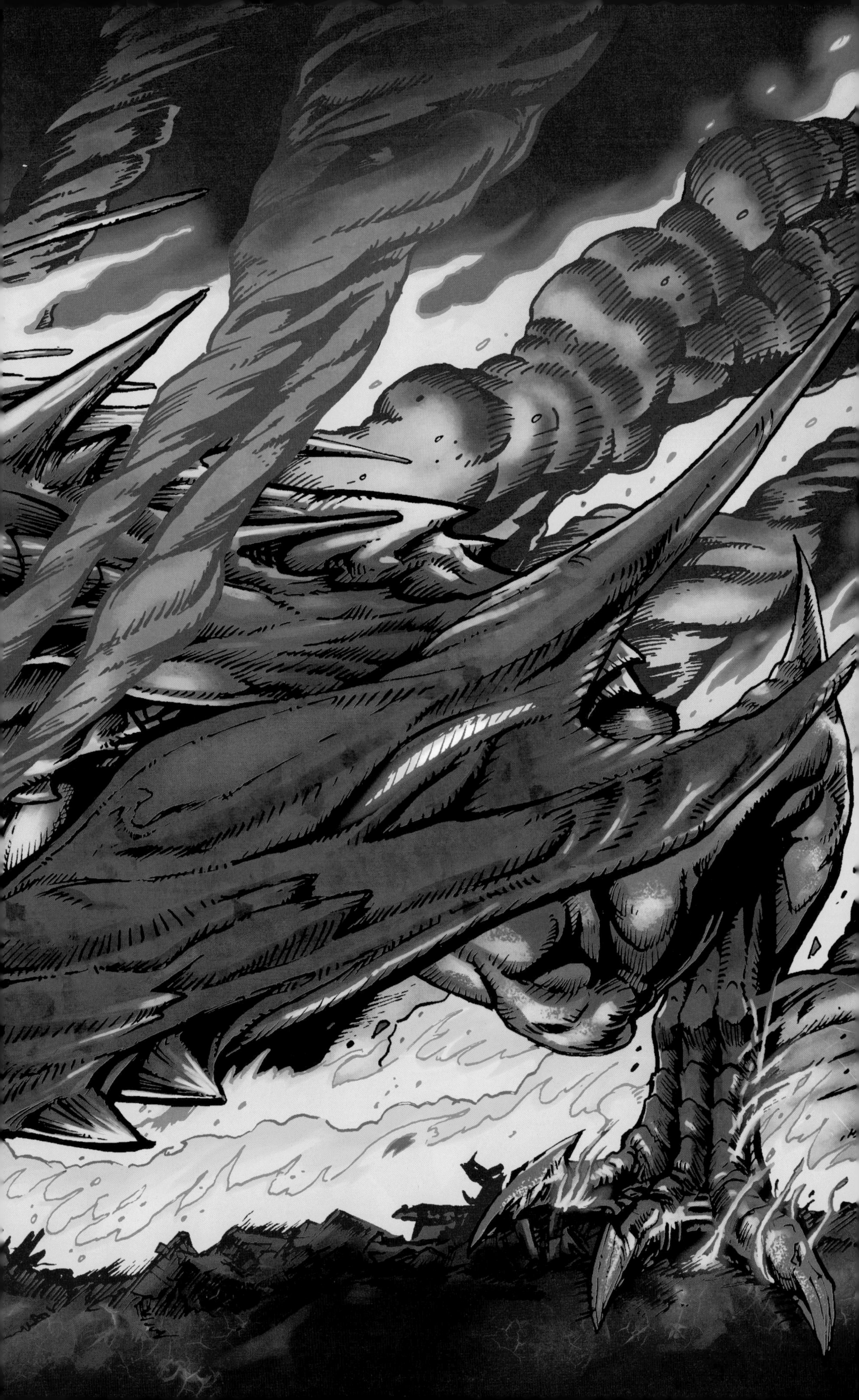

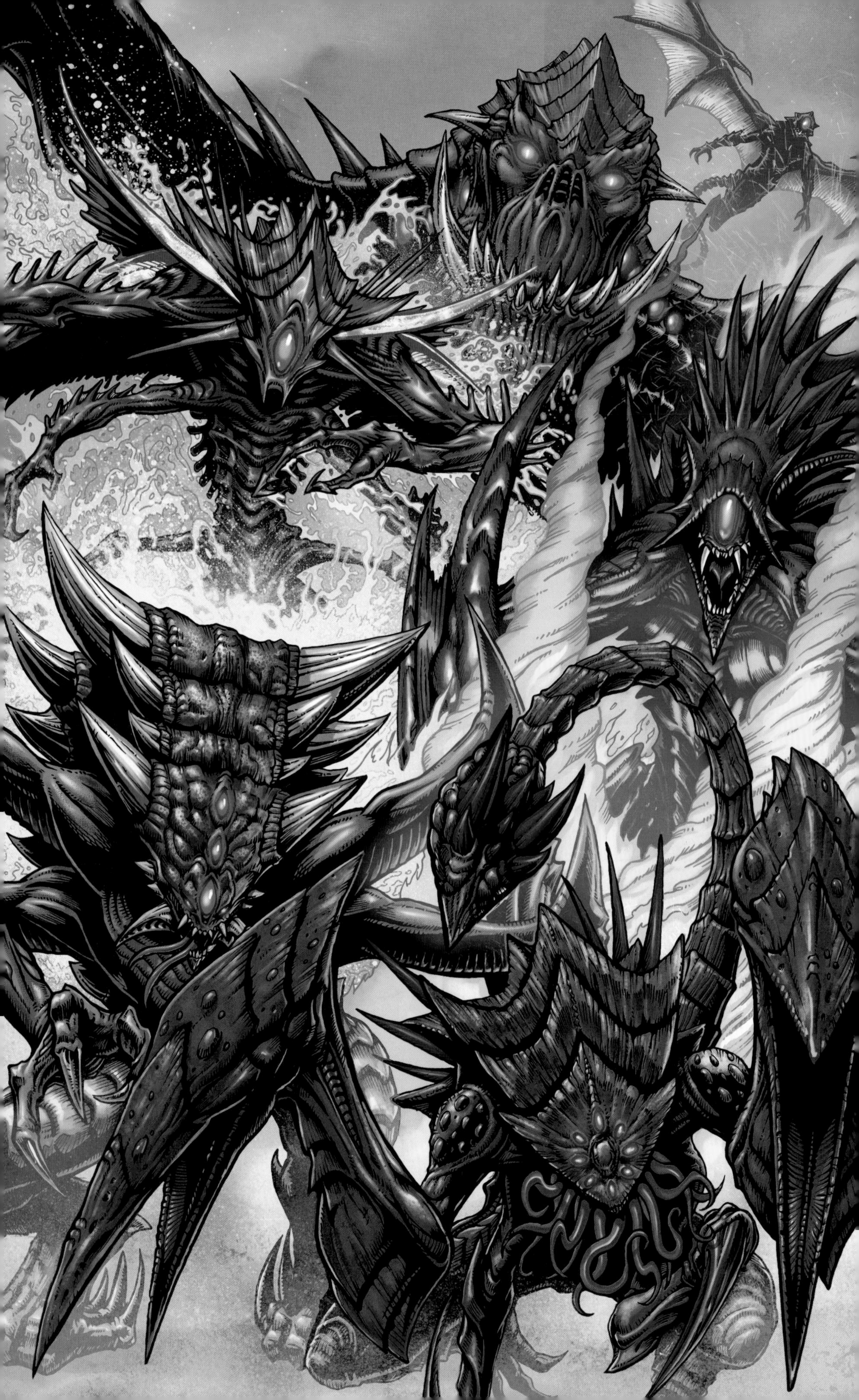

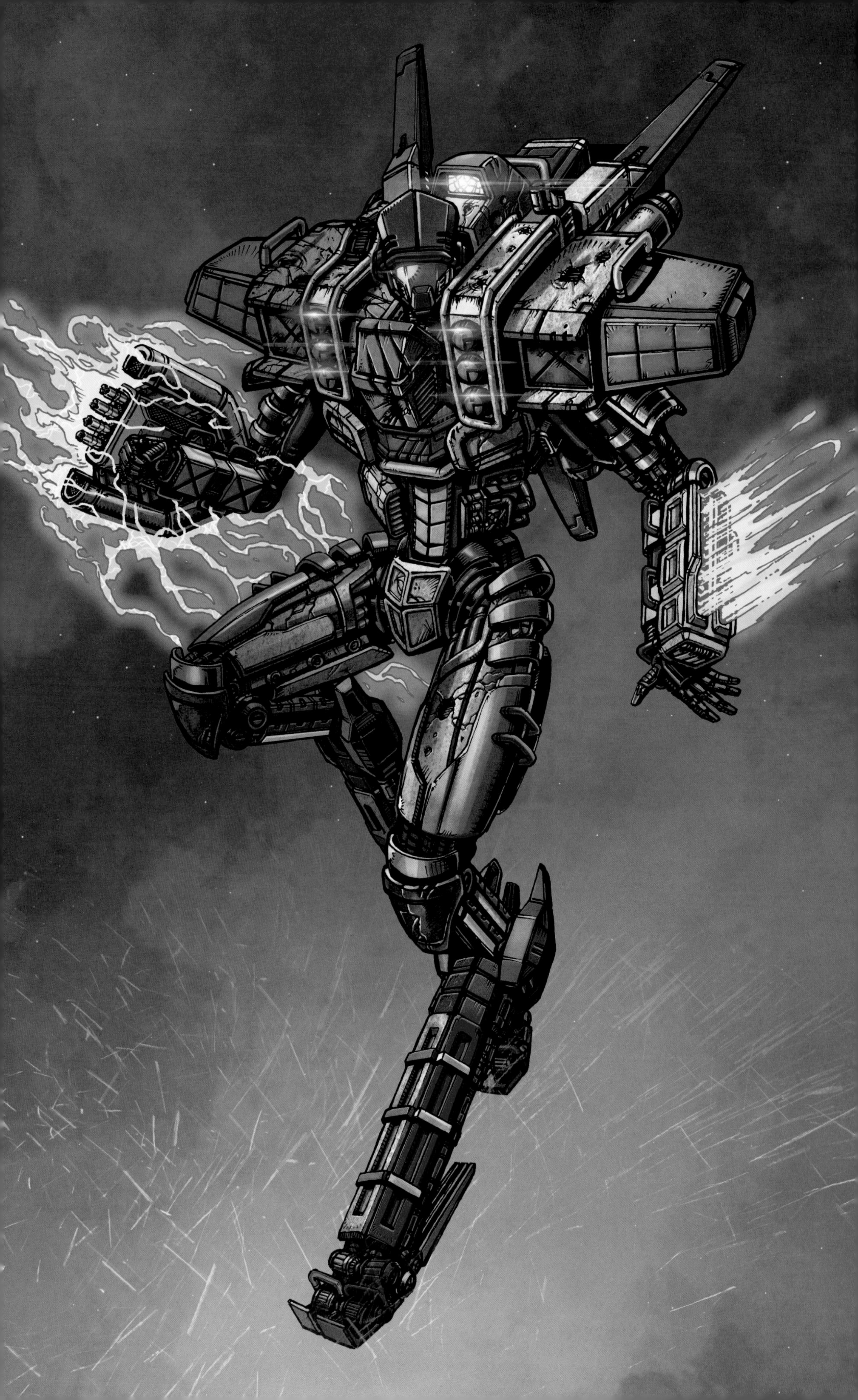

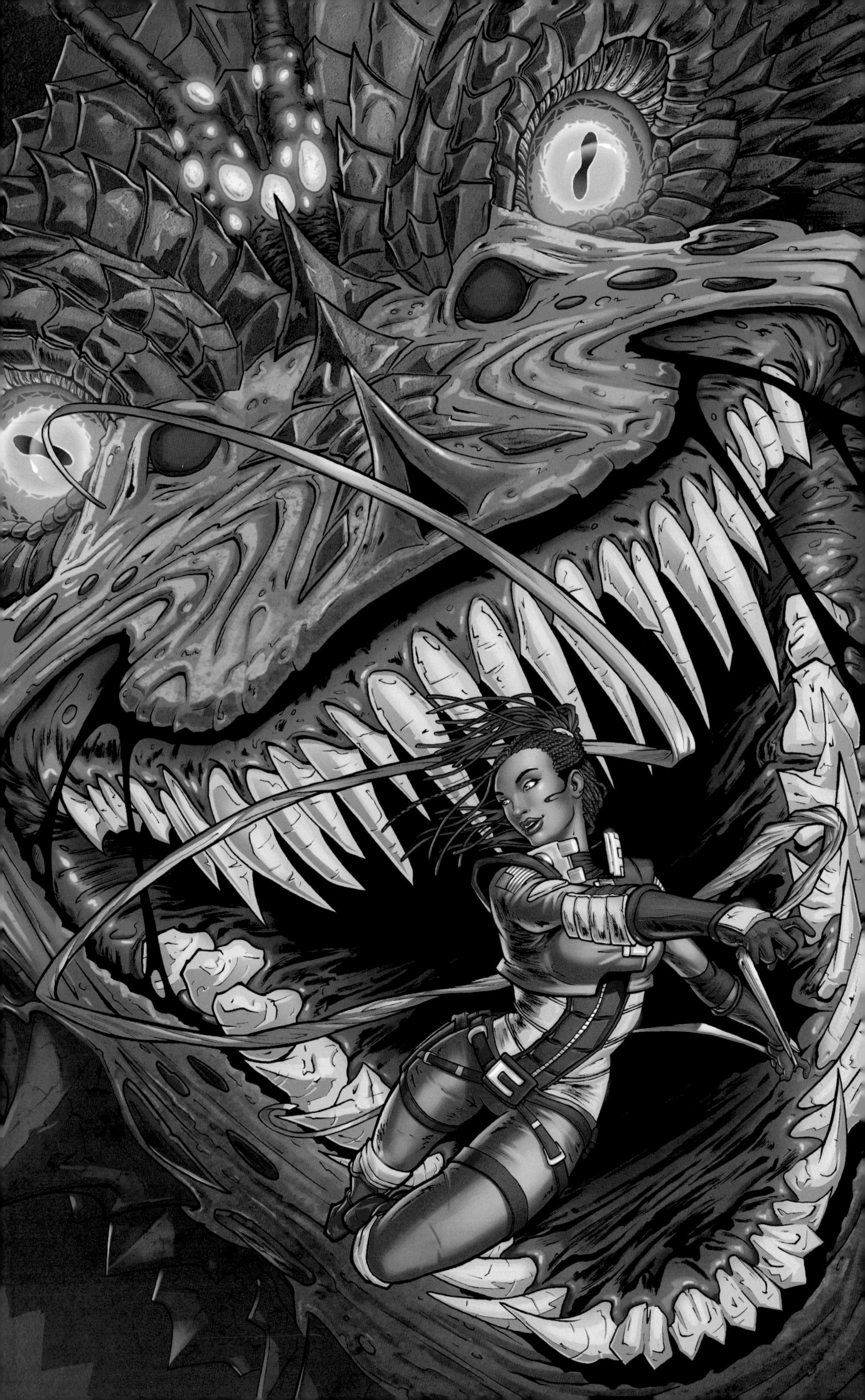

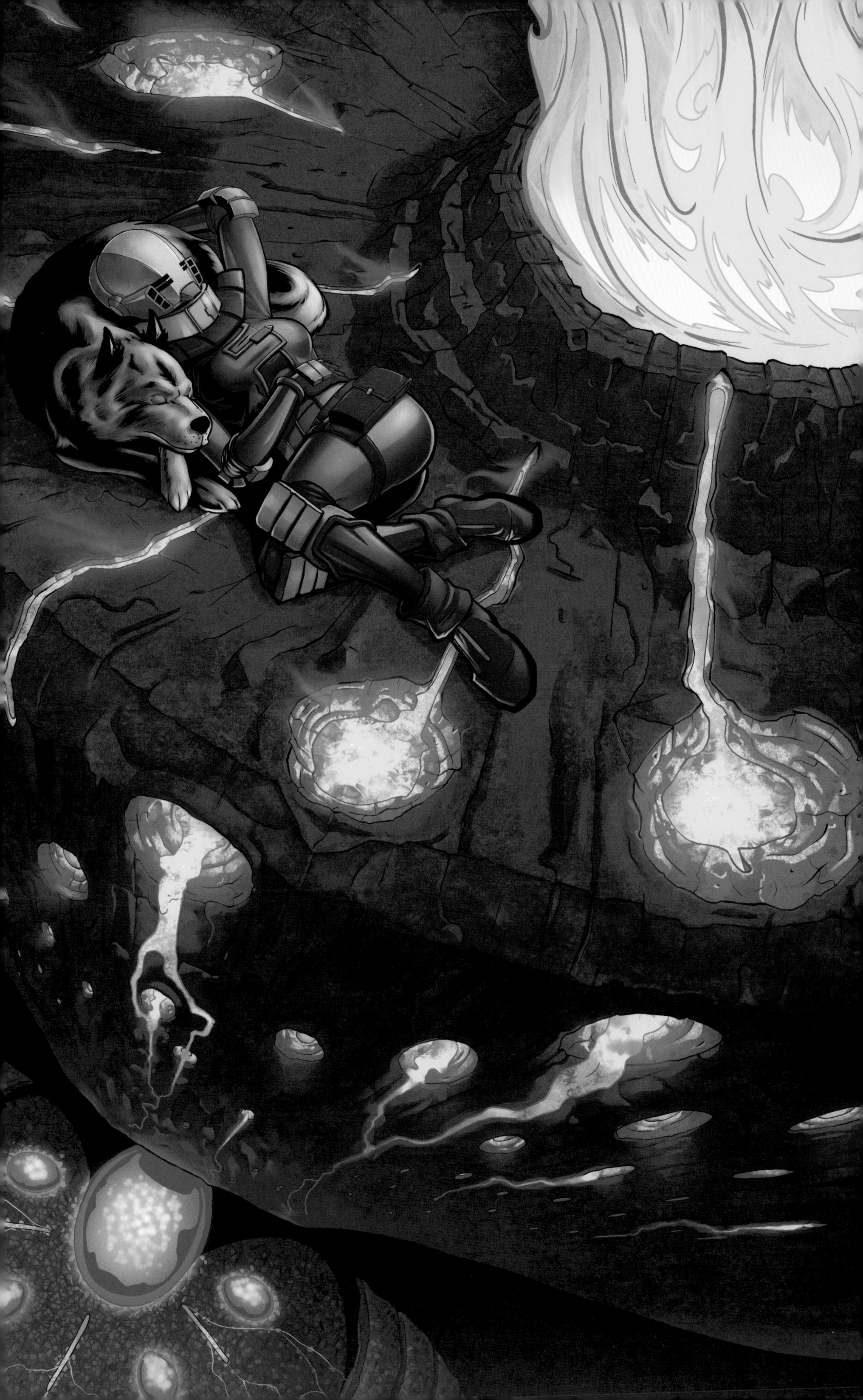

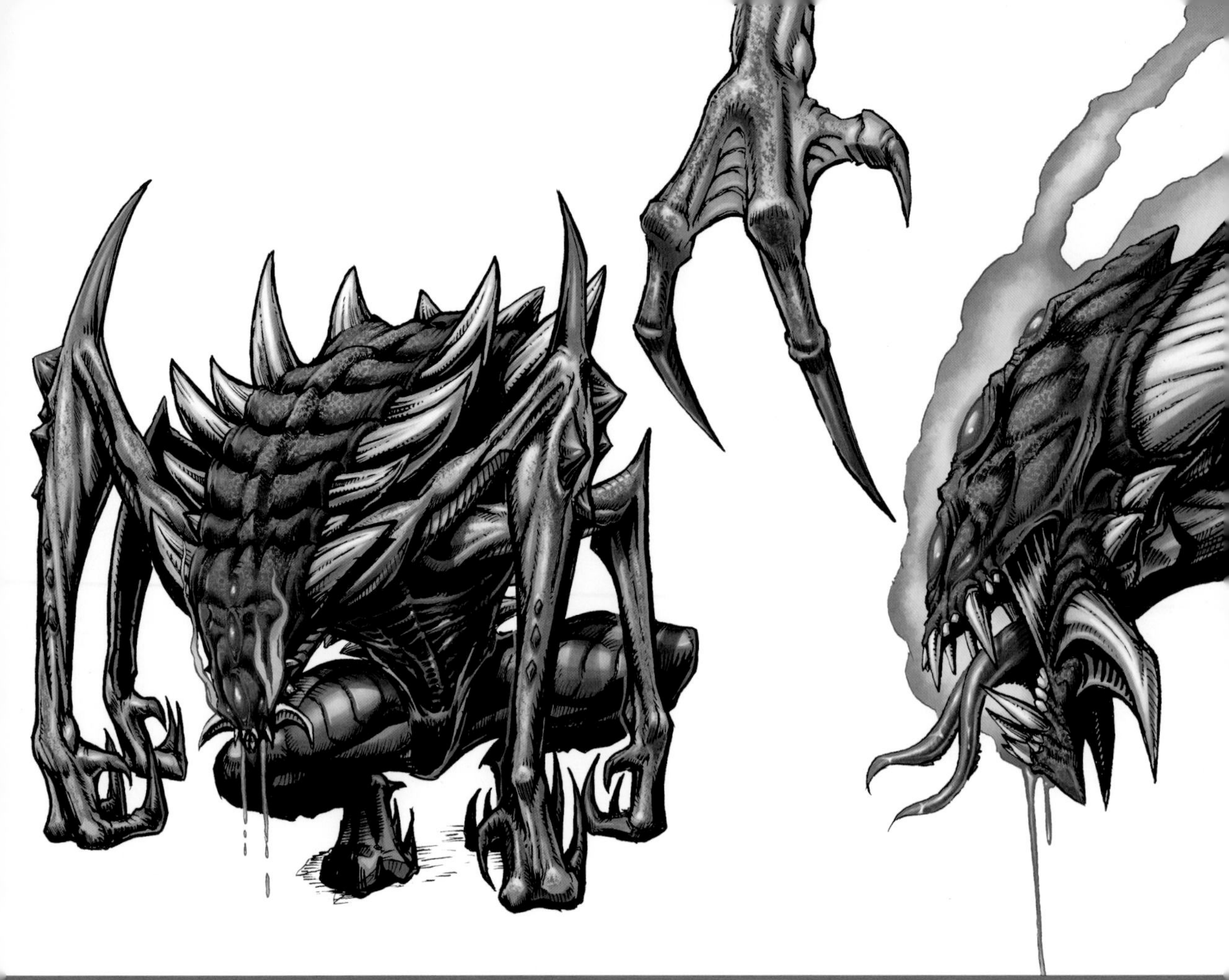

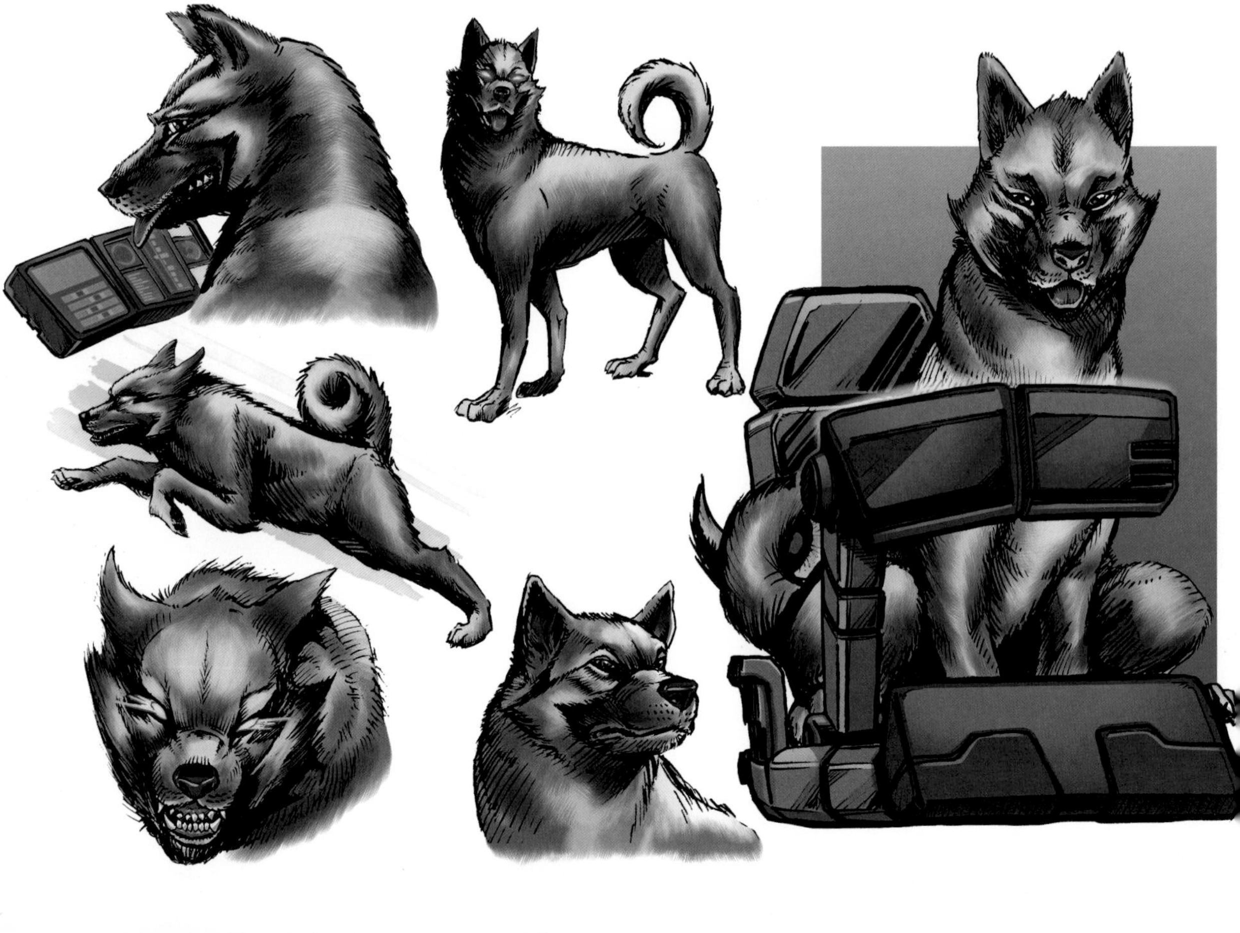